ראיתי את הקונטריסים שהרב נתן יוסף מיללער שליט"א
הדפיס בשמי ועברתי בין בתריו וראיתי שהם הם הדברים
שאמרתי בהגידי שעורים לפני בני הישיבה הקדושה ישיבת
נר ישראל בבאלטימאר במוצאי שבתות. אין כוונת הקונטרס
הזה לפרש כל הדינים של הלכות עניני רופאים ורפואה חיובי
האם עניני מיתה נחלה ואבילות רק אלו הם תשובות של
השאלות ששאלוני. וע"ז אני מכיר טובה להרב הנ"ל על
הטרחה המרובה לסדר הדברים לדפוס וגם הכרת טוב
להישיבה שנתנה לי האפשרות להפיץ דיני התורה ברבים
לתלמידים הגונים ומבחבבי תורת השי"ת. על זה באתי עה"ח
בשלישי בשבת לסדר קטנתי מכל החסדים ומכל האמת אשר
עשית את עבדך י"ב יום לחודש כסליו שנת תש"פ לפ"ק

משה בן החבר ר' ברוך גדליה למשפחת היינעמאן

Please note this קונטרוס was compiled based on the שיעורים of Rav Heinemann שליט"א, given at Yeshivas Ner Yisroel of Baltimore. Recordings of the שיעורים were provided by the Audio Library of Yeshivas Ner Yisroel. Although the קונטרוס was reviewed and revised by the Rav, any questions or errors are due to my חסרונות alone.

May this collection of insights and stories gathered from Rav Heinemann's שיעורים serve as a springboard for a more profound understanding of רצון ה', a greater appreciation for these intricate הלכות, and a tremendous קידוש שם שמים.

With boundless gratitude to the רבונו של עולם, the Rav, R' Dovid Rowshanshad for reviewing the content, the Yeshiva, my clinical mentors at TA and RCC, and my family – especially my wife

נתן יוסף מיללער

For Comments, Questions, or Suggestions, please email:
60SecondSpark@gmail.com

Table of Contents

Chapter 1: Preventative Medicine

Q1. Is it permitted to take vitamin D that has non-kosher ingredients?

A: (5779) In general, if it's not possible to obtain a medicine which you need which has a *hechsher* or is kosher, then you are allowed to eat it if it's forbidden *m'drabanan* because it's considered *shelo k'derech achila* (Shulchan Aruch YD 155:3)[1]. Of course, if it's a question of a danger to your health – like if you would die tomorrow if you don't take the medicine – then there is no doubt that you are allowed to take the medicine even if it is forbidden by the Torah. There is a benefit to having the medicine put in a capsule or tablet form because there are two parts of the issue of eating something *treif:* One is the הנאת גרונו – the pleasure of swallowing the food and the second is הנאת מעיו – the pleasure of the food being good for your health (Chullin 103b)[2]. Although you might not be able to do anything about the second issue, you can put the medicine into a veggie-capsule to avoid the first issue. I'm not so sure if Vitamin D is a medicine for everyone since there are some people who get the necessary Vitamin D from the sun. Maybe you don't actually need Vitamin D. However, there are tests which doctors can utilize to see if you need it. If you do need Vitamin D, then it's important for your health and considered a necessary medicine – especially if you live in a country where there is not so much sunlight, such as further north or you're a *frum* woman who covers herself modestly and doesn't obtain those benefits from the sun. Nonetheless, you are obligated to obtain the kosher form of any medicine if it is available. Needing medicine is not a blanket *heter* if the medicine you need is available in a kosher form. If the only kosher form of

---

[1] Shulchan Aruch YD (155:3) - בשאר איסורים מתרפאים במקום סכנה בשאר איסורים מתרפאים במקום סכנה אפי' דרך הנאתן ושלא במקום סכנה כדרך הנאתן אסור שלא כדרך הנאתן מותר חוץ מכלאי הכרם ובשר בחלב שאסורים אפילו שלא כדרך הנאתן אלא במקום סכנה: הגה י"א דכל איסורי הנאה מדרבנן מותר להתרפאות בהן אפילו חולה שאין בו סכנה

[2] Chullin (103b) - אלא אי בתר גרונו אזלינן אי בתר מעיו אזלינן

4

this medicine is in New York, which will take a few days to reach you, and you need the medicine now, then you can start taking the non-kosher medicine until the kosher medicine arrives. Moreover, if the kosher medicine is available in your town but is more expensive than the non-kosher form of medicine, you are obligated to pay extra for the kosher one.

Q2. Can one take vitamin D on Shabbos?

A: (5779) Although you cannot take medicine on Shabbos (Shulchan Aruch 328:1)[3], if a person is considered a *choleh kol gufo* – which is quite possible due to a lack of vitamin D – then it is permitted on Shabbos (Shulchan Aruch 328:17)[4]. Even though you might not see the illness so clearly, if the person is tired and not able to focus properly, then that's considered *choleh kol gufo*. Such an individual can take vitamin D on Shabbos if those symptoms are occurring due to the vitamin D deficiency.

Q3. Is it *hashkafically* correct to take vitamins?

A: (5779) The Torah requires a person to do whatever is necessary to promote good health. If vitamins promote better health, then they should be taken. We rely on the doctors of our time to decide whether vitamins are better for our health or not.

Q4. Is there a problem with getting vaccinated? If not, is one obligated to get vaccinated?

A: (5779) When I was young, we were vaccinated for three things: 1) Pertussis - whooping cough 2) Diphtheria 3) Tetanus. That's all we received when we were younger. I had measles when I was younger, and whatever else people had back then –

---

[3] Shulchan Aruch (328:1) - מי שיש לו מיחוש בעלמא והוא מתחזק והולך כבריא אסור לעשות לו שום רפואה ואפי' ע"י עכו"ם גזירה משום שחיקת סמנים

[4] Shulchan Aruch (328:17) - חולה שנפל מחמת חלי למשכב ואין בו סכנה הגה או שיש לו מיחוש שמצטער וחלה ממנו כל גופו שאז אע"פ שהולך כנפל למשכב דמי אומרים לעכו"ם לעשות לו רפואה אבל אין מחללין עליו את השבת באיסור דאורייתא

Chapter 1: Preventative Medicine

I had it. In my days, parents whose children didn't yet have measles would send their children to play with those who had measles because it's better to have it when you're young. The main issue with getting vaccinated which we need to consider is not so much the question for yourself – if you don't mind getting the disease, then that's your choice. You have a right to make that choice. However, the main question is spreading the disease to someone else who has a compromised immune system. If you contract a disease which spreads to such an individual, then you're damaging them and putting the other individuals in a life-threatening situation. Seventy years ago, we didn't have as many people with compromised immune systems who would be in danger by you not getting vaccinated. Consequently, the entire question of vaccination has changed into putting other people in danger. If a pregnant mother develops German measles, then it could be very dangerous to the fetus. The child might have trouble hearing, have compromised eyesight, all kinds of things which affect the child which wouldn't have happened if other people were vaccinated for measles. Therefore, I say there is an obligation to receive vaccinations.

Q5. Is there also an element of chillul Hashem caused by not being vaccinated?

A: (5779) If becoming vaccinated will prevent a chillul Hashem, then you should get vaccinated for that reason as well. I'm not sure if what we do will make such a difference in the way the world looks at us, but if you can stop a chillul Hashem from having the nations upset with us for not being vaccinated then that is enough of a reason to get vaccinated.

Q6. Can parents say they don't want to be vaccinated because of a threat to their own children?

A: (5779) If parents feel they have a medical reason why their child should not be vaccinated, then they should go to their medical doctor to ask for guidance. The doctor can decide whether or not a particular vaccination is dangerous for your child – but I'm not talking about a doctor who says you shouldn't vaccinate anyone. Their medical judgment on the matter doesn't mean anything for your child. However, if a doctor does vaccinate patients and is pro vaccination but says it would be a danger for your child, then you should trust their medical judgment.

Q7. Can a community pressure people to vaccinate their children by not allowing those who don't vaccinate their family to *daven* in their shuls or attend their schools?

A: (5779) I'm not going to say in my shul that someone who isn't vaccinated cannot come to our shul because then I wouldn't be allowed to come to shul myself. Saying others cannot enter your shul without proper vaccinations is not practical – you're going to ask for people's vaccination records before *davening*? Schools can implement such a policy – and they should do so.

Q8. Is Lasek eye surgery permitted?

A: (5779) What options do you have? You can wear glasses for the rest of your life. Medical wisdom doubles every five years. That means whatever was considered the Cadillac surgery five years ago might be discarded completely today. Therefore, it's always better to push off your surgery as much as you can. A lot of people living in third world countries who can afford to come to America will fly here for surgery because their countries are further behind.

Q9. Must one *bench gomel* after emerging from anesthesia?

A: (5779) If it's not considered a danger to our life, then you don't *bench gomel* (Shulchan Aruch 219:8)[5]. Most people survive anesthesia even though they endured the complex

---

[5] Shulchan Aruch (219:8) - בכל חולי צריך לברך אפילו אינו חולי של סכנה ולא מכה של חלל אלא כל שעלה למטה וירד מפני שדומה כמי שהעלוהו לגרדום (פי' מעלות שעושין דיינים לשבת כשדנין) לידון אין הפרש בין שיש לו מיחוש קבוע ובא מזמן לזמן ובין שאינו קבוע: הגה ויש אומרים דאינו מברך רק על חולי שיש בו סכנה כגון מכה של חלל

situation. I'm just saying that there is more of a danger with the anesthesia than there is with the surgery itself.

Q10. Should one do genetic testing to see if he is the carrier of a disease?

A: (5779) This isn't a yes or no question. The first question you should ask yourself is if there's anything you can do about you being a carrier. If there's nothing you can do about being a carrier, then there's no reason to find out whether you are a carrier or not – it'll just make you nervous. There are sometimes where - depending on whether you are carrying a dominant or recessive gene for a disease - that you need to know before getting married. Some recessive gene diseases might mean that three out of four children won't have the disease, but one of them will. If the genetic testing reveals that you have a 60% chance of developing cancer, then you must share that information during *shidduchim*. If you don't know whether you have a possibility of developing a disease, then you're not obligated to find out. Not knowing whether you have the possibility of developing a disease later in life is the same doubt that everyone enters marriage with. If you're engaged and now want to test your genetics together as to how the combination might affect your children, then it might be a cause of breaking up the engagement – which isn't too positive. Nonetheless, if your genetics will affect future children then it's not fair to bring children into the world who will be hurt. It's unnecessary pain because the chosson and kallah can part ways and have children with other people. There is an organization called Dor Yesharim which will not tell you the results of your genetic testing for your personal records. This way, you don't know if you have any recessive genes for diseases which would require you to tell future dates. They will tell you whether the product of you and your prospective spouse will likely produce children will health problems. Dor Yesharim did a phenomenal job as seen by the fact that Tay-Sachs Disease – common among Eastern European Ashkenazim – dropped dramatically to the extent that it is almost eliminated. Tay-Sachs Disease is where a child can be born completely normal, behave as every other child for the first months, and then dies at three years old. It's a very traumatic experience for everyone involved.

Q11. Is it permitted to clone another human being?

A: (5779) I don't know if it's possible at this time whether this question is even practical for humans. I know scientists did clone a sheep, but it wasn't a healthy animal. You don't want to clone another human being without any *seichel*. It's not fair to this individual to be brought into the world in such a state. Moreover, I don't think it's right to mix into the creation of the Ribono Shel Olam – whether the clone is a Jew or non-Jew.

Q12. Is there a problem with gene modifications?

A: (5779) If the gene modifications are needed for a *refuah*, then I have no problem with it. They're not sophisticated enough today to know whether there will be negative side effects of the gene modifications. There are some countries which will not allow food which has been genetically modified because they're worried about what kind of diseases or fertility problems it might cause. There is no halachic problem of gene modification. In regards to modifying chickens, statistically speaking *frum* Jews like the bottoms of chickens more than tops while the more modern Orthodox groups of Jews like the tops better. Consequently, Chassidish *hechsherim* would rather certify the bottoms of chickens in order to sell the chicken for a higher price to *frum yidden*, and don't care too much for the chicken tops. For that reason, you can get the tops of chickens at a cheaper price from those *hechsherim* than you would from other companies like Empire which are more geared to the broader Jewish community. So what do companies like Empire do? Empire developed chickens which produce larger tops and smaller bottoms because their clientele wanted the tops more. How did they develop such a chicken? They found one chicken with a large top and used it to fertilize a lot of other eggs. Then those chickens had larger tops. That is a form of gene modification – though you're not performing it in the lab. I once asked my son when he was about five years old – when he knew not to eat *milchigs* with *fleishigs* – "Where does meat come from?" He answered, "A cow." Then I asked where milk comes from. "A cow." So I asked him how it's possible to have milk and meat from the same cow. He thought for a minute and then said, "There are two types of cows: cows which give meat and cows which give milk." He's right! The cows which give milk do not produce meat, and the cows which give meat do not produce milk. They have developed Holstein cows – the white and black cows – to produce milk. They give about 30 pounds of milk every milking - which is over 3 gallons - and can be milked three times a day depending on various factors. On the other hand, the cows which we eat are called beef cows and do not have big utters. They really just produce enough milk for their calves and that's it, while Holstein cows produce enough milk for ten calves – and it's very unusual for a cow to have more than one calf at a time. The meat from Holstein cows is too tough to eat, so it's really only edible by grinding it up for hamburgers. They developed these cows over a couple hundred years by specifically breeding cows which produce more milk or better meat. That's really genetic modification through years of breeding. They also created a beefalo which had a lot of benefits like feeding them less to produce more meat. Chickens will produce one pound of meat from two pounds of feed. They spent a lot of time trying to develop beefalo – about 30 years of working on it – and then they opened up the first beefalo stand in Texas. It wasn't too successful, and today you don't even hear about it anymore. Why? The meat didn't taste as juicy and people didn't like it, so all of their work went down the drain. I think the first beefalo made cost them $150,000 since they believed it was going to be the best meat available. Now they're working on creating meat in a laboratory through genetic engineering. As far as I'm concerned, such meat is considered *fleishigs* because it still tastes like meat. Gene modification isn't a problem when done in a natural way. It's only a problem when it's done through unnatural means. Rav Elyashiv was very much against genetic modification, especially when dealing with modifying human beings.

Q13. May one go on a diet purely for the purpose of looking skinnier if he will starve himself?

Chapter 1: Preventative Medicine

A: (5779) If going on a diet to look skinny won't affect your health and you'll be able to learn the same way while doing all the *mitzvos* of serving Hashem the same way before and after your diet, then I have no problem with that. I don't know if there is a benefit to being skinny – as long as it doesn't harm your health then you can do whatever you want for dieting. However, if dieting will negatively affect your health then you should not do so. Ask your doctor regarding what diet would be good for your health and whether you should diet or not. I saw a report from Johns Hopkins University saying that it's better to be fatter than skinnier – not obese. Why? They said that although there are certain diseases from high blood pressure or diabetes *chas v'shalom* which arise from being overweight, they have a way to deal with all of those diseases. On the other hand, someone who is skinnier is less likely to survive an operation than those who are larger because he doesn't have enough nutritional resources in his body to survive an operation. I'm not going to get involved in the discussion whether it's better to be fatter or skinnier, but it seems to be the consensus of medical opinion that being obese isn't healthy. If you can't help yourself because your hormones won't allow your body to lose weight from dieting, then it wouldn't help to go on a diet – and might even become dangerous. Therefore, don't do anything with asking your doctor first.

(5755) If you have a tendency to eat because you like to eat, then it's questionable if you're allowed to go on a diet because Rav Eliezer Hakapar says that a nazir should bring a *korban* אשר חטא לנפש since he pained himself by not drinking wine. Therefore, Rav Eliezer Hakapar (Taanis 11a)[6] says we see the Ribono Shel Olam will hold everyone accountable for not enjoying a permitted pleasure available to him. We see the Gemara (Taanis 11a)[7] says יושב בתענית נקרא חוטא because you

---

[6] Taanis (11a) - תניא ר' אלעזר הקפר ברבי אומר מה תלמוד לומר (במדבר ו:יא) וכפר עליו מאשר חטא על הנפש וכי באיזה נפש חטא זה אלא שציער עצמו מן היין והלא דברים קל וחומר ומה זה שלא ציער עצמו אלא מן היין נקרא חוטא המצער עצמו מכל דבר ודבר על אחת כמה וכמה

[7] Taanis (11a) - אמר שמואל כל היושב בתענית נקרא חוטא

pained yourself by not eating. The Mishna Avos (6:4)[8] פת במלח
תאכל is referring to your willingness to accept sleeping on the
ground, drinking only water, and eating only bread in order to
learn Torah (Rashi Avos 6:4)[9]. Chazal aren't saying that you
are only supposed to eat bread, drink water, and sleep on the
floor. However, if you are going on a diet for medical reasons
then there is no question that it's permitted. In fact, it would be
recommended to promote your health – and it's a *mitzva* to do
so (Kitzur Shulchan Aruch 32:1)[10]. The question is if you want
to go on a diet just to look nicer. There was a doctor in
Philadelphia – Dr. Askowitz – who was a big tzadik and called
"The Chofetz Chaim of Philadelphia." He was an eye doctor
with two massive bookcases from the floor to the ceiling and
maybe five or six feet wide. One was filled with *seforim* and
the other was filled with medical books. He said the difference
between the two is that the older the medical books are, the
more obsolete they become, but the older the *seforim* are the
more valuable they become. Medical textbooks write one
opinion today and change it tomorrow. Doctors used to say
those who go on a diet by eating less food become larger
because the fasting slows down their metabolism. I saw a report
from a study in Hopkins which shows that people above 60 who
are fat live longer than those who are thin, so they're starting to
rethink their entire understanding of the healthiness of being
thin. Rav Moshe (Igros Moshe CM 2:65)[11] wrote in a *teshuva*

---

[8] Avos (6:4) - כָּךְ הִיא דַּרְכָּהּ שֶׁל תּוֹרָה, פַּת בְּמֶלַח תֹּאכַל, וּמַיִם בִּמְשׂוּרָה תִשְׁתֶּה,
וְעַל הָאָרֶץ תִּישַׁן, וְחַיֵּי צַעַר תִּחְיֶה, וּבַתּוֹרָה אַתָּה עָמֵל, אִם אַתָּה עֹשֶׂה כֵן, (תהלים
קכח) אַשְׁרֶיךָ וְטוֹב לָךְ. אַשְׁרֶיךָ בָּעוֹלָם הַזֶּה וְטוֹב לָךְ לָעוֹלָם הַבָּא
[9] Rashi Avos (6:4) - לֹא עַל הֶעָשִׁיר הוּא אוֹמֵר שֶׁיַּעֲמֹד בְּחַיֵּי צַעַר כְּדֵי לִלְמֹד
תּוֹרָה, אֶלָּא הָכִי קָאָמַר, אֲפִלּוּ אֵין לְאָדָם אֶלָּא פַּת בְּמֶלַח וְכוּ' וְאֵין לוֹ כַּר וְכֶסֶת לִישֹׁן
אֶלָּא עַל הָאָרֶץ, אַל יִמָּנַע מִלַּעֲסֹק בָּהּ, דְּסוֹפוֹ לִלְמֹד אוֹתָהּ מֵעֹשֶׁר
[10] Kitzur Shulchan Aruch (32:1) - הוֹאִיל וֶהֱיוֹת הַגּוּף בָּרִיא וְשָׁלֵם מִדַּרְכֵי
הַשֵּׁם הוּא, שֶׁהֲרֵי אִי אֶפְשָׁר שֶׁיָּבִין אוֹ יֵדַע דָּבָר מִידִיעַת הַבּוֹרֵא וְהוּא חוֹלֶה, לְפִיכָךְ
צָרִיךְ הָאָדָם לְהַרְחִיק אֶת עַצְמוֹ מִדְּבָרִים הַמְאַבְּדִין אֶת הַגּוּף, וּלְהַנְהִיג אֶת עַצְמוֹ
בִּדְבָרִים הַמַּבְרִין וְהַמַּחֲלִימִים אֶת הַגּוּף. וְכֵן הוּא אוֹמֵר, וְנִשְׁמַרְתֶּם מְאֹד לְנַפְשֹׁתֵיכֶם
[11] Igros Moshe (CM 2:65) - ושאר ממון הרוחת שבשביל פשוט דדבר
הנאות מותר להצטער במניעה משתיית יין משום דלא נחשב זה מצטער כלל מאחר
דהוא שמח אדרבה מהממון שמרויח ומשאר הנאות שאית לו עי"ז מאחר דכל
הצער הוא מצד שמתאוה ליין והרי מתאוה יותר להרויח כדחזינן שבשביל זה הוא

that going on a diet to lose weight without medical necessity is forbidden because it's considered injuring oneself. However, he says that if you would feel worse about yourself by being fat than you would feel with the pain of not eating, then it would permitted to go on a diet. For most people, the pain of being fat isn't as much as the pain of not eating – and you see most people don't succeed with keeping off the weight after dieting. A person is allowed to refrain from eating something if the spiritual pleasure of being able to hold oneself back is greater than the pain of not eating the food – like Rebbi Yehuda said (Kesubos 104a)[12] he didn't obtain pleasure from food in this world (Tosfos Kesubos 104a)[13].

Q14. Is it permitted to skip breakfast in order to learn?

A: (5755) A person has the right to make the decision that his learning is more important right now than eating breakfast. It would be permitted to miss breakfast if the pleasure of learning is more than eating, but it might lead to other *bittul torah* issues later (Mishna Berura 155:11)[14].

Q15. Is it permitted to eat dessert after a meal?

A: (5755) Anything which is considered normal is permitted regarding eating food. Dessert isn't just eating extra in addition

---

נמנע מיין והוא פשוט וברור וממש כן הוא הנאת האשה ממה שתהיה יותר נאה
ויפה לא מבעיא בפנויות שרוצות להנשא אלא אפילו נשואות כדי להתחבב על
בעליהן יותר בהדייעט ולא משגיחות על שמצטערות מזה בשביל הנאתם מהנוי
אבל היתר זה הוא מצער המניעה מדברים מתוקים שהצער הוא רק ממניעת הנאה
שנחשב הנאה כנגד הנאה ובוחרת בהנאת הנוי שגדולה לה ביותר

[12] Kesubos (104a) - כלפי מעלה בשעת פטירתו של רבי זקף עשר אצבעותיו
אמר רבש"ע גלוי וידוע לפניך שיגעתי בעשר אצבעותי בתורה ולא נהניתי אפילו
באצבע קטנה

[13] Tosfos Kesubos (104a) - דאמרינן במדרש עד שאדם מתפלל שיכנס תורה
לתוך גופו יתפלל שלא יכנסו מעדנים לתוך גופו

[14] Mishna Berura (155:11) - וטוב שירגיל בו - כדאמרינן בגמרא שמונים
ושלשה מיני חלאים תלויים במרה וכולם פת במלח וקיתון של מים שחרית
מבטלתן ומצוה להנהיג עצמו במדה טובה והנהגה טובה לשמור בריאותו כדי
שיהיה בריא וחזק לעבודת הבורא יתעלה

to the meal, but it's part of the *kinuach haseuda* which helps digest the food by putting a good taste in your mouth (Rashi Pesachim 119a)[15]. On the other hand, if you don't feel like you're weak or missing food after a meal, then the ice cream dessert is not recommended (Rambam De'os 4:2)[16].

Q16. Is receiving food intravenously considered eating?

A: (5755) No, receiving food through IV is not considered eating, so it's not forbidden for someone to receive food intravenously on Yom Kippur (Igros Moshe OC 4:101:3)[17]. The brain tells the body that it should be hungry when there aren't enough nutrients in the bloodstream. Therefore, the nutritional fluids given through the veins will not make the patient feel hungry. Nonetheless, if a sick person is in danger if he fasts on Yom Kippur, then Rav Moshe (Igros Moshe OC 3:90)[18] says there is no obligation not to eat rather than receive fluids intravenously since it's not normal. The Torah doesn't obligated us to do anything not normal to get ourselves out of the *issur*. It wasn't considered normal in former times to stick yourself with a needle since it was a question of *sakanas nefashos* since it might become infected or other kinds of

---

[15] Rashi Pesachim (119a) - לרב דשמואל - כגון ארדילאי לי וגוזליא לאבא הוה רגיל לאכול בקינוח סעודה כמהין ופטריות ורב רגיל לאכול אחר סעודתו גוזלות

[16] Rambam De'os (4:2) - לֹא יֹאכַל אָדָם עַד שֶׁתִּתְמַלֵּא כְּרֵסוֹ אֶלָּא יִפְחֹת כְּמוֹ רְבִיעַ מִשָּׂבְעָתוֹ

[17] Igros Moshe (OC 4:101:3) - נראה שרשאי לאכול אף כשצריך לאכול הרבה ואף כשאפשר ליתן לו האינטרע ווינעס בעיו״כ כי לבד שודאי אינו דומה לאכילה ממש שדרך אינטרע ווינעס לא מיתבא דעתא כאכילה ואצל חולה גם צער וכאב בעלמא אפשר לגרום לו סכנה מצד חולשתו הנה יש לחוש על כל דבר שאינו כפי הטבע שיקלקל לאיזה דבר ולא שייך לסמוך על הרופאים בזה שאין לידע זה בברור אלא בהשערה בעלמא ובמשך הזמן אפשר שיראו מה שנתקלקל מזה וכן אירע בכמה דברים שבמשך זמן גדול נודעו הרופאים שאיכא גם היזק והפסד להגוף ממה שנתנו לו לרפאותו יש להחולה לחוש לזה ואם יכול לאכול אין לעשות לו אינטער ווינעס

[18] Igros Moshe (OC 3:90) - ובדבר אחד שאסור לו לצום ואם יעשו לו זריקת איזו רפואה ע״י תחיבת מחט בגופו יוכל לצום פשוט לע״ד שאינו מחוייב לעשות זה ולא מצד שאין לחייבו כיון שהוא פטור להכניס עצמו לחיוב

medical problems. Even though nowadays they've developed the technology to avoid most of these medical issues with needles, we still say you're not obligated to do that to avoid eating on Yom Kippur. In fact, even in the times of Chazal people could be fed through putting food into the body through the rectum, however since it's not the normal way of eating Chazal didn't obligate anyone to do that to get around the *issur* of eating on Yom Kippur. Also, you don't make a *beracha* for food received through the IV even though you receive nutrients through it.

Chapter 2: Doctors in Halacha

Q1. What is the doctor's responsibility to serve his patients?

A: (5755) The doctor is charged with the responsibility of doing his work *b'emunah* – just like every worker. If you undertake to do the work, like a carpenter who agrees to a price to make new cabinets for your kitchen, then he must make sure to do quality work ensuring the cabinets stay up properly and last as long as people in the region expect new cabinets to last for. If the carpenter doesn't do a proper job with his cabinets, then he's considered a thief. He was paid to perform a service but didn't follow through on what he was paid to do. Doctors are no different – if you hire a doctor, then he must give you proper service based on what's considered normal for the amount of money that he's taking.

Q2. Can a doctor administer extra medical tests to a patient "just in case" at the expense of the insurance company?

A: (5755) There's a very big problem today which the non-Jews are also trying to grapple with since they have what they call medical ethics. If you have a cough, then you can go to the doctor – who knows what the cough could be? So the doctor takes the stethoscope, listens to the sound in your chest, and says "it's nothing – *gornisht.*" Since you're in the office anyway, he suggests you have an x-ray taken of your lungs just to be sure there's nothing. When the doctor sees there's nothing in your x-ray which is concerning, then he says, "Since you're here already, we'll take an electrocardiogram just to make sure everything is alright." When he sees your heart is OK too, then he'll suggest you take a CT-scan just in case. Eventually you leave with a bill over $2,500 which is mostly paid for by the insurance, and you feel really healthy since all the tests came back with a good report. The doctors say they are obligated to perform all these tests because if a patient comes in with a cough and then half a year later, they find out he developed

16

cancer in his lungs *rachmana litzlan*, then he'll sue the doctor. The patient can say, "Had I known I had something more serious six months ago, I might've been able to do something about it." Doctors get sued for malpractice, so insurance companies are happy to have all of the tests done for the patient since they're the ones who will have to pay the most if a lawsuit occurs. Doctors are really practicing defensive medicine because they are worried about being sued for malpractice. An *ehrliche* doctor asked me if he could administer those extra tests to cover himself. I asked him if the patient must pay for the extra tests or is the insurance agency charged. He said the insurance company pays for it because they would rather cover themselves as well since they'll have to come up with the money if a lawsuit occurs. I told him that if the insurance company is willing to pay for the tests, then there's no problem with giving the extra tests. However, the doctor should tell the patient, "I feel there's nothing wrong with you, but just to be on the safe side we'll only know if we perform a couple more tests." Then he can't sue the doctor later because the choice was the patient's – though it's still not so simple that he can't sue because the patient can claim if the doctor really pressed him to take an x-ray or CT-scan then he would have went through with it. The doctor should just convey to the patient that he doesn't think there are any issues, but that there is always a possibility that there's something underneath and a series of tests will help confirm or reject that.

Q3. Should one perform surgery to separate Siamese twins?

A: (5755) This question arose during Rav Moshe's lifetime, and the Jewish Siamese twins shared a heart with six chambers. A normal heart has four chambers, so these twins had an attached heart. The doctors said if they don't perform any surgery on the twins, then they'll both die since the heart would not be strong enough to supply enough blood for both of them. On the other hand, the surgery would only allow the twin who received the four-chamber heart to survive while the other twin would die. This is a halachic question as well as a medical ethics question since the doctor performing the surgery might be guilty of manslaughter. If the twins die on their own, then the doctors aren't held accountable. The legal department gave the OK that the medical team would be protected from malpractice, so they asked Rav Moshe about whether they could perform the surgery halachically. He explained that in the case of a mother who is having difficulty in childbirth and is in danger, then you may kill the fetus before its born to save the mother. Why? The child is considered a *rodef* chasing after the mother to kill her, so we say it is permitted to save her at the expense of the child (Sanhedrin 72a)[19]. Once the child is already born, we don't say the child is a *rodef* (Rambam Rotze'ach 1:9)[20]. In this case of the Siamese twins, each one is trying to kill the other one because they both cannot live while the other one is using part of the six-chamber heart. Therefore, the doctor is allowed to kill either one of the Siamese twins since they are both considered *rodfim* (Care of the Critically Ill 1: "So One May Live")[21]. Rav Moshe said that whichever twin the doctors believe will be more likely to survive is the one they should save during the surgery. The doctors at this Catholic hospital had the *psak* translated for them, they thought it made sense, and performed the operation. I remember it was a big Kiddush Hashem at that time because they saw the *yidden* have a logical approach to these kinds of complex medical questions and even the Catholic doctors accepted the *psak*.

Q4. What should a Jewish doctor do if the patient is someone who causes problems for Klal Yisroel?

---

[19] Sanhedrin (72a) - התורה אמרה אם בא להורגך השכם להורגו

[20] Rambam Rotze'ach (1:9) - אַף זוֹ מִצְוַת לֹא תַעֲשֶׂה שֶׁלֹּא לָחוּס עַל נֶפֶשׁ הָרוֹדֵף לְפִיכָךְ הוֹרוּ חֲכָמִים שֶׁהָעֻבָּרָה שֶׁהִיא מַקְשָׁה לֵילֵד מֻתָּר לַחְתֹּךְ הָעֻבָּר בְּמֵעֶיהָ בֵּין בְּסַם בֵּין בְּיָד מִפְּנֵי שֶׁהוּא כְּרוֹדֵף אַחֲרֶיהָ לְהָרְגָהּ וְאִם מִשֶּׁהוֹצִיא רֹאשׁוֹ אֵין נוֹגְעִין בּוֹ שֶׁאֵין דּוֹחִין נֶפֶשׁ מִפְּנֵי נֶפֶשׁ וְזֶהוּ טִבְעוֹ שֶׁל עוֹלָם

[21] Rav Moshe Tendler Care of the Critically Ill (1): "So One May Live" - אם אי אפשר דמיתציל העובר אז באמת הוי כיחדו למיתה דמי שא"א לחיות לפי הבנתינו בחוקי הטבע והמדע הרפואי הוי כנגמר דינו ע"י ב"ד של מעלה למיתה והנה להתאום בעלת מומין פנימיים אין שום אפשרות שתתשאר בחיים יותר מכמה שבועות א"כ הוי כיחדה למיתה וחייבת מיתה דמותר לכתחילה למסורה כדי להציל אחותה

Chapter 2: Doctors in Halacha

A: (5755) Although there is an element to treat anyone who needs medical help because of רַחֲמָיו עַל־כָּל־מַעֲשָׂיו (Tehillim 145:9)[22], for a wicked individual who causes trouble for Klal Yisroel a doctor can be passive and שב ואל תעשה (Avoda Zara 26a)[23] if it's possible. However, it's not always possible to be passive with such an individual – and if the patient survives then he can cause even worse problems for Klal Yisroel. I remember when Stalin was sick after he had already killed millions of people, he had ten of the best doctors in Russia treating him – and all ten were Jews. When he died under their care, all ten doctors were put to death. I guess the message was made clear to them: Either you save Stalin or die. They decided to treat Stalin as good as they could. However, they were not successful and were put to death. Nonetheless, a doctor can never actively kill someone unless there was a Beis Din (which we do not have today) which decided the person should die – or it's a question of this patient putting other people in danger. It's a very complex question which cannot be decided on your own. In the concentration camps, if someone would be מלשין other Jews hoping to get favors from the Germans, then the inmates would take care of him. The Shulchan Aruch (158:1)[24] which says not to treat such a patient doesn't mean that the doctor can actively kill the patient, rather it means that you can let the person remain in the pit without helping him. Even so, the Chazon Ish (Yoreh De'ah 2:16)[25] says that *din* doesn't

---

[22] Tehillim (145:9) - טוֹב־ה' לַכֹּל וְרַחֲמָיו עַל־כָּל־מַעֲשָׂיו

[23] Avoda Zara (26a) - סבר רב יוסף למימר הא דתניא העובדי כוכבים ורועי בהמה דקה לא מעלין ולא מורידין

[24] Shulchan Aruch (158:1) - עובדי עבודת כוכבים מז' עממין שאין בינינו וביניהם מלחמה ורועי בהמה דקה מישראל בארץ ישראל בזמן שהיו רוב השדות של ישראל וכיוצא בהן אין מסבבים להם המיתה ואסור להצילם אם נטו למות כגון שראה א' מהם שנפל לים אינו מעלהו אפילו אם יתן לו שכר לפיכך אין לרפאותן אפילו בשכר אם לא היכא דאיכא משום איבה

[25] Chazon Ish YD (2:16) - ונראה דאין דין מורידין אלא בזמן שהשגחתו גלויה כמו בזמן שהיו נסים מצויין ומשמשת בת קול וצדיקי הדור תחת השגחה פרטית הנראית לעין כל והכופרין אז הם בנליזות מיוחדת בהטיית היצר לתאוות מיוחדות והפקרות ואז היה בעיבור רשעים גדרו של עולם שהכל ידעו כי הדחת הדור מביא פורעניות לעולם ומביא דבר וחרב ורעב בעולם אבל בזמן ההעלם שנכרתה האמונה מן דלת העם אין במעשה הורדה גדר הפרצה אלא הוספת הפרצה

19

apply nowadays since it only applied when all of Klal Yisroel were *tzadikim* and we were dealing with one wicked person. However, since we're not on such a high level, it's like taking your suit to the cleaners to remove many stains – that's not possible.

Q5. Must a doctor treat someone if the patient cannot pay?

A: (5755) The *issur* of לֹא תַעֲמֹד עַל־דַּם רֵעֶךָ (Vayikra 19:16)[26] and the *mitzva* of רַפֹּא יְרַפֵּא (Shemos 21:19)[27] – maybe it's only a *reshus* (Bava Kamma 85a)[28] but it's certainly a *mitzva* to help those in trouble – have nothing to do with money. You have the right to charge for your services, but you're not exempt from the *mitzva* just because someone cannot pay. Not only that, but doctors must take upon themselves to treat patients for free if they are unable to pay.

Q6. Can a patient say that he doesn't want to pay for medical care since the doctor has an obligation to help him?

A: (5755) We as a community have an obligation to provide poor people with their needs. What should the community do if a wealthy individual doesn't want to use his money because he would rather save it and rely on the community funds? The Gemara (Kesubos 67b)[29] says tell him "goodbye" - אֵין נִזְקָקִין לוֹ. However, this only applies to the wealthy individual himself, but his children aren't held accountable for their father's incorrect actions. Therefore, in such a case the children become the ward of the Beis Din who can then force their father to pay for their needs. The father cannot say, "I don't want anything

---

שֶׁיִּהְיֶה בְּעֵינֵיהֶם כְּמַעֲשֶׂה הַשְׁחָתָה וְאָלִימוּת ח"ו וְכֵיוָן שֶׁכָּל עַצְמֵנוּ לְתַקֵּן אֵין הַדִּין נוֹהֵג בְּשָׁעָה שֶׁאֵין בּוֹ תִּיקּוּן וְעָלֵינוּ לְהַחֲזִירָם בַּעֲבוֹתוֹת אַהֲבָה וְלַעֲמִידָם בְּקֶרֶן אוֹרָה בְּמַה שִׁידֵינוּ מַגַּעַת

[26] Vayikra (19:16) - לֹא־תֵלֵךְ רָכִיל בְּעַמֶּיךָ לֹא תַעֲמֹד עַל־דַּם רֵעֶךָ אֲנִי ה'

[27] Shemos (21:19) - אִם־יָקוּם וְהִתְהַלֵּךְ בַּחוּץ עַל־מִשְׁעַנְתּוֹ וְנִקָּה הַמַּכֶּה רַק שִׁבְתּוֹ יִתֵּן וְרַפֹּא יְרַפֵּא

[28] Bava Kamma (85a) - דְּתַנְיָא דְּבֵי ר' יִשְׁמָעֵאל אוֹמֵר (שמות כא:יט) וְרַפֹּא יְרַפֵּא מִכָּאן שֶׁנִּיתַּן רְשׁוּת לָרוֹפֵא לְרַפֹּאות

[29] Kesubos (67b) - וְהכ"א יֵשׁ לוֹ וְאֵינוֹ רוֹצֶה לְהִתְפַּרְנֵס אֵין נִזְקָקִין לוֹ

to do with you" if he has the money to provide for his children but chooses not to help. Now as for demanding free medical care, a doctor has an obligation to help a patient in need – but the doctor doesn't have to bring him into the hospital or provide anesthesia during treatment since those are all medical luxuries. The doctor just needs to provide the necessary care without the other luxuries. Similarly, if due to insurance reasons the hospital doesn't allow the doctor to treat a patient, the doctor may still have an obligation to help the patient but would only be able to fulfill his obligation to the patient by providing his medical needs at home.

Q7. Does a doctor have to give up his job to avoid doing a forbidden action like abortion or pulling the plug?

A: (5779) Not every abortion is forbidden. For instance, if the mother is in danger due to the fetus, then we say the fetus is a *rodef* (Rambam Rotze'ach 1:9)[30]. If someone tries to kill you, you kill them first (Sanhedrin 72a)[31] – and the doctor would be allowed to do an abortion in such a case. Additionally, there are times when pulling the plug is permitted as well. For instance, if the patient cannot breathe under his own power and is only being kept alive by the respirator which is pumping air into him, Rav Moshe *poskins* based on the *posuk* כֹּל אֲשֶׁר נִשְׁמַת־רוּחַ חַיִּים בְּאַפָּיו מִכֹּל אֲשֶׁר בֶּחָרָבָה מֵתוּ (Bereishis 7:22) that the breath of a person is his life, and if an individual cannot breathe on his own then you're allowed to pull the plug attached to the respirator. It's not always so simple to figure out if an individual is breathing on his own or not, but there are ways which you can utilize to examine whether the patient can breathe on his own or not. If you see the patient cannot currently breathe on his own, then Rav Moshe (Igros Moshe

---

[30] Rambam Rotze'ach (1:9) - אַף זוֹ מִצְוַת לֹא תַעֲשֶׂה שֶׁלֹּא לָחוּס עַל נֶפֶשׁ הָרוֹדֵף לְפִיכָךְ הוֹרוּ חֲכָמִים שֶׁהָעֻבָּרָה שֶׁהִיא מַקְשָׁה לֵילֵד מֻתָּר לַחְתֹּךְ הָעֻבָּר בְּמֵעֶיהָ בֵּין בְּסַם בֵּין בְּיָד מִפְּנֵי שֶׁהוּא כְּרוֹדֵף אַחֲרֶיהָ לְהָרְגָהּ וְאִם מִשֶּׁהוֹצִיא רֹאשׁוֹ אֵין נוֹגְעִין בּוֹ שֶׁאֵין דּוֹחִין נֶפֶשׁ מִפְּנֵי נֶפֶשׁ וְזֶהוּ טִבְעוֹ שֶׁל עוֹלָם

[31] Sanhedrin (72a) - התורה אמרה אם בא להורגך השכם להורגו

YD 3:132)[32] says you can pull the plug on the respirator because there is no hope he will breathe on his own in the future. However, if you are the doctor in a situation where it is forbidden to pull the plug or abort a child, then you must give all of your money to prevent yourself from transgressing the *issur*. For a *mitzva*, you are not obligated to spend more than one-fifth of your property (Kesubos 50a)[33], but you are obligated to give up your job and all your money to not transgress a negative commandment (Rema 656:1)[34]. The same thing applies to a situation where you need to desecrate Shabbos to keep your job – you must keep Shabbos and leave your job.

Q8. If you see a doctor going to turn off a respirator, are you obligated to kill him as a *rodef* (Shulchan Aruch CM 425:1)[35]?

---

[32] Igros Moshe YD (3:132) - הנה בדבר ידיעת מיתת האדם מפורש בגמ׳ יומא דף פ״ה ע״א בנפל מפולת על האדם שמפקחין את הגל אפילו בשבת ובודקין עד חוטמו ואיפסק כן ברמב״ם פ״ב משבת הי״ט ובש״ע או״ח סימן שכ״ט סעי׳ ד׳ שאם לא הרגישו שום חיות הוא בדין מת שהוא בבדיקת הנשימה שאף אם הנשימה קלה מאד נמי הוא בדין חי שרואין זה ע״י נוצה וע״י חתיכת נייר דקה שמשימין אצל החוטם אם לא מתנדנד הוא בחזקת מת אבל צריך שיבדקו בזה איזה פעמים כדבארתי באגרות משה ח״ב דיו״ד סימן קע״ד ענף ב׳ בבאור דברי הרמב״ם בפ״ד אבל ה״ה שכתב ישהא מעט שמא נתעלף שהוא זמן דאי אפשר לחיות בלא נשימה והוא דוקא כשהסתכלו כל זמן זה בלא היסח הדעת אף לרגע קטן וראו שלא נשם כל העת אבל כיון שאי אפשר לאינשי להסתכל אף משך זמן קצר בלא היסח הדעת שיש לחוש שמא נתחזק מעט ונשם איזה נשימות ונחלש עוד הפעם וחזר ונתחזק אי אפשר לידע אלא שיבדקו איזה פעמים ואם יראו שאינו נושם זהו סימן המיתה שיש לסמור על זה ואין להרהר

[33] Kesubos (50a) - א״ר אילעא באושא התקינו המבזבז אל יבזבז יותר מחומש תניא נמי הכי המבזבז אל יבזבז יותר מחומש שמא יצטרך לבריות ומעשה באחד שבקש לבזבז [יותר מחומש] ולא הניח לו חבירו ומנו רבי ישבב ואמרי לה רבי ישבב ולא הניחו חבירו ומנו רבי עקיבא

[34] Rema (656:1) - מי שאין לו אתרוג או שאר מצוה עוברת אין צריך לבזבז עליה הון רב וכמו שאמרו המבזבז אל יבזבז יותר מחומש אפי׳ מצוה עוברת ודוקא מצות עשה אבל לא תעשה יתן כל ממונו קודם שיעבור

[35] Shulchan Aruch CM (425:1) - הרודף אחר חבירו להרגו והזהירוהו והרי הוא רודף אחריו אפי׳ היה הרודף קטן הרי כל ישראל מצויים להצילו באבר

22

A: (5779) It's not so easy to know in each case whether the doctor is allowed to turn off the respirator or not. As we explained before, you need to conduct the test to examine whether you can pull the plug or not. Nonetheless, even if you're a fellow doctor and you know the patient is able to breathe under his own power, you're not allowed to kill the doctor pulling the plug.

Q9. Is a doctor obligated to refer a patient to a bigger expert if he himself is able to perform the same procedure, but the other expert can do it better?

A: (5779) There are different ways to perform an operation. For instance, the old way they would remove a gallbladder, they would cut open the stomach area, remove the gallbladder, stitch it up, and it would take about six weeks to recover. Another way to do it is by making a couple of holes, inserting a movie camera through a pipe, use one hole for the camera to see precisely where the gallbladder is and the other hole to remove the gallbladder. That procedure is what they call laparoscopic surgery. It's much easier to surgically remove the gallbladder when everything is open with lights on in contrast to the darker laparoscopic surgery. The biggest risk in surgery is the anesthesia since if the anesthesiologist gives too much anesthesia then the patient will die and if there's too little anesthesia then the patient will create some trouble by waking up in the middle of the operation. The operation is typically done better if everything is open, and it's difficult to develop yourself into a skilled laparoscopic surgeon. Just because you don't have the ability to perform the surgery using laparoscopic methods doesn't mean you shouldn't perform the surgery in the way you know best. My understanding is that the operation of removing a gallbladder is done better using the old methods, so I don't know if you are obligated to send a patient elsewhere. The right thing for a doctor to do would be to inform the patient that there are alternative methods of performing the surgery and that you're not the expert in the different methods other than

---

מאברי הרודף ואם אינם יכולים לכוין ולא להצילו אלא א"כ יהרגו לרודף הרי אלו הורגים אותו אע"פ שעדיין לא הרג

the one you're good at. Then let the patient make their own decisions.

Q10. Is there a preference to go to a male or female doctor?

A: (5779) If you have something serious, you should go to the best doctor there is. It doesn't make any difference if the doctor is a man, woman, gorilla – it doesn't make any difference as long as the doctor is the best available (Rema EH 21:5)[36].

Q11. If the halacha for a non-Jew is לא מעלין ולא מורידין (Avoda Zara 26a)[37] (Shulchan Aruch 158:1)[38], why is it permitted for a Jewish doctor to treat a non-Jewish patient (who is an idol worshipper)?

A: (5779) First of all, the Chazon Ish says that the halacha of לא מעלין ולא מורידין does not apply nowadays. He says it is similar to a *mashal* where someone has a white suit which is covered with black stains. Even if you give it to the cleaners, it's not going to fix the entire suit. If there are just one or two stains on your suit, then the dry cleaners could get rid of the stains. Nowadays since there are so many people who do bad things, לא מעלין doesn't apply. Even when the halacha did apply

---

[36] Rema EH (21:5) - וי"א דכל שאינו עושה דרך חבה רק כוונתו לשם שמים ואין נראה - (195:20) and Shach YD מותר לכן נהגו להקל בדברים אלו דודאי אף להרמב"ם ליכא איסור דאורייתא אלא כשעושה כן דרך תאוה וחיבת ביאה כמש"ל סי' קנ"ז ס"ק י' מה שאין כן הכא וכן המנהג פשוט שרופאים ישראלים ממששים הדפק של אשה אפילו אשת איש או עובדת כוכבים אע"פ שיש רופאים אחרים עובדי כוכבים וכן עושים שאר מיני משמושים ע"פ דרכי הרפואה אלא הדבר פשוט כמ"ש וזה נראה דעת הרב דלעיל בסי' קנ"ז משמע מדבריו כהרמב"ם וכמו שכתבתי שם בס"ק י' וכאן התיר מישוש הדפק מ"מ באין סכנה אסור לבעלה למשש הדפק כשהיא נדה

[37] Avoda Zara (26a) - סבר רב יוסף למימר הא דתניא העובדי כוכבים ורועי בהמה דקה לא מעלין ולא מורידין אסוקי בשכר שרי משום איבה

[38] Shulchan Aruch (158:1) - עובדי עבודת כוכבים מז' עממין שאין בינינו וביניהם מלחמה ורועי בהמה דקה מישראל בארץ ישראל בזמן שהיו רוב השדות של ישראל וכיוצא בהן אין מסבבים להם המיתה ואסור להצילם אם נטו למות כגון שראה א' מהם שנפל לים אינו מעלהו אם יתן לו שכר לפיכך אין לרפאותן אפילו בשכר אם לא היכא דאיכא משום איבה

in former times, that was only talking about those who served לְהַעֲבִיר גִּלּוּלִים מִן הָאָרֶץ וְהָאֱלִילִים כָּרוֹת יִכָּרֵתוּן לְתַקֵּן עוֹלָם בְּמַלְכוּת שַׁקִי. The non-Jews of today believe in the Ribono Shel Olam – even if they believe in someone else also. The Rema (156:1)[39] says only we are commanded in not having other gods, while the other nations of the world aren't commanded in לֹא יִהְיֶה־לְךָ אֱלֹהִים אֲחֵרִים עַל־פָּנַי (Shemos 20:3). Nonetheless, the Protestants and Martin Luther reformed the Catholic religion and no longer believe in their founder as a god. They might consider him like an intermediary like the golden calf (Ramban Shemos 32:1)[40] – I'm not exactly sure and I don't know if they're so sure either – but they believe in the Ribono Shel Olam so there is no halacha of לא מעלין ולא מורידין. Not only is it permitted for a Jewish doctor to treat a non-Jewish patient, but if he doesn't treat the non-Jewish patient then he can cause a lot of animosity towards Klal Yisroel. In fact, Rav Moshe (Igros Moshe OC 4:79)[41] says a Jewish doctor can desecrate Shabbos to treat a non-Jew because it's a danger for Jews since

---

[39] Rema (156:1) - ויש מקילין בעשיית שותפות עם העכו"ם בזמן הזה משום שאין העכו"ם בזה"ז נשבעים בע"א ואע"ג דמזכירין העבודה זרה מ"מ כוונתם לעושה שמים וארץ אלא שמשתתפים שם שמים ודבר אחר ולא מצינו שיש בזה משום לפני עור לא תתן מכשול דהרי אינם מוזהרים על השתוף

[40] Ramban Shemos (32:1) - אבל הענין כמו שאמרתי שלא בקשו העגל להיות להם לאל ממית ומחיה וקבלו עבודת אלהותו אבל ירצו שיהיה להם במקום משה מורה דרכם וזהו התנצלותו של אהרן טען כי לא אמרו לי רק שאעשה להם אלהים אשר ילכו לפניהם במקומך אדני שלא ידעו מה היה לך ואם תשוב אם לא ולכן הם היו צריכין למי שיורה להם דרכם כל זמן שלא תהיה אתה עמהם ואם אולי תשוב יעזבוהו וילכו אחריך כבראשונה

[41] Igros Moshe OC (4:79) - אבל כשנזדמן שהוא מוכרח להיות שבת בבית החולים או כשהוא כבר רופא קבוע שאף שהמשרד שלו סגור בשבת בא דוקא אליו נכרי חולה בדבר שהוא סכנה הוא מוכרח להזדקק לו אף בחלול שבת באיסור דאורייתא וכ"ש כשנזדמן איזה אסון סמוך לביתו שקורין לרופא הסמוך יותר מאחר דלא מתקבל במדינותינו הדחיים שאמר אביי הוא סכנה ממש בעצם לגופו ממש מקרובי החולה וגם אם הוא אינו חושש שתהא סכנה לו בעצמו יש לחוש לאיבה גדולה כל כך מצד אנשי המדינה וגם מהממשלה שיש ודאי לחוש גם לעניני סכנה מתוצאות זה ואף שהתוס' שם ד"ה סבר תמהין איך אפשר להתיר משום איבה איסורא דאורייתא כפי המצב במדינותינו בזמן הזה איכא מצד איבה סכנה גדולה אף במדינות שהרשות לכל אדם מישראל להתנהג בדיני התורה שהוא עכ"פ שלא כשע"י זה לא ירצה להציל נפשות

that will rouse more anti-Semitism. Today throughout Europe they have police officers outside every shul because they don't know what's going to happen – אם ירצה השם we don't need to come onto that in America, but the anti-Semitism in America seems to be getting worse.

Q12. If a doctor is called on Shabbos for a non-Jewish patient, is he allowed to order an Uber to take him to the hospital?

A: (5779) Yes, a doctor is allowed to call an Uber to take him to the hospital for a non-Jewish patient (Igros Moshe OC 4:79)[42].

Q13. May one go to a non-religious Jewish doctor? Is it better to avoid them?

A: (5779) You should go to the best doctor available – whether he's religious, not religious, or not Jewish. If you have two equal doctors who are both trustworthy, then I would say it's better to go to the Jewish doctor even if he's not religious.

Q14. If two patients enter the emergency room – one is certainly an emergency and will live a few more months with treatment while the second is unsure if it's an emergency but he'll naturally live a full life after treatment – who should a doctor treat first?

---

[42] Igros Moshe OC (4:79) - אבל כשנזדמן שהוא מוכרח להיות שבת בבית החולים או כשהוא כבר רופא קבוע שאף שהמשרד שלו סגור בשבת בא דוקא אליו נכרי חולה בדבר שהוא סכנה הוא מוכרח להזדקק לו אף בחלול שבת באיסור דאורייתא וכ"ש כשנזדמן איזה אסון סמוך לביתו שקורין לרופא הסמוך יותר מאחר דלא מתקבל במדינותינו הדחוים שאמר אביי הוא סכנה ממש גם בעצם לגופו ממש מקרובי החולה וגם הוא אם אינו חושש שתהא סכנה לו בעצמו יש לחוש לאיבה גדולה כל כך מצד אנשי המדינה וגם מהממשלה שיש ודאי לחוש גם לעניני סכנה מתוצאות זה ואף שהתוס' שם ד"ה סבר תמהין איך אפשר להתיר משום איבה איסורא דאורייתא, כפי המצב במדינותינו בזמן הזה איכא מצד איבה סכנה גדולה אף במדינות שהרשות לכל אדם מישראל להתנהג בדיני התורה שהוא עכ"פ שלא כשע"י זה לא ירצה להציל נפשות

Chapter 2: Doctors in Halacha

A: (5755) Rav Moshe (Igros Moshe CM 2:73:1)[43] says that there are two different factors to consider in this question. If both patients arrive at the same time, then the patient who will live a full life is given preference for treatment because *chayei olam* precedes *chayei sha'ah*. However, if the patient who will live a couple months after treatment arrives before the patient who can live a full life, then you should continue treating the first patient despite the fact that it will prevent you from treating the patient who will live a full life if treated. This entire *shailah* is only a question for the doctor as opposed to the patients since the patients themselves have no obligation to relinquish their right to treatment for another patient. Even if the first patient will only live another couple months isn't paying for treatment because he's a charity case, once the doctors already begin working with him he acquires the *zechus* of being treated in the emergency room. In fact, the first patient is not even allowed to give up his *chayei sha'ah* for another patient's *chayei olam*.

Q15. Based on the previous question of two patients – one who will live for a couple months and another who will live a full life – which patient do you treat first if they are both

---

[43] Igros Moshe CM (2:73:1) - ועדיין והכניסוהו אחד רק כשבא ובדיעבד
לא התחילו לטפל בו ובא השני הנה נראה לע"ד שאם באו שניהם בבת אחת היינו
קודם שהכניסו האחד מהם צריך להכניס בתחלה את מי שלדעת הרופאים
הנמצאים שם יכולין לרפאותו אם גם לחולה זה צריך להתחיל תיכף אם יש צורך
אף מספק ואם כבר הכניסו שם את החולה שלדעתם הוא רק לחיי שעה אין מוציאין
אותו משם בין שהכניסוהו כדין מחמת שעדיין לא היה שם חולה השני ובין שעשו
שלא כדין בין שוגגין או מזידין אין מוציאין אותו משם והטעם פשוט דודאי חיי
הראוי להתרפא ולחיות כל ימי חייו הראוין שיחיה כדרך סתם אינשי עדיפא מאלו
שעומדין למות מצד חולי שלהן שלא ידוע להרופאים רפואה למחלתן אבל זה הוא
לעלמא דלהחולה עצמו ליכא חיוב להציל נפש אחרים בנפשו וכיון שהכניסוהו
להיחידה לרפאותו כבר זכה במקום לא מיבעיא כשהוא משלם בעד הזמן שנמצא
בבית החולים בין שאינו משלם שמרפאין שם בחנם ואף אם רק לעניים בחנם
והוא עני מ"מ כבר קנה במה שהובא שם להיות שם הזמן שצריך להיות שם
והשעבודים שיש על ביה"ח והרופאים דשם לרפאותו ואינו מחוייב ואולי גם אסור
שיתן את זכותו שעי"ז יהיה החיי שעה שהוא הזמן קצר שאפשר לו לחיות לחולה
אחר אף שראוי לחיות כשיתרפא כל ימיו הקבועים לו

27

waiting in the ER yet the first patient arrived first in the waiting room?

A: (5755) Rav Moshe (Igros Moshe CM 2:74:1)[44] explains that if the doctors decide to start treating the second patient who can live a full life before treating the first patient who arrived in the ER first, then he'll think the doctors have given up home on him. "Why else would the medical staff have taken this other patient when I came here first?" The doctors will be crushing his spirit making him think there's no hope – and doing that is forbidden since you might be causing his death. They say all the people who gave up hope in the concentration camps died but those who made it through were the ones who still held onto the hope of leaving. Some of them couldn't hold out, but those who gave up hope were certainly as good as dead. Therefore, Rav Moshe says you cannot make the first patient believe there is no hope for him. Moreover, even if the patient knows he has a terminal illness but might feel hopeless if you skip over treating him before another patient, you must treat him if he came to the emergency room first. If the two patients arrive at the same time, you always take the patient who will live a long life.

Q16. What precautions must a Jewish medical student take when dealing with a cadaver in anatomy class (granted the student is not a Kohen)?

---

[44] Igros Moshe CM (2:74:1) - ואף ענין קדימה ליכא אלא במה שתנן במתני׳ דסוף הוריות (י״ג) ואף באלו קשה לעשות מעשה בלא עיון גדול. ואף באופן שיודעין שלפי הדין יש קדימה ודאי הוא דוקא כששוין בזמן ויש להרופא לילך למי שנקרא קודם שהרי תיכף נתחייב לילך לשם ולהשני שלא נקרא עדיין לא נתחייב עד שנקרא. ורק אם השני הוא חולה מהראשון יש לו לילך להשני מאחר שהוא חולה ביותר והכרעת דבר זה תלוי בדעת הרופא וכן אם לחולה השני יודע הרופא איך לרפאותו ולחולה הראשון אינו יודע אלא שהוא להשקיט רוחו היה מסתבר לכאורה שיש לו לילך תחלה להחולה שיודע לו רפואה אבל ודאי לפעמים יש להרופא לילך קודם למי שהוא רק להשקיט רוחו כשיבין מזה שהוא חולה גדול ומיואש מהרופאים כיון שלפי הדרך היה צריך הרופא לילך אצלו קודם ומזה יש לחוש שיסתכן וצריך הרופא לעיין בהכרעתו היטב ולשם שמים לחיוב שעליו לרפא מאחר שהוא הרופא בעיר ובסביבתה ובעיר גדולה כששני החולים הם מאלו שמחזיקין אותו לרופא שלהם

Chapter 2: Doctors in Halacha

A: (5779) It is very difficult to find out whether the cadaver is a Jew. If someone tells you that the individual is a Jew, you have to wonder whether or not this person can be believed for this. Moreover, even if the cadaver has a *bris*, that doesn't mean anything since they often perform circumcisions in hospitals too. Even if his last name is Horowitz, that doesn't mean he's Jewish since his father might be Jewish while his mother isn't. I don't think it's likely for a medical student to find out whether the cadaver is Jewish or not. If you're working on a non-Jewish cadaver, then there aren't too many questions about working on the body as part of medical school. We're not talking about a case where the individual is clinically dead yet might not be considered dead according to the Torah. Killing such an individual – whether Jewish or not – would be considered murder and transgress לא תרצח (Shemos 20:13)[45]. Nonetheless, assuming they took this cadaver out of the freezer for you to work on, then the cadaver is considered dead. He might not have been put into the freezer dead according to the standards of the Torah, but he's certainly dead now. If somehow you know the cadaver is Jewish, then there's a question of *bizayon hameis* – degrading the deceased (Noda B'Yehuda YD 210)[46]. However, when a person dies suddenly without any known illness, then the state he was living in will very likely have a law which requires conducting medical tests and an autopsy to find out whether he was murdered or not. Was he poisoned to death, did he inhale poisonous gas, or the like? Someone who is sick with heart problems generally isn't investigated by the state, but someone who is considered perfectly healthy yet dies

---

[45] Shemos (20:13) - לֹא תִּרְצָח לֹא תִּנְאָף לֹא תִּגְנֹב לֹא־תַעֲנֶה בְרֵעֲךָ עֵד שָׁקֶר

[46] Noda B'Yehuda YD (210) - אבל בנדון דידן אין כאן שום חולה הצריך לזה רק שרוצים ללמוד חכמה זו אולי יזדמן חולה שיהיה צריך לזה ודאי דלא דחינן משום חששא קלה זו שום איסור תורה או אפילו איסור דרבנן שאם אתה קורא לחששא זו ספק נפשות א"כ יהיה כל מלאכת הרפואות שחיקת ובישול סמנים והכנת כלי איזמל להקזה מותר בשבת שמא יזדמן היום או בלילה חולה שיהיה צורך לזה ולחלק בין חששא לזמן קרוב לחששא לזמן רחוק קשה לחלק. וחלילה להתיר דבר זה ואפילו רופאי האומות אינם עושים נסיון בחכמת הניתוח ע"י שום מת כי אם בהרוגים ע"פ משפט או במי שהסכים בעצמו בחייו לכך ואם אנו ח"ו מקילים בדבר זה א"כ ינתחו כל המתים כדי ללמוד סידור אברים הפנימים ומהותן כדי שידעו לעשות רפואות להחיים

29

suddenly raises red flags. Then they hold onto the person for a couple weeks to determine the cause of death. Rav Moshe (Igros Moshe YD 2:151)[47] says that if you are investigating the cause of death for a Jewish individual, you are allowed to draw blood with a syringe for a blood test because that is a normal procedure done for people who are alive too. That's not considered degrading the *meis*. Depending on the doctor in charge of the morgue, very often this is sufficient to determine whether there is any suspicion of murder. They might require performing MRIs or CT scans to see if there was any internal trauma, but that is also permitted because it's done to live people as well. In fact, the Agudah of Maryland worked with the medical facilities to have them satisfied with the results of blood tests and MRI/CT scans to investigate whether a murder took place.

Q17. What should a Jewish medical student do in Israel?

A: (5779) Most of the people living in Israel are Jewish, so a medical student would need to assume he's working on a Jew. However, I'm sure they have Rabbonim in Eretz Yisroel who *poskin* these *shailos* for them. Chazal say that if you find a child on the street but don't know whether he's a Jew or not, then you follow the majority of people in that neighborhood (Kesubos 15b)[48]. Rav Yehuda says you follow the majority of people who cast their children away (Mishna Machshirim 2:7)[49]. A Jew doesn't ordinarily throw a child onto the street. Even if most people living on the street are Jews, Rav Yehuda

---

[47] Igros Moshe YD (2:151) - אבל נראה לע"ד דאם לא יחתכו האברים ולא יפתחו צוארו ובטנו רק רוצים לתחוב לנידעל להוציא ממנו איזה לחלוחית להודע מזה איזו דברים הנוגעים להמחלה שזה אין להחשיב לניוול שהרי דבר כזה מצוי טובא בזמננו שעושים כן גם לחיים ויש להתיר בפשטות וכן להוציא מעט דם לבדוק וכדומה ע"י נידעל אינו ניוול ויש להתיר

[48] Kesubos (15b) - מצא בה תינוק מושלך אם רוב עובדי כוכבים עובד כוכבי' אם רוב ישראל ישראל מחצה על מחצה ישראל ואמר רב לא שנו אלא להחיותו אבל ליוחסין לא ושמואל אמר לפקח עליו את הגל

[49] Mishna Machshirim (2:7) - מָצָא בָהּ תִּינוֹק מֻשְׁלָךְ אִם רֹב נָכְרִים נָכְרִי. וְאִם רֹב יִשְׂרָאֵל יִשְׂרָאֵל מֶחֱצָה לְמֶחֱצָה יִשְׂרָאֵל רַבִּי יְהוּדָה אוֹמֵר הוֹלְכִין אַחַר רֹב הַמַּשְׁלִיכִין

says the child is still considered a non-Jew under the assumption that his non-Jewish parents threw him out. This makes a difference regarding whether you follow most people who live in the community where this individual was murdered or the majority of people who are murdered. Either way, we don't *poskin* like Rav Yehuda and just follow the majority.

Q18. What should a Kohen do in medical school?

A: (5779) A Kohen is allowed to be in the same room as a non-Jewish cadaver, but is not allowed to touch or move a non-Jewish cadaver (Rambam Tumas Meis 1:13)[50]. The Mechaber didn't want to *poskin* that a non-Jew isn't *metameh b'ohel* (Shulchan Aruch YD 372:2)[51], but *b'dieved* he's lenient that a non-Jew isn't *metameh b'ohel* and would only be *metameh* through *maga u'masa*. I don't think a person can learn to be a doctor by just watching other people involved in the practice of medicine. He needs to get involved with it himself. The way the medical school system is in place right now in America, it doesn't really work for a Kohen to become a doctor. There might be other countries which don't require medical students to touch cadavers, but I wouldn't want to use a doctor who only learned through virtual learning. There are some medical schools which are starting to use synthetic cadavers, and I have no problem with that.

Q19. Is a person allowed *lechatchila* to choose a residency or field of medicine that will force him to desecrate Shabbos?

A: (5779) If he knows he must desecrate Shabbos, then he is not allowed to choose such a residency. If it's possible for him to change his schedule with another resident to allow him to be Shomer Shabbos, then that is fine – but he should choose the

---

[50] Rambam Tumas Meis (1:13) - וְאֵין הָעַכּוּ"ם מְטַמֵּא בְּאֹהֶל וְדָבָר זֶה קַבָּלָה הוּא וַהֲרֵי הוּא אוֹמֵר בְּמִלְחֶמֶת מִדְיָן (במדבר לא:יט) כֹּל נֹגֵעַ בֶּחָלָל וְלֹא הַזְכִּיר שָׁם אֹהֶל

[51] Shulchan Aruch YD (372:2) - קברי עובדי כוכבים נכון ליזהר הכהן מלילך עליהם (אע"פ שיש מקילין) ונכון להחמיר

residency which allows him to become the best doctor that he possibly can without desecrating Shabbos. If you are unable to maneuver your residency schedule to avoid desecrating Shabbos, you still cannot be *mechalel* Shabbos. There are residencies where you can switch around your Shabbos and Yom Tov schedule with other people. If you can't figure that out, you might be able to figure out a way not to desecrate Shabbos by just staying close to the hospital on Shabbos or Yom Tov, hire a nurse to insert your patients' information into the computer, etc. A lot of things doctors do in the hospital do not require desecrating Shabbos. For instance, if you need to check inside the patient's ears, then you can tell the patient to press the light button to look inside. The patient is doing it for himself because he's the one being tested (Shulchan Aruch 244:1)[52]. Alternatively, you can have your nurse turn on the light for you. The doctor cannot draw blood himself since that is forbidden on Shabbos *m'doraysa* (Shulchan Aruch 328:48)[53], so you would need to have your nurse do that. You cannot desecrate Shabbos for a residency, but you can probably figure out ways around it so that you're not *mechalel* Shabbos yourself.

Q20. What does one do when medical protocol conflicts with halacha?

A: (5779) Let's say the patient is considered brain dead, and medical protocol is to pull the plug on such an individual. These kinds of questions depend on what you consider dead. If a person has a stroke, the left arm might work while the right one doesn't – we don't say the person is dead. Similarly, when the

---

[52] Shulchan Aruch (244:1) - פוסק אדם [פי' מתנה] עם העכו"ם על המלאכה וקוצץ דמים והעכו"ם עושה לעצמו ואע"פ שהוא עושה בשבת מותר

[53] Shulchan Aruch (328:48) - אסור להניח בגד על מכה שיוצ' ממנו דם and Mishna Berura 147 - מפני שהדם יצבע אותו ואסור להוציא דם מהמכה שאסור לדחוק בידיו על המכה כדי להוציא דם או כשצורך איזה דבר על המכה [אפילו בדבר דלית ביה משום צביעה] אסור להדקה כדי שיצא דם דהוא חובל והוי אב מלאכה ויש שסוברין דה"ה אם מניח על המכה דבר שמושך ליחה ודם [כגון צו"ק זאל"ב וכיו"ב] ג"כ הוי מלאכה דאורייתא כיון שנתכוין לזה ועכ"פ איסור בודאי יש

brain stops working but the heart is still pumping, why would we consider the person dead? It's not as simple as I'm making it out to be. The brain has three parts. One part controls the muscles by sending messages to various parts of the body to move. All the muscles are hooked up to the nervous system which the brain uses to make the muscles expand or contract. Then there's a part of the brain which is connected to eyesight, reasoning, memory, etc. I don't want to confuse you with the fancy names for each part of the brain. Rav Moshe has a *teshuva* (Igros Moshe YD 2:146)[54] discussing what is considered death according to the Torah. Although others may disagree with it, Rav Moshe was the Rav of America. He explains that it says in the Mishna (Yoma 83a)[55], "If a building collapsed on top of an individual and he is somewhere in this building where we don't know whether he's alive or not, you are allowed to desecrate Shabbos or Yom Kippur to remove all the lumber and bricks with a crane until you reach his nose. Then you can see whether he's breathing or not." (Yoma 85a)[56] If he's still breathing then you are allowed to continue desecrating Shabbos to save him, but if he is no longer breathing then you must stop desecrating Shabbos. It seems that according to the Mishna, we focus on whether the person is

---

[54] Igros Moshe YD (2:146) - אבל ברור ופשוט שאין החוטם האבר שהוא נותן החיות בהאדם וגם אינו מאברים שהנשמה תלויה בו כלל אלא דהמוח והלב הם אלו הנותנים חיות להאדם וגם שיהיה לו שייך לנשום ע"י חוטמו ורק הוא האבר שדרך שם נעשה מעשה הנשימה שבאין ע"י המוח והלב ואית לנו הסימן חיות רק ע"י החוטם אף שלא הוא הנותן ענין הנשימה משום שאין אנו מכירים היטב בלב ובטבור וכ"ש שאין מכירין במוח וכוונת הקרא דנשמת רוח חיים באפיו לא על עצם רוח החיים שזה ודאי ליכא בחוטם אלא הרוח חיים שאנו רואין איכא באפיו אף שלא נראה באברים הגדולים אברי התנועה וגם אחר שלא ניכר גם בדפיקת הלב ולא ניכר בטבור שלכן נמצא שלעניין פקוח הגל בשבת תלוי רק בחוטם

[55] Yoma (83a) - מי שנפלה עליו מפולת ספק הוא שם ספק אינו שם ספק חי ספק מת ספק כותי ספק ישראל מפקחין עליו את הגל מצאוהו חי מפקחין ואם מת יניחוהו

[56] Yoma (85a) - תנו רבנן עד היכן הוא בודק עד חוטמו ויש אומרים עד לבו בדק

breathing or not (Shulchan Aruch 329:4)[57]. Now breathing is an action which takes place automatically without thoughts – just as you blink without thinking. Those actions which don't require thought on your part are governed by the brain stem. If a person's brain stem (medulla) is dead, then he can no longer breathe and is considered dead. Hence, Rav Moshe says that even if the other parts of the brain are still functioning – he can still think and see – he is considered dead. The heart has its own ability to continue pumping even without the brain. That's why it's possible for the heart to continue functioning even though the brain may be dead. The heart is a muscle, and the muscle requires oxygen in order for it to move. Since lungs provide the oxygen for the heart, if the lungs are not working then the heart no longer receives oxygen and will only work for another minute or two after the brain dies. Nowadays, it's possible to insert an artificial heart to pump blood throughout the body – like during certain types of heart surgery. Even though you can separate the brain and the heart, Rav Moshe says a person who cannot breathe is considered dead according to halacha. Once he's considered dead according to halacha, you can take him off the respirator.

Q21. May a woman training to be a nurse or a doctor wear pants scrubs for surgery if it is all that is available?

A: (5779) If this is required by the hospital – and there is no other way (wearing a lab coat on top of the scrubs) – then it is permitted.

Q22. What do Chazal mean when they say the best of doctors go to Gehinnom (Kiddushin 82a - טוב שברופאים לגיהנם)?

A: (5779) Many doctors transgress לא תרצח quite often (Shemos 20:13)[58]. As a matter of fact, it's the opinion of most

---

[57] Shulchan Aruch (329:4) - אפי' מצאוהו מרוצץ שאינו יכול לחיות אלא לפי שעה מפקחים ובודקים עד חוטמו אם לא הרגישו בחוטמו חיות אז ודאי מת לא שנא פגעו בראשו תחלה לא שנא פגעו ברגליו תחילה

[58] Shemos (20:13) - לֹא תִּרְצָח לֹא תִּנְאָף לֹא תִּגְנֹב לֹא־תַעֲנֶה בְרֵעֲךָ עֵד שָׁקֶר

hospitals that if the patient is no longer worth keeping alive, they take care of him. This stems from insurance issues because the United States government (Medicare) used to pay for a patient to be in the hospital for as long as the hospital staff said he needed to stay there. I'm not talking about Medicaid. Now the government pays a set amount of money per hospital visit for each patient. If they're able to send the patient out of the hospital faster, then they get to keep all the money which enables them to open up a hospital bed for another patient. This way they can potentially double their income. However, they made a new law that if the patient returns to the hospital due to the lesser quality medical care, then the hospital must pay for the treatment out of the original sum of money given at the beginning of the treatment. There's only one way the hospitals can ensure the patient doesn't come back to complain that he is still suffering from the heart problem they attempted to treat.

Q23. Are there androgynous or *tumtum* nowadays? Can they be changed medically?

A: (5779) Yes, there are certainly still androgynous and *tumtum* individuals nowadays.

Q24. If someone with a DNR (do not resuscitate) collapses, are you obligated to save him even if the patient will sue?

A: (5779) If you can save such a person, then you are obligated to save the patient. How can he sue you for saving him? Either way, I'm not so sure if he can sue you – even if he can sue you, you need to give up one fifth of your money to save him (Rema 656:1)[59]. Nonetheless, that doesn't mean that you need to give up your livelihood. Also, if the patient is a non-Jew with a DNR then you do not need to save him.

Q25. If a person writes a DNR but he would probably live after CPR, should we save the patient?

---

[59] Rema (656:1) - מי שאין לו אתרוג או שאר מצוה עוברת אין צריך לבזבז עליה הון רב וכמו שאמרו המבזבז אל יבזבז יותר מחומש אפי' מצוה עוברת ודוקא מצות עשה אבל לא תעשה יתן כל ממונו קודם שיעבור

A: (5755) If the patient would be so upset after regaining consciousness finding out that you performed CPR on him against his will – and his aggravation might cause his death – then you should not perform CPR. However, if he can be calmed down after successfully administering CPR and he would be willing to want to live longer, then it would be a *mitzva* to save him. Nonetheless, if he is conscious and says not to resuscitate him, then you should not save the patient because the aggravation of being saved against his will might actively cause his death as opposed to passively allowing him to die.

Q26. Can a doctor perform tests on a fetus to see if it's healthy?

A: (5755) If a family has a medical history of certain illnesses like Tay-Sachs Disease, then they would likely want the doctors to test the fetus so they can make an intelligent decision on what to do if the fetus will be sick. Rav Moshe (Igros Moshe CM 2:69:3)[60] says that the doctors cannot perform these tests on the fetus because there's nothing you can do to alleviate the fetus' situation at this point anyway since you're not allowed to abort the fetus just because it won't live for more than 3 or 4 years – the general life expectancy for a child with Tay-Sachs Disease (Igros Moshe CM 2:69:3)[61]. Therefore, it's better for the couple not to put themselves into the *nisayon* of aborting their child when performing such a procedure isn't permitted. Additionally, Rav Moshe says that the doctors themselves cannot say with certainty what will happen to the fetus. I know a story of a woman who had German Measles when she was pregnant. Ordinarily, if a pregnant woman contracts German

---

[60] Igros Moshe (CM 2:69:3) – שלכן נשתוממתי בראותי תשובה מחכם אחד בא"י הנכתב למנהל ביה"ח שערי צדק ונדפס בחוברת אסיא י"ג המתיר הולדות שע"י בחינות תרופאיס כשהוא עובר יותר מג"ח שהעובר הוא במחלת תיי-סקס להפילו...ועל שו"ת רב פעלים שג"כ היה ירא לפסוק בזה שלכן מסיק להתיר בתיי-סקס להפיל עד שבעה חדשים ולא מובן זמן זה שלא מצינו כלל

[61] Igros Moshe (CM 2:69:3) - וברור ופשוט כדכתבתי הלכה הברורה ע"פ רבותינו הראשונים המפרשים והפוסקים ממש שאסור בדין רציחה ממש כל עובר בין כשר בין ממזר בין סתם עוברים ובין הידועים לחולי תיי-סקס שכולן אסורין מדינא ממש

Measles during the first trimester of pregnancy, it will likely cause a deformity in the fetus as the child might not be able to see, hear, talk, etc. Therefore, the parents asked Rav Moshe what to do since the mother contracted German Measles. He told them that they certainly were not allowed to abort the fetus and that they shouldn't worry because the child will be OK. And so it was. How did Rav Moshe know the child would be OK? He said that most children born whose mothers had German Measles in the first trimester were born without any deformities. On the other hand, doctors tell the parents that their child will likely develop a deformity and that they should abort the fetus in order to take themselves legally off the hook. Anything Rav Moshe wrote in his *teshuvos* was written after discussions with doctors. His own son-in-law Rav Tendler is a biochemist who knows a lot about medicine, and Rav Moshe himself would speak with many medical professionals.

Q27: What must you ensure is provided for a patient?

A: (5778) Rav Moshe (Igros Moshe CM 2:75) says you must provide air, nutrition, hydration for patients. You cannot starve a patient to death. Sometimes a patient will just stop eating and aspirate the food you insert in their stomach. Often these occasions lead to the food entering the lungs. At that point, the Ribono Shel Olam decided the person will no longer accept food and by giving him food you might be the cause of his death by having the food enter his lungs. You must ask the doctor what will happen if the patient will receive food. Don't ask him whether they should save the patient or not. Nowadays, there is a push on the side of most hospitals to get rid of their patients – not because they want to kill the patient. It's all money driven. If someone has a heart attack today, there's a certain amount of money insurance will cover, a certain amount Medicare will cover, and a certain amount Medicaid will cover – which might only be 5 days of heart care. If the hospital wants to discharge the patient after only 4 days, they'll get the same money too. Therefore, the faster the hospital can send their patients out the better. However, on the other hand if the patient is there for 7 days, the hospital still gets paid the same amount. Worse, if the patient returns for the same issue, then the hospital must take the patient without additional payment from the insurance company. The most effective way of preventing the patient from returning again is by having him buried. Doctors will tell you "No one would want to live under these circumstances or pain," but we believe in the Ribono Shel Olam and realize it's a *zechus* to be alive every single moment.

Q28: What happens if someone has an abnormality where the doctors say the patient will only live 3 months according to the current knowledge of medicine if left untreated but an operation can give the patient a normal lifespan with the risk of potentially killing him on the operating table? Should you let him live 3 months or take the risk?

A: (5778) The Shulchan Aruch (Shulchan Aruch 329:4)[62] clearly says we're not *choshesh* for *chayei sha'ah* versus *chayei olam*, but this question is more complex (Yoma 85a)[63]. I heard a story which I feel is true. Rav Moshe (Igros Moshe YD 2:58) says if there is a 5% chance to live through a surgery, you are allowed to do it. Even if there is a 95% chance of failure, you can do it. Rav Elyashiv says you can only do it with a 51% chance of success or higher, which is easier to understand. Nonetheless, Rav Moshe's talmidim brought him a *teshuva* where he wrote (Igros Moshe YD 3:36) that a procedure with a 40% chance of success was allowed. Rav Moshe said it's not a contradiction explaining that one case was where the individual had a 5% chance of living, so he permitted the medical procedure. In the other case, the patient had a 40% chance of the operation being successful – which meant that despite the patient dying, the operation itself was considered successful but the person died by another medical issue. These questions are very serious where people's lives are at stake. I can testify that there was someone who was in his 80s where the doctors gave up on him, yet he lived another two years and had the pleasure

---

[62] Shulchan Aruch (329:4) - אפי' מצאוהו מרוצץ שאינו יכול לחיות אלא לפי שעה מפקחים ובודקים עד חוטמו אם לא הרגישו בחוטמו חיות אז ודאי מת לא שנא פגעו בראשו תחלה לא שנא פגעו ברגליו תחילה

[63] Yoma (85a) - מצאוהו חי מפקחין מצאוהו חי פשיטא לא צריכא דאפי' לחיי דאפי' לחיי שעה

of seeing a few grandchildren's weddings. It's not always so easy to trust doctors because their agenda is not necessarily the same agenda as our own.

Chapter 3: Patient's Perspective

Q1. Is one obligated to learn CPR and first aid?

A: (5779) It's not an obligation, but if someone feels that he would administer CPR if necessary, then it would be a *middas chassidus* to learn CPR.

Q2. Is optional surgery (like plastic surgery) permitted?

A: (5779) There is a *machlokes haposkim* regarding a woman who wants to have plastic surgery to look nicer. Rav Moshe (Igros Moshe CM 2:66)[64] is lenient, however the Tzitz Eliezer (11:41)[65] is stringent. Laser eye surgery is not necessarily optional since there are times when you need it. You're certainly allowed to have a surgery to see better. If you have an issue with your knee and are in a lot of pain whenever you walk, are you obligated to endure that suffering for the rest of your life because it's an "optional" surgery? No, of course you can have the surgery. Optional really means that there is another way of producing the same results as the surgery without having to go through with such a procedure – or if you don't have the surgery then life wouldn't be too difficult (Tosfos Shabbos 50b)[66]. In general, if you don't need the surgery then you shouldn't have it – that's considered *chovel b'atzmo*

---

[64] Igros Moshe CM (2:66) - צריך לומר דכיון שהוא לנוי שלכן הוא לטובתו שרוצה בזה ליכא איסור דחובל והוי מזה ראיה ממש לעובדא דידן שכל שכן בנערה שהיפוי יותר צורך וטובה לה מלאיש דהא איתא בכתובות נט: תני ר"ח אין אשה אלא ליופי שודאי יש להחשיב שהוא לטובתה ומותרת לחבול בשביל להתיפות

[65] Tzitz Eliezer (11:41) - בנוגע לניתוחים פלסטיים שמבצעים כעת הרופאים אצל הרבה בני אדם לשם יפוי אבריהם וכדו' באין שום מחלה או כאב ויש מקום גדול לטעונה זאת שלא על כגון דא הוא שנתנה תורה רשות לרופא לרפאות [אם אפילו נקרא זה בשם לרפאות] ואין רשות לבני אדם לתת לרופאים לחבול בעצמם לשם מטרה זאת וגם אין רשות לרופא לבצע זאת ויש לדעת ולהאמין כי אין צייר כאלקינו והוא ית"ש צר והטביע לכאו"א מיצוריו בצלמו ובדמותו ההולמת לו ועליו אין להוסיף וממנו אין לגרוע

[66] Tosfos Shabbos (50b) - בשביל צערו - ואם אין לו צער אחר אלא שמתבייש לילך בין בני אדם שרי דאין לך צער גדול מזה

40

which is forbidden (Rambam Chovel u'Mazik 5:1)[67]. As a piece of advice, I would say that if you don't need surgery then you should stay away from it because there are certain problems which can arise during surgery. Before having such a medical procedure done, you need to sign waivers in case you die during surgery that you won't sue the hospital or doctors. Although if there was medical negligence then you can still sue, if you can't prove medical negligence then the waiver protects the hospital. In fact, the most dangerous part of the surgery isn't the procedure – it's the anesthesia. If the individual administering the anesthesia isn't careful, the patient can die just from the anesthesia alone. The patient might even become paralyzed from the anesthesia or not come out of it 100%. Even though everyone is very careful about finding the best surgeon possible, they aren't so careful about getting the greatest anesthesiologist because they don't realize the greater danger involved with the anesthesia. Besides for that reason, it's worth staying away from surgery if you can because of the potential risk of infection – even when the staff makes sure the surgical instruments are sterile. The worst place for a person to get sick is in the hospital because hospitals are filled with all types of viruses and bacteria in the air. The best place to have an operation would be at home, but it's not so practical to have it at home because they would need to bring all the equipment which probably won't even fit through the door. When the Lubavicher Rebbe got sick, he made sure that he didn't go to the hospital – and they did bring the hospital to his home and probably broke down the wall to make space for all the equipment. If you can avoid surgery, then you should try to do so. If you can't avoid surgery, then you should have the procedure done.

Q3. May one accept plastic surgery to look nicer?

A: (5755) If a person wants to fix his nose or other facial appearances which he feels don't look nice, there is a question of injuring oneself by accepting surgery. It is a *machlokes haposkim*

---

[67] Rambam Chovel u'Mazik (5:1) - אָסוּר לְאָדָם לַחֲבֹל בֵּין בְּעַצְמוֹ בֵּין בַּחֲבֵרוֹ

as the Tzitz Eliezer (11:41)[68] forbids this elective surgery completely, while Rav Moshe (Igros Moshe CM 2:66)[69] says it's permitted to accept such a surgery if the pain of feeling you don't look nice is more than the pain of the surgery. There is a *chachmas hapartzuf* where some people can tell what kind of person you are based on your facial features (Rabbenu Bachya Shemos 18:21)[70]. For instance, someone with a longer nose is a more patient person than a person with a shorter nose. That character trait is part of the person's nature and won't change just because a doctor changes the patient's external appearance. If a person with smaller ears is considered a cruel person, lengthening the ears through surgery isn't going to change his nature. There are exceptions to every rule, but generally people with similar facial features share common natures.

Q4. Is there any problem with having a surgery to remove a birthmark or prevent balding?

A: (5779) If the surgery for removing a birthmark is only being done to look nicer, then it might be considered injuring yourself for a woman. For a man, it might also be considered *lo yilbash*

---

[68] Tzitz Eliezer (11:41) - בנוגע לניתוחים פלסטיים שמבצעים כעת הרופאים אצל הרבה בני אדם לשם יפוי אבריהם וכדו' באין שום מחלה או כאב ויש מקום גדול לטעונה זאת שלא על כגון דא הוא שנתנה תורה רשות לרופא לרפאות [אם אפילו נקרא זה בשם לרפאות] ואין רשות לבני אדם לתת לרופאים לחבול בעצמם לשם מטרה זאת וגם אין רשות לרופא לבצע זאת ויש לדעת ולהאמין כי אין צייר כאלקינו והוא ית"ש צר והטביע לכאו"א מיצוריו בצלמו ובדמותו ההולמת לו ועליו אין להוסיף וממנו אין לגרוע

[69] Igros Moshe (CM 2:66) - צריך לומר דכיון שהוא לנוי שלכן הוא לטובתו שרוצה בזה ליכא איסור דחובל והוי מזה ראיה ממש לעובדא דידן שכן בנערה שהיפוי יותר צורך וטובה לה מלאיש דהא איתא בכתובות נט: תני ר"ח אין אשה אלא ליופי שודאי יש להחשיב שהוא לטובתה ומותרת לחבול בשביל להתיפות

[70] Rabbenu Bachya (Shemos 18:21) - או יאמר ואתה תחזה בהכרת פנים מכח חכמת הפרצוף שהיה משה יודע ובקי בה בהיותו שלם שבשלמים גדול שבנביאים וחכם הרזים ולכך הזהירו במלת ואתה כלומר ואתה בעצמך ולא על ידי צווי

(Devarim 22:5)[71]. If the operation is medically indicated, then it's not considered injuring yourself – like if the birthmark might become cancerous. However, if the birthmark is just being removed for cosmetic purposes, then it's a *machlokes* between Rav Moshe (Igros Moshe CM 2:66)[72] and the Tzitz Eliezer (11:41)[73] whether it is permitted to have such a surgery. Having such a surgery done is not *lechatchila*. Regarding balding, what exactly is the treatment? If it's just taking a medicine, then you would be allowed to do so depending on the side effects. If there are no *shailos* about the side effects, then you would be allowed to take the medicine to prevent balding.

Q5: What kind of side effects must one be concerned for?

A: (5779) Some of the questions you have to ask about side effects is whether the medicine will make you sterile. If it's a question of you risking your life, then you have to even worry about the side effects in 1 in 10,000 cases. However, in other cases you can follow the majority of people.

Q6. If nowadays *metzitza* could cause an infection, then shouldn't we stop doing it?

---

[71] Devarim (22:5) - לֹא־יִהְיֶה כְלִי־גֶבֶר עַל־אִשָּׁה וְלֹא־יִלְבַּשׁ גֶּבֶר שִׂמְלַת אִשָּׁה כִּי תוֹעֲבַת ה' אֱלֹקֶיךָ כָּל־עֹשֵׂה אֵלֶּה

[72] Igros Moshe CM (2:66) - צריך לומר דכיון שהוא לנוי שלכן הוא לטובתו שרוצה בזה ליכא איסור דחובל והוי מזה ראיה ממש לעובדא דידן שכן בנערה שהיפוי יותר צורך וטובה לה מלאיש דהא איתא בכתובות נט: תני ר"ח אין אשה אלא ליופי שודאי יש להחשיב שהוא לטובתה ומותרת לחבול בשביל להתיפות

[73] Tzitz Eliezer (11:41) - אולם אם כנידון של השערי צדק פשוט להתיר כפי מנהגן של ישראל בזה אבל יש לדעתי השלכות לחידושו זה בנוגע לניתוחים פלסטיים שמבצעים כעת הרופאים אצל הרבה בני אדם לשם יפוי אבריהם וכדו' באין שום מחלה או כאב ויש מקום גדול לטעון זאת שלא על כגון דא הוא שנתנה תורה רשות לרופא לרפאות [אם אפילו נקרא זה בשם לרפאות] ואין רשות לבני אדם לתת לרופאים לחבול בעצמם לשם מטרה זאת וגם אין רשות לרופא לבצע זאת ויש לדעת ולהאמין כי אין צייר כאלקינו והוא ית"ש צר והטביע לכאו"א מיצוריו בצלמו ובדמותו ההולמת לו ועליו אין להוסיף וממנו אין לגרוע

A: (5779) The Teshuvos Chasam Sofer writes that if the *mohel* has a disease which can infect the baby, then he can no longer be a *mohel* until the disease is taken care of. Maybe the *mohel* can use a pipe since according to many *poskim* this is considered *metzitza b'peh* (Biur Halacha 331:1)[74]. Alternatively, you can have someone other than a *mohel* do the *metzitza* as long as he knows what he's doing.

Q7. Are you allowed to undergo experimental surgery?

A: (5779) If they say there are no statistics regarding how successful a particular surgery is, then that usually means the procedure helps in less than 25% of the cases. If you don't have any option other than dying, then you are allowed to undergo such an experimental surgery (Shulchan Aruch YD 155:1)[75]. However, if the surgery is completely experimental and they really don't have any statistics, then you should not undergo such a procedure. Rav Elyashiv holds that if you have two months left to live and can undergo a surgery which would either end up prolonging your life or causing your death, then you're only allowed to accept the surgery if 51% of the time the patients live through the surgery. The patient is not obligated to take on such a procedure, but he is allowed to.

Q8. What should you do regarding such a surgery if the patient can't communicate his feelings for whatever reason?

A: (5779) We assume that a person would want to take the risk of living a long, normal life in exchange for the two months he has left to live.

---

[74] Biur Halacha (331:1) - עיין בתשו' בנין ציון סימן כ"ג וכ"ד דהמציצה דוקא בפה ולא ע"י דבר אחר שהמציאו הרופאים החדשים ובתשובת יד אליעזר סי' מתיר למצוץ בספוג דבדוקה דיותר טוב ממציצה בפה ואפילו בשבת יש להתיר בספוג ע"ש

[75] Shulchan Aruch YD (155:1) - כל מכה וחולי שיש בהם סכנה שמחללין עליהם שבת אין מתרפאים מעובד כוכבים שאינו מומחה לרבים (וכל המקיזים דם הוו מומחים לענין הקזה) דחיישינן לשפיכת דמים ואפילו הוא ספק חי ספק מת אין מתרפאים ממנו אבל אם הוא ודאי מת מתרפאים ממנו דלחיי שעה לא חיישינן בהא

Q9. Can you donate blood for money?

A: (5755) The Red Cross actually has blood insurance where if you donate blood, they will guarantee if someone in your immediate family needs blood then they will provide you with blood for free. Rav Moshe has a *teshuva* (Igros Moshe CM 1:103)[76] where he discusses donating blood due to the issue of injuring yourself. The Torah's perspective is that our body does not belong to us. The Ribono Shel Olam gave us a body to do *mitzvos* with it, and we must take care of the body He gave us. Since the Ribono Shel Olam gave us blood to live, do we have the right to sell or donate it? Rav Moshe said that although allowing yourself to be injured is forbidden, the Gemara says, "The head of all diseases is through the blood." (Bava Basra 58b)[77] In former times, people would let their blood at the barber shops. That's the reason why the barbers' polls were red and blue – in addition to cutting hair, they would also let blood by putting heated up cups on a person's back to draw out blood as a form of *refuah*. Therefore, Rav Moshe says that since they used to let blood for health reasons in the times of Chazal, we can't say donating blood is certainly considered injuring yourself. You can say that in former times it was healthy to let your blood and nowadays it's

---

[76] Igros Moshe (CM 1:103) - אבל בחבלה זו להוציא דם על פי השגחת הרופאים יש טעם גדול שלא לאסור דהא מצינו שבדורות הקודמים היו נוהגין להקיז דם אף רק לאקולי כמפורש בשבת דף קכ"ט וגם איתא שם אמר שמואל פורסא דדמא כל תלתין יומין בנעוריו עד ארבעים שנים ואחר כך עד ששים שנה אחת לשני חדשים ואף אחר ששים אחת לג' חדשים עיי"ש ברש"י ובהגהות מיימוניות פ"ד מדעות בשם רבינו חננאל איתא גירסא אחרת דלא כברבינו חננאל הנדפס ולכן אף שנשתנה אחר כך כמו בזמן הרמב"ם כדכתב בפ"ד מדעות הלכה י"ח שיקיז רק בצריך לזה ביותר ואחר חמשים שנה לא יקיז כלל ועיין בכסף משנה ועתה נשתנה עוד יותר שאין מניחין להקיז כלל מכל מקום ודאי גם עתה איכא גם רפואה בזה דלא יהי' שינוי גדול כל כך וגם היום מוציאין הרופאים כמעט בלא צער ולכן אפשר אין לאסור בחבלה זו דהקזת דם והרוצה להקל אין למחות בו כיון שהיא סברא גדולה

[77] Bava Basra (58b) - חזא דכתיב בראש כל מותא אנא דם בראש כל חיין אנא חמר אלא מעתה דנפיל מאיגרא ומית ודנפיל מדיקלא ומית דמא קטליה ותו מן דדרכיה למימת משקו ליה חמרא וחיי אלא הכי בעי למכתב בראש כל מרעין אנא דם

not so helpful, but not enough to say that it is damaging to your health or forbidden due to *chovel b'atzmo*. I know Rav Ruderman זכר צדיק לברכה allowed an organization to come to Yeshiva for a blood drive, though I don't know if they still do that in Yeshiva today.

Q10. Should one involve himself in a bone marrow drive?

A: (5755) About seven years ago there was a *frum* person in Detroit who developed Leukemia *lo alenu*. In order to keep him alive, they needed someone to donate a similar type of bone marrow which they would transplant into this patient. The odds were 1-in-28,000 that they would find someone with the same type of bone marrow. They made a major blood drive in Detroit to see if anyone would be a match for this person, and then wanted to come to Baltimore because they needed more people. The doctor in charge asked me if I would support the drive here, and I asked him who was funding the drive. The doctor told me the Young Israel in Detroit was funding it, and wondered why I wanted to know. I told him that I wouldn't allow the drive if the Red Cross was behind it. The day of the blood drive, I saw the Red Cross was here too, so I asked the doctor what was going on. He told me that the Young Israel didn't have enough money to support the entire drive and the Red Cross was willing to do it for free. I was very upset with him for allowing that, but once they were already here I wasn't going to stop it. The doctor asked me why I was upset, and I told him that now the Red Cross has the records of all the *frum* Jews in Baltimore. If the Red Cross eventually finds another bone marrow match from these records, then if the *yid* doesn't want to donate his bone marrow it will cause a chillul Hashem. "You only want to give for your people, but you don't want to give to others." About two years later, they called me saying that I might be a match for someone with Leukemia, so they wanted to test me further. I felt that since there was a possibility I might be a match for another *frum yid* – they won't tell you who you might be a match for – then I needed to do it in order for it not to be a chillul Hashem. In the end I wasn't a match for this patient, but I think I would have needed to go through with the operation if I was a match in order to avoid the terrible chillul Hashem. It's painful for the person who has the bone marrow removed and he will need to leave work for a few days, but this other person is dying. Therefore, it's an obligation for me to get involved in order to save this person. However, if I would have never gotten involved in the first place with the Red Cross then it would have been better. There is a big *inyan* to go to such a blood drive, but you're not obligated to go because the chances are slim that you will be a match for saving this person's life. Also, if no *yidden* will get involved then it would be a terrible chillul Hashem.

(5779) Rav Moshe Feinstein has a *teshuva* (Igros Moshe CM 1:103)[78] about this since a person is not allowed to be injure himself unless he is going to do the *mitzva* of saving someone's life. It is certainly permitted to give blood or bone marrow and is a *middas chassidus* to do so. This leniency applies both to a Jew and a non-Jew since there is a kiddush Hashem involved in this as well as the fact that non-Jews are also created in the image of the Ribono Shel Olam (Bereishis 1:27)[79]. The only question would be if the non-Jew is an idol worshipper, but in America nowadays I don't really think there any idol worshippers as they believe in the Ribono Shel Olam (Rema 156:1)[80]. Therefore, it's a *mitzva* to give blood or bone marrow when needed.

---

[78] Igros Moshe CM (1:103) - אבל בחבלה זו להוציא דם על פי השגחת הרופאים יש טעם גדול שלא לאסור דהא מצינו שבדורות הקודמים היו נוהגין להקיז דם אף רק לאקולי כמפורש בשבת דף קכ"ט וגם איתא שם אמר שמואל פורסא דדמא כל תלתין יומין בנעוריו עד ארבעים שנים ואחר כך עד ששים שנה אחת לשני חדשים ואף אחר ששים אחת לג' חדשים עיי"ש ברש"י ובהגהות מיימוניות פ"ד מדעות בשם רבינו חננאל איתא גירסא אחרת דלא כברבינו חננאל הנדפס ולכן אף שנשתנה אחר כך כמו בזמן הרמב"ם כדכתב בפ"ד מדעות הלכה י"ח שיקיזו רק בצריך לזה ביותר ואחר חמשים שנה לא יקיז כלל ועיין בכסף משנה ועתה נשתנה עוד יותר שאין מניחין להקיז כלל מכל מקום ודאי גם עתה איכא גם רפואה בזה דלא יהי' שינוי גדול כל כך וגם היום מוציאין הרופאים כמעט בלא צער ולכן אפשר אין לאסור בחבלה זו דהקזת דם והרוצה להקל אין למחות בו כיון שהיא סברא גדולה

[79] Bereishis (1:27) - וַיִּבְרָא אֱלֹקִים אֶת-הָאָדָם בְּצַלְמוֹ בְּצֶלֶם אֱלֹקִים בָּרָא אֹתוֹ זָכָר וּנְקֵבָה בָּרָא אֹתָם

[80] Rema (156:1) - ויש מקילין בעשיית שותפות עם העכו"ם בזמן הזה משום שאין העכו"ם בזה"ז נשבעים בע"א ואע"ג דמזכירין העבודה זרה מ"מ כוונתם לעושה שמים וארץ אלא שמשתתפים שם שמים ודבר אחר ולא מצינו שיש בזה משום לפני עור לא תתן מכשול דהרי אינם מוזהרים על השתוף

Chapter 3: Patient's Perspective

Q11. May a Kohen who needs an organ transplant accept an organ from a *meis*?

A: (5755) There are various factors in this question. If the Kohen needs a heart or kidney transplant, then we're dealing with a life-threatening situation which is permitted if there is no other way to obtain the organ other than through the dead person. Tumas Kohen is not something you are required to give your life for. Additionally, once the organ is transplanted into the Kohen's body, he really isn't touching the organ of the *meis* anymore since the organ is in the *beis hastarim* where there is no *din* of *maga hameis*. Touching a *meis* is only forbidden when a Kohen touches the *meis* with his revealed limbs. The halacha by *orlah* is that if you graft a branch from a two-year-old tree which still has a *din* in *orlah* to a 30-year-old tree, the new branch is subordinate to the older tree and is now permitted (Sotah 43b)[81]. The same thing applies in the opposite case where you graft a 30-year-old tree branch onto a 2-year-old tree that the branch is subordinate to the younger tree and would become forbidden until the tree loses its *orlah* status. We learn from this that if you transplant the organ of a *meis* into a live person, the organ is now subordinate to the live person. There is no issue of being in the same room as the organ before the transplant since it is a case of *pikuach nefashos*.

(5779) The halacha is that the first three years of a tree's fruits are considered *orlah* and you cannot use them (Shulchan Aruch YD 294:1)[82]. What happens if you take the branch of a tree which was only one year old, and you grafted it onto a tree which is five years old – are the fruits from this branch still obligated in *orlah* or do we say it becomes a part of the main part of the tree which has passed the years of *orlah* already. The Gemara says we look at the

---

[81] Sotah (43b) - 'האי הרכבת היתר היכי דמי אילימא ילדה בילדה תיפוק לי
דבעי מיהדר משום ילדה ראשונה אלא ילדה בזקינה והאמר רבי אבהו ילדה
שסיבבה בזקינה בטלה ילדה בזקינה ואין בה דין ערלה

[82] Shulchan Aruch YD (294:1) - הנוטע עץ מאכל מונה לו ג' שנים מעת
נטיעתו וכל הפירות שיהיו בו בתוך ג' שנים אסורין בהנאה לעולם

grafted branch as part of the main tree (Sotah 43b)[83]. Similarly, we say that once the organ is transplanted into a Kohen's body, the organ becomes a part of his body and no longer considered from a *meis*. The only issue would be that the surgeon touches the Kohen with the organ before completing the procedure, so there might be a question about that point in time. Nonetheless, Rav Moshe (Igros Moshe YD 1:230)[84] says that since the Kohen is strapped down and cannot move it's fine. This is all where the understanding is that the organ is from an *akum* whose organs are not *metameh* in an *ohel* – only *b'maga u'bmasa*.

Q12. Is a Kohen allowed to go to the hospital for a non-life-threatening situation?

A: (5755) The only way it would be forbidden for a Kohen to be in the hospital is if the *meis* is in the same *ohel* as the Kohen or סוף טמאה לצאת (Shulchan Aruch YD 371:4)[85] – meaning that the *meis* is going to be removed from the hospital via that path. The Kohen is not allowed to be in the same corridor where the *meis* will eventually pass through since they will use that hallway when the *meis* is moved. If the Kohen is in one of the other rooms where the door is closed and there is no issue of סוף טמאה לצאת, then he won't become *tameh* since his room creates a barrier against the

---

[83] Sotah (43b) - האי הרכבת היתר היכי דמי אילימא ילדה בילדה תיפוק לי' דבעי מיהדר משום ילדה ראשונה אלא ילדה בזקינה והאמר רבי אבהו ילדה שסיבכה בזקינה בטלה ילדה בזקינה ואין בה דין ערלה

[84] Igros Moshe YD (1:230) - ולכן לדינא כיון שהרופאים חותכין ועושין נקב בתוך הרגל ושם מדביקין את בשר המת ותופרין אח"כ את החתך יש להתיר לא מביא כשתתכסה כולו בעודו בלוע שהיא טומאה ממש אלא אף אם נשאר בשר המת גלוי מקצתו לחוץ נמי נבטל להגוף ונטהר. אבל צריכין לקשור את רגלו באופן שלא יוכל להזיזו קודם שיתפרו כל התפירות ואם אפשר לעשות באופן שגם הרופאים לא יזיזו צריך לעשות דוקא באופן זה ואם א"א להתיר כיון שהוא בשר מת עכו"ם מצד ס"ס אף כשהרופאים יזיזו אבל הוא לא יוכל להזיז זהו הנלע"ד למעשה

[85] Shulchan Aruch YD (371:4) - חצר המוקפת זיזין ואכסדראות וטומאה באחד מהבתים אם כל פתחי הבתים והחלונות נעולים טומאה יוצאת לתחת הזיזין והאכסדראות (והטעם משום דהואיל וסוף הטומאה לצאת דרך שם רואין כאלו יצאה ולכן יש מחמירין לכהנים לילך דרך שער העיר שסוף המת לצאת משם ויש מתירין והמקיל לא הפסיד במקום שלא נהגו להחמיר

tumah. Therefore, practically speaking the only reason a Kohen wouldn't be allowed to go to a hospital would be if you are concerned that there might be a *meis* in one of the rooms which will use the same corridor which the Kohen is walking through. The corridors and stairways from one floor to another are closed off throughout the hospital, and usually each department is closed off from one another for fire regulations, so you don't need to suspect that one of the hallways which you are walking through will be used right now for a *meis* – especially since most of the patients in the hospital are non-Jews who are not *metameh b'ohel* (Nazir 61b)[86] according to many *poskim* (Rambam Tumas Meis 1:13)[87]. Therefore, the Shulchan Aruch (YD 372:2)[88] says that when there is a need for the Kohen to be in the same *ohel* as a non-Jew then we are lenient. If the Kohen knows there is a *meis* in the corridor, then he would not be allowed to enter the hallway until the *meis* is removed. Generally, the hospital staff takes the *meis* out of the room down to the morgue in the basement which is sealed off from the other floors. Then they take the *meis* out from the morgue directly to the funeral home rather than through the hospital.

Q13. After not having children for a few years, is it permitted for a man to be *motzi zera* in order for a doctor to see whether he can have children or not?

A: (5755) *Hashchasas zera* is a very severe *issur* in the Torah saying *er v'onan* were *ra b'einei* Hashem (Bereishis 38:10)[89]. The language of evil in the eyes of Hashem isn't something normally said in the Torah. Things which people didn't feel were so important became much more revealed to the public as the Zohar

---

[86] Nazir (61b) - יצא עובד כוכבים שאין לו טומאה מנלן דלית להו טומאה דאמר קרא (במדבר יט:כ) ואיש אשר יטמא ולא יתחטא ונכרתה הנפש ההיא מתוך הקהל במי שיש לו קהל יצא זה שאין לו קהל

[87] Rambam Tumas Meis (1:13) - וְאֵין הָעַכּוּ"ם מְטַמֵּא בְּאֹהֶל וְדָבָר זֶה קַבָּלָה הוּא וַהֲרֵי הוּא אוֹמֵר בְּמִלְחֶמֶת מִדְיָן (במדבר לא:יט) כֹּל נֹגֵעַ בֶּחָלָל וְלֹא הַזְכִּיר שָׁם אֹהֶל

[88] Shulchan Aruch YD (372:2) - קברי עובדי כוכבים נכון ליזהר הכהן מלילך עליהם (אע"פ שיש מקילין) ונכון להחמיר

[89] Bereishis (38:10) - וַיֵּרַע בְּעֵינֵי ה' אֲשֶׁר עָשָׂה וַיָּמֶת גַּם־אֹתוֹ

began to spread after the times of the Rishonim. The Gemara (Yevamos 76a)[90] says that a person is allowed to be *motzi zera* to test whether he is able to marry a *bas Yisroel* (Igros Moshe EH 2:18)[91]. I don't want to get involved too much in this question, but essentially *hashchasas zera* is only forbidden when it is *l'vatala*. If the whole purpose of the *hotzaas zera* is in order to have children, then it's not considered *hashchasas zera* (Igros Moshe EH 4:32:5)[92]. Nonetheless, there are other *shailos* involved in such a medical procedure which must be taken care of, so it's important to speak with a Rav beforehand.

Q14. If a man had his *beitzim* removed due to an illness like cancer, may he still get married?

A: (5755) This is similar to the question of a vasectomy where a man who medically cannot have children is not allowed to marry a *bas Yisroel*. He might be able to marry a convert who already has children and doesn't want more children. The general rule in the Gemara (Yevamos 75b)[93] is that a person who cannot have children *bidei shamayim* is allowed to marry a *bas Yisroel* while a person who cannot have children because of a procedure done

---

[90] Yevamos (76a) - שלח ליה רבא בריה דרבה לרב יוסף ילמדנו רבינו היכי עבדינן א"ל מייתינן נהמא חמימא דשערי ומנחינן ליה אבי פוקרי ומקרי וחזינן ליה

[91] Igros Moshe (EH 2:18) - שאף שהוא בשביל להוליד בנים שמסתבר שאין בזה משום איסור הוצאת זרע לבטלה והוא כ"ש ממה שמותר למי שניקב הגיד שלו וסתמו שבודקין אותו בהוצאת זרע לראות אם נסתם היטב ביבמות דף ע"ו אף שהתם הוא ספק אלמא דכיון שהוא כדי לראות אם מותר ליקח אשה אין זה לבטלה כ"ש הכא שהוא כמו ודאי שיוליד עי"ז שלא הוי לבטלה

[92] Igros Moshe (EH 4:32:5) - לזרוק זרע הבעל לגוף אשתו כשאומרים הרופאים שמה שלא מתעברת הוא מצד שבביאתו לא בא הזרע להרחם מצד איזה חולשה ממנו או מצד שיום שהאשה ראויה להריון הוא משונה שרק ביום העשירי וי"א לראיית דמי נדותה ראויה אשה זו להריון ודאי יכולים לזרוק בבטנה ע"י רופאים זרע בעלה ואם הצורך הוא משום שע"י ביאה לא בא הזרע לרחמה הרי היא טהורה ויוציא הזרע ע"י תשמיש וכו

[93] Yevamos (75b) - אמר רב יהודה אמר שמואל פצוע דכא בידי שמים כשר אמר רבא היינו דקרינן פצוע ולא קרינן הפצוע

by the hands of man is not allowed to (Shulchan Aruch EH 5:10)[94]. Consequently, if a person develops a sickness which disintegrates his beitzim, then that is considered *bidei shamayim* and he would be allowed to marry a bas Yisroel. On the other hand, bidei adam refers to if someone hits this man or another unnatural occurrence, then he cannot marry a bas Yisroel. The *poskim* say that if a person has a sickness which requires the doctors to remove the beitzim, then that is still considered *bidei shamayim* since the Ribono Shel Olam allowed this procedure to be done for pikuach nefesh (Pischei Teshuvos EH 5:7)[95]. When men get older, it is common for the prostate glands to swell and prevent them from going to the bathroom. Therefore, doctors remove the gland and must cut through the tubes which allow the *zera* to flow through – and makes the person become a פְּצוּעַ דַּכָּא (Yevamos 75a)[96]. Up until recently doctors didn't have a remedy for this, so people knew that once it became difficult going to the bathroom then their days were numbers. Rav Meir Simcha had this sickness of an enlarged prostate and knew his days were numbered, so he told Slobodka not to say Tehillim for him because he felt it was a tefillas shav (Berachos 54a)[97]. Everyone knew it was the sign of the end, so there was no eitza for him. Today doctors are able to perform this

---

[94] Shulchan Aruch (EH 5:10) - כל פיסול שאמרו בענין זה כשלא היה בידי
שמים כגון שכרתו אדם או הכהו קוץ וכיוצא בדברים אלו אבל אם נולד כרות
שפכה או פצוע דכא או שנולד בלא ביצים או שחלה מחמת גופו ובטלו ממנו
איברים אלו או שנולד בהם שחין והמסה אותו או כרתן הרי זה כשר לבא בקהל
שכל אלו בידי שמים להרמב"ם אבל לרש"י והרא"ש לא מקרי בידי שמים אלא
ע"י רעמים וברד או ממעי אמו אבל ע"י חולי חשיב בידי אדם ופסול וכתב הרא"ש
דהכי משמע בירושלמי

[95] Pischei Teshuvos (EH 5:7) - אבל בשהרופא ריפא וסתם הנקב
בתחבושת לית דין ולית דיין דאי מחמת חולי הוי ביד"ש דכשר לבא בקהל ואי
נימא ניחוש לדעת הרא"ש דחולי לא הוה ביד"ש מ"מ הא נסתם לפנינו וזה פסול
שחוזר להכשרו ודעת ר"א ממיץ דאמר דאינו מועיל אלא להכשיר זרעו
ולא אותו הרי חלקו עליו כל הפוסקים ולכל הפחות הוא ס"ס להקל כו' ולכן הריני
מסכים להכשיר

[96] Yevamos (75a) - איזהו פצוע: תנו רבנן איזהו פצוע דכא כל שנפצעו ביצים
שלו ואפילו אחת מהן ואפי' ניקבו ואפילו נמוקו ואפילו חסרו

[97] Berachos (54a) - והצועק לשעבר הרי זו תפלת שוא היתה אשתו מעוברת
ואומר יהי רצון שתלד אשתי זכר הרי זו תפלת שוא היה בא בדרך ושמע קול
צוחה בעיר ואומר יהי רצון שלא תהא בתוך ביתי הרי זו תפלת שוא

operation and it is certainly permitted to have it done, but the question is whether you are allowed to remain married to your wife. The מנהג follows the Chazon Ish (Chazon Ish EH 12:7) who *poskins* that the whole issue of פְּצוּעַ דַּכָּא only applies to the outer *chutim*. Also, this procedure is necessary to save his life which means it's *bidei shamayim*, so it would be permitted for him to remain married or marry a bas Yisroel. You don't need to wait until the enlarged prostate becomes a life-threatening situation to have the procedure done. As long as the prostate issue will eventually become a question of life and death then you may have the procedure done. This also applies to *shailos* on Shabbos like someone who broke his bone where he might want to wait until after Shabbos to drive to be driven to the hospital to reset it. It's not simple to wait at all – someone with a broken arm or broken leg is really a life-threatening issue. There was a story here where someone broke an arm, didn't want to go to the hospital on Shabbos, and then went to the doctor after Shabbos. The doctor told him that his life was in danger throughout Shabbos because the bone might have cut a vein or artery and cause him to bleed to death internally.

Q15. Is it permitted to donate a kidney?

A: (5779) Regarding donating your kidney to someone else, there's a *teshuva* from the Radvaz where someone is told, "Either let me cut off your hand or I'm going to kill another *yid*." The Radvaz (Shailos U'teshuvos HaRadvaz 2:1052)[98] answered that

---

[98] Shailos U'teshuvos HaRadvaz (2:1052) - זו מדת חסידות אבל לדין יש תשובה מה לסכנת אבר דשבת שכן אונס דאתי משמיא ולפיכך אין סכנת אבר דוחה שבת אבל שיביא הוא האונס עליו מפני חבירו לא שמענו ותו דילמא ע"י חתיכת אבר אעפ"י שאין הנשמה תלויה בו שמא יצא ממנו דם הרבה וימות ומאי חזית דדם חבירו סומק טפי דילמא דמא דידיה סומק טפי ואני ראיתי אחד שמת ע"י שסרטו את אזנו שריטות דקות להוציא מהם דם ויצא כ"כ עד שמת והרי אין לך באדם אבר קל כאוזן וכ"ש אם יחתכו אותו ותו דמה לשבת שכן הוא ואיבריו חייבין לשמור את השבת ואי דאמר קרא וחי בהם ולא שימות בהם הוה אמינא אפילו על חולי שיש בו סכנה אין מחללין את השבת תאמר בחבירו שאינו מחוייב למסור עצמו על הצלתו על אע"ג דחייב להצילו בממונו אבל לא בסכנת איבריו ותו דאין עונשין מדין ק"ו ואין לך עונש גדול מזה שאתה אומר שיחתוך אחד מאיבריו מדין ק"ו והשתא ומה מלקות אין עונשין מדין ק"ו כ"ש חתיכת אבר ותו דהתורה

the Jew is not obligated to have his own hand cut off, but it's a *middas chassidus* to save another's life. When someone gives blood or bone marrow, there are probably no lasting effects on the body, so it's a completely different story than having an arm cut off since not having a hand for the rest of your life is a tremendous impediment. If you can't use a computer, then you'll already be out of most jobs. In general, not having both hands makes things difficult. Maybe it doesn't make such a difference if you're a singer, but most jobs require you to pick things up or use both hands. Therefore, the Radvaz says you're not obligated to give your hand even to save the life of another person, though it is a *middas chassidus* to do so. I think donating a kidney is more similar to this case than donating blood since when you get older often your kidneys don't function 100%. Sometimes they don't even function at 50% when you get older, so it's not so simple if you only have one kidney. Additionally, there is a question of *pikuach nefesh* for the person donating the kidney – albeit unusual, but possible – so it's not the same as giving blood or bone marrow. Maybe you'll be in pain for a few days after giving bone marrow, but after that you get back to normal.

Q16. Is it a good thing to donate blood and organs?

A: (5779) In former times, people used to let out blood on a monthly basis because they considered it healthy (Shabbos 129a)[99]. The reason it was so healthy was because it lowered the blood pressure of people with high blood pressure. The halacha was that if you see an animal isn't acting as it normally does on

---

אמרה פצע תחת פצע כויה תחת כויה ואפ"ה חששו שמא ע"י הכוייה ימות והתורה אמרה עין תחת עין ולא נפש ועין תחת עין ולכך אמרו שמשלם ממון והדבר ברור שיותר רחוק הוא שימות מן הכויה יותר מעל ידי חתיכת אבר ואפ"ה חיישינן לה כ"ש בנ"ד תדע דסכנת אבר חמירא דהא התירו לחלל עליה את השבת בכל מלאכות שהם מדבריהם אפילו ע"י ישראל ותו דכתיב דרכיה דרכי נעם וצריך שמשפטי תורתינו יהיו מסכימים אל השכל והסברא ואיך יעלה על דעתנו שיניח אדם לסמא את עינו או לחתוך את ידו או רגלו כדי שלא ימיתו את חבירו הלכך איני רואה טעם לדין זה אלא מדת חסידות ואשרי חלקו מי שיוכל לעמוד בזה ואם יש ספק סכנת נפשות הרי זה חסיד שוטה דספיקא דידיה עדיף מוודאי דחבריה

[99] Shabbos (129a) - תלתין כל דדמא פורסא שמואל אמר הפרקים ובין יומין ימעט ובין הפרקים יחזור וימעט

Yom Tov, then there are ways that you are allowed to let its blood out (Shulchan Aruch 332:4)[100]. High blood pressure can lead to a stroke and heart attacks, so it was healthy for people to let out their blood. Nowadays, they lower people's blood pressure through medication instead of letting blood – it's not necessarily better, just more convenient. Therefore, if you want to know whether it's a good thing to donate blood, I think it may be helpful for the donor if he has high blood pressure. On the other hand, I don't think donating organs is helpful for the donor, but it is a *middas chassidus* to do so – especially if you know that the organ will be used for another person (Igros Moshe YD 2:174). Sometimes hospitals will take your blood and store it in blood bank, so it isn't used for anyone since it doesn't last forever. They just want people to get used to donating blood for when the hospital really does need blood. If your blood isn't being used, then I don't think it's such a good thing to donate your blood. Nonetheless, I don't think it's considered injuring yourself if it's being done for *refuah*.

Q17. Is it a good thing to donate your organs before dying?

A: (5755) - In order for the donated organ to be as viable as possible, the doctors want to remove it as close as possible to the time of death. For instance, if a kidney isn't removed immediately after a patient dies, then it is essentially useless. Therefore, they remove the kidney when such a person dies on the operating table. In order to ensure the kidney is good, doctors don't wait until a person is considered clinically dead – they only wait until the patient is legally dead. Once the law considers a patient dead, there are no repercussions if a person kills the patient. For example, there was a wealthy fellow who had nothing else to do with his money so he traveled the world as a vacation to Bermuda, Tibet, Jamaica, the Philippines – all around the world. He didn't tell anyone where he was going, so after three years of not hearing from him his inheritors said that they can assume he's dead. The court agreed that the wealthy man could be presumed dead after no one heard from him for three years, so the family divided all of his property. After a couple more years, the man returned and

---

[100] Shulchan Aruch (332:4) - אם אחזה דם יכול להעמידה במים כדי שתצטנן ואם הוא ספק שאם לא יקיז לה דם תמות מותר לומר לעכו"ם להקיזה

asked what happened to all of his money. They told him, "You're dead!" so he went to the court to reverse the order, but they replied, "You're legally dead. It was your responsibility to inform your family that you weren't dead, and the law is that after not hearing from a family member for three years you can assume he is dead. Although injustice may have been done in this case, the law does not change." Additionally, once the main body deteriorates to such an extent that the person cannot continue, then the patient is considered legally dead as well. I don't know the exact laws of when a person is considered clinically dead, but it comes after being legally dead and before being halachically dead. When the doctors say there are no brainwaves, then the kidneys are allowed to be removed. Once the hospital pronounces a person is legally dead, they will not be reimbursed from the insurance company for any medicine administered because they are legally treating a dead person. The patient might be still be moving, but the insurance company won't pay for the medical care which will inspire the hospital not to provide medical services. That can cause a lot of problems. You can only donate your organs to save someone else's life if one can be assured that the organs will only be removed after he is halachically dead.

(5779) - This is a different story completely in contrast to everything we've discussed thus far. If a person dies in an automobile crash, people feel they might as well use their salvageable organs for others. However, there is a very serious issue involved in such a question since there are three levels of death: 1) someone who is legally dead 2) someone who is clinically dead 3) someone who is actually dead. This question of donating organs only applies to a case where the hospital is taking someone's organs when the person is considered actually dead. At the same time, the faster the kidneys are removed closer to the time of death, the more effective they are going to be. Although they are most effective when removed immediately after the person dies, it's not really so practical to know when someone will precisely leave this world. First of all, the only way the hospital can remove the kidneys immediately after the patient dies is if they have him on the operating table with his body already open ready to remove the kidney as they wait for the person to die. However, they might be killing the patient from the operation itself since once a person is nearing his final moments of life, the anesthesia can negatively affect his brain and breathing – thereby killing him. The hospital might not care whether the anesthesia affects the patient's breathing because he's already considered legally dead to them anyway. Usually, hospitals remove organs from people who are dying when they are considered legally dead rather than actually dead. Then they're killed during the surgery. If you allow the hospital to harvest your organs in a case of an automobile crash or the like, then you are placing a stumbling block in front of the doctors since even non-Jews are commanded (Rambam Melachim 9:1)[101] not to commit murder (Shemos 20:13)[102]. The doctor is helping you commit suicide – that's completely different than donating a kidney to help another person live. The hospital wants to do everything they can to make sure you survive the surgery while you donate your kidney otherwise people won't want to donate kidneys anymore. If you really know that there is another person who can use your organs and you are really on the verge of dying, then theoretically it's not a bad thing to allow doctors to eventually give your organs to the other patient. However, it's not so simple to successfully donate your organs to another person. You can't just take anyone's kidney and have the surgery work. There are different types of kidneys which work with different types of blood and other factors, so the hospital needs to test various things before performing the surgery. Therefore, even if you want to donate your kidneys to a particular person, it's not so simple that you'll be a good match. Although it is degrading the honor of the *meis* to take his organs, he is allowed to be *mochel* on his honor if he wants to. Nonetheless, after the individual dies, his body belongs to the inheritors – so they need to give permission for the organs to be given as well. If they agree to it, then it is permitted. Since there's a *mitzva* to fulfill the words of

---

[101] Rambam Melachim (9:1) - עַל שִׁשָּׁה דְּבָרִים נִצְטַוָּה אָדָם הָרִאשׁוֹן עַל עֲבוֹדָה זָרָה וְעַל בִּרְכַּת הַשֵּׁם וְעַל שְׁפִיכוּת דָּמִים וְעַל גִּלּוּי עֲרָיוֹת וְעַל הַגֵּזֶל וְעַל הַדִּינִים אַף עַל פִּי שֶׁכֻּלָּן הֵן קַבָּלָה בְּיָדֵינוּ מִמֹּשֶׁה רַבֵּנוּ וְהַדַּעַת נוֹטָה לָהֶן מִכְּלַל דִּבְרֵי תּוֹרָה יֵרָאֶה שֶׁעַל אֵלּוּ נִצְטַוָּה הוֹסִיף לְנֹחַ אֵבֶר מִן הַחַי שֶׁנֶּאֱמַר (בראשית ט:ד) אַךְ בָּשָׂר בְּנַפְשׁוֹ דָמוֹ לֹא תֹאכֵלוּ נִמְצְאוּ שֶׁבַע מִצְוֹת

[102] Shemos (20:13) - לֹא תִרְצָח לֹא תִנְאָף לֹא תִגְנֹב לֹא־תַעֲנֶה בְרֵעֲךָ עֵד שָׁקֶר

the *meis* (Taanis 21a)[103], the inheritors will likely agree with whatever he said to do. Rav Moshe (Igros Moshe YD 2:174) says there is an *inyan* to give your organs after dying – as long as they're donated after he is considered dead according to halacha.

Q18. If donating a kidney might lower your lifespan, would it still be permitted to give a kidney?

A: (5779) If the doctors are not sure whether donating your kidney will negatively affect you but are sure it will help the recipient, then there is still an *inyan* to donate your kidney. You're not obligated to do so, but it's a *middas chassidus*.

Q19. If one got a tattoo and then became a *ba'al teshuva*, is he obligated to have it removed?

A: (5779) No, he is not obligated to remove a tattoo he received earlier. The Torah doesn't say you cannot have a tattoo – it only says you are not allowed to make a tattoo on your body (Vayikra 19:28)[104]. Although you're not obligated to have your tattoo removed, if people are able to see it then you're advertising to the whole world that you're a *ba'al teshuva* – which I don't know if that's something everyone wants to do. You are allowed to have a tattoo removed medically - even though it involves injuring your body - because the procedure is being done to remove your embarrassment (Tosfos Shabbos 50b)[105].

Q20. Should one carry around a card with directives on it what a hospital should do if *chas v'shalom* he is unable to give his directives?

---

[103] Taanis (21a) - אם אמר מתו ירשו אחרים תחתיהם בין שאמר תנו בין שאמר אל תתנו אין נותנין להם אלא שקל א"ל הא מני ר"מ היא דאמר מצוה לקיים דברי המת

[104] Vayikra (19:28) - וְשֶׂרֶט לָנֶפֶשׁ לֹא תִתְּנוּ בִּבְשַׂרְכֶם וּכְתֹבֶת קַעֲקַע לֹא תִתְּנוּ בָּכֶם אֲנִי ה

[105] Tosfos Shabbos (50b) - בשביל צערו - ואם אין לו צער אחר אלא שמתביייש לילך בין בני אדם שרי דאין לך צער גדול מזה

Chapter 3: Patient's Perspective

A: (5779) Most of the time if you need to give directives to the doctor but you're unable to do so, then you're not going to be able to give them the card with your directives either. It's not going to help – even if the hospital might check the patient's wallet.

Q21. Is it permitted to request a DNR?

A: (5779) The Gemara Nedarim (Nedarim 40a)[106] says, "It's a *mitzva* to visit a sick person because anyone who doesn't visit a sick person won't *daven* for him to live or die." I can understand that if you don't visit the patient then you won't *daven* for him to live, but why would he *daven* that the patient should die? The Ran (Nedarim 40a)[107] explains that there are times when the patient is in pain and you should pray he should die. Such a case is where the individual cannot live and had a condition which will not allow him to live according to current medical science. For instance, if the person developed pancreatic cancer, then I don't believe medical knowledge today can help him. Why would you keep him in pain? Of course you're not allowed to kill him *chas v'shalom*, but you're not doing him any favors by saving him. If he wants to be saved and live for as long as he can, then he has the right to make that decision for himself. However, he also has the right to say, "Do not resuscitate." The Chachamim learned a lot of things from Rebbi's maidservant just by virtue of the fact that she was around Rebbi Yehuda HaNasi. For instance, they didn't know what the word וטאטאתיה meant, but one time they heard Rebbi's

---

[106] Nedarim (40a) - כי אתא רב דימי אמר כל המבקר את החולה גורם לו שיחיה וכל שאינו מבקר את החולה גורם לו שימות מאי גרמא אילימא כל המבקר את החולה מבקש עליו רחמים שיחיה וכל שאין מבקר את החולה מבקש עליו רחמים שימות שימות ס"ד אלא כל שאין מבקר חולה אין מבקש עליו רחמים לא שיחיה ולא שימות

[107] Ran Nedarim (40a) - - אין מבקש עליו רחמים לא שיחיה ולא שימות נראה בעיני דה"ק פעמים שצריך לבקש רחמים על החולה שימות כגון שמצטער החולה בחליו הרבה ואי אפשר לו שיחיה כדאמרינן בפרק הנושא (כתובות קד) דכיון דחזאי אמתיה דרבי דעל כמה זימנין לבית הכסא ואנח תפילין וקא מצטער אמרה יהי רצון שיכופו העליונים את התחתונים כלומר דלימות רבי ומש"ה קאמר דהמבקר חולה מועילו בתפלתו אפי' לחיות מפני שהיא תפלה יותר מועלת ומי שאינו מבקרו אין צריך לומר שאינו מועילו לחיות אלא אפי' היכא דאיכא ליה הנאה במיתה אפי' אותה זוטרתי אינו מהנהו

59

maidservant says "get the טאטיתא and sweep the house (Rosh Hashana 24a)[108]" – so they were able to understand it meant a broom. The Gemara (Kesubos 104a)[109] explains elsewhere that when Rebbi Yehuda was sick, he was in a lot of pain and the Yeshiva *davened* for him to live. The maidservant' asked the Ribono Shel Olam that the upper Bais Din should overpower the lower Bais Din to allow him to die. We see that there are times when there is a *mitzva* for us to *daven* for someone to die so they are no longer in pain. If a person has a certain type of disease that makes it not naturally possible for him to emerge from the sickness alive, then it's a *mitzva* to *daven* for him to die if he's in pain. Rav Moshe (Igros Moshe YD 2:174) says it doesn't make any sense for it to be a *mitzva* to *daven* for the patient to die yet we should try to save him. Therefore, it must be that we don't have an obligation to save such a patient. That's the essential criteria for having a DNR. You cannot assume anyone in the hospital is at such a point where they warrant having such a DNR. The issue nowadays is that the hospitals feel that the faster we can kill everyone who is sick, the better it is for society. It's not that the hospitals don't like people. Rather, they feel that they're being merciful for this patient because they say he won't have a good quality of life. However, the real reason is because of money. It used to be that insurance companies would pay a certain amount of money for every day the patient was in the hospital. Therefore, if the hospital accepts your insurance, then they need to follow the laws of your insurance company. They changed the laws so that the insurance agencies tell the hospital, "We are going to pay your $2,500 for our client's stay in the hospital for ten days" – or whatever the numbers are. If the hospital is able to have the patient

---

[108] Rosh Hashana (24a) - לא הוו ידעי רבנן מאי (ישעיהו יד:כג) וטאטאתיה במטאטא השמד יומא חד שמעוה לאמתא דבי רבי דהוות אמרה לחבירתה שקולי טאטיתא וטאטי ביתא

[109] Kesubos (104a) - ההוא יומא דנח נפשיה דרבי גזרו רבנן תעניתא ובעו רחמי ואמרי כל מאן דאמר נח נפשיה דר' ידקר בחרב סליקא אמתיה דרבי לאיגרא אמרה עליוני' מבקשין את רבי והתחתוני' מבקשין את רבי יהי רצון שיכופו תחתונים את העליונים כיון דחזאי כמה זימני דעייל לבית הכסא וחלץ תפילין ומנח להו וקמצטער אמרה יהי רצון שיכופו עליונים את התחתונים ולא הוו שתקי רבנן מלמיבעי רחמי שקלה כוזא שדייא מאיגרא [לארעא] אישתיקו מרחמי ונח נפשיה דרבי

leave earlier, then they still keep the money, while if the hospital needs to continue treating the patient beyond the ten days, they still only get the same amount of money given originally. The hospitals want to get you out as quickly as possible so they can take the sum of money and open up another available bed. However, the issue arises with the second part of the law: if the patient returns to the hospital later due to a complication form the same medical issue as before, the hospital must continue treating the patient based on the original payment. Now if the patient returns for another ten days after being discharged early from the hospital the first time, the hospital loses out money on all the days. There's only one way a hospital can stop a patient from returning again to complain about the work done in the hospital.

Q22. Is one permitted to go to an area where people aren't *tznius* if it's for medical reasons?

A: (5755) Rav Moshe (Igros Moshe EH 1:56)[110] addresses a similar question where doctors tells a person that he should go swimming to promote his health and rehabilitate his strength. However, there were no private swimming pools in this person's area, so his only option was going to the beach where women swim as well. The Gemara (Eruvin 18b)[111] says כל העובר אחורי אשה בנהר אין לו חלק לעולם הבא - that if a woman is going across the river and a man walks behind her, then he loses his portion in Olam Haba because he will look at her as she needs to lift up her clothing a little. Why do he lose his Olam Haba? He could have waited a minute until she crossed the river so he wouldn't need to see her, but since he put himself in this situation then he loses his Olam Haba. Similarly, Rabbenu Yonah (Shaarei Teshuva 3:22)[112] says

---

[110] Igros Moshe (EH 1:56) - וכן אם צריך לרפואה להיות אצל הים נמי אם סובר שלא יבוא לידי הרהור מותר להיות שם אם אינו מוצא מקום ושעות שאין שם נשים ואם אינו בטוח צ"ע לדינא

[111] Eruvin (18b) - אמר רב נחמן בר יצחק מסתברא דגברא סגי ברישא דתניא לא יהלך אדם אחורי אשה בדרך ואפילו אשתו נזדמנה לו על הגשר יסלקנה לצדדין וכל העובר אחורי אשה בנהר אין לו חלק לעולם הבא

[112] Shaarei Teshuva (3:22) - ועל מצות ציצית אמרו רבותינו זכרונם לברכה בספרי שהציצית מוספת קדושה שנאמר (במדבר ט"ו:מ) למען תזכרו ועשיתם את כל מצותי והייתם קדושים לאלקיכם וגם (פי' כמו אף על פי) כי אין מצות ציצית

that someone who doesn't wear *tzitzis* transgresses a very serious *aveira* because it's an easy *mitzva* to fulfill (Pesachim 113b)[113]. How much does it cost already? If someone has a chance to perform an inexpensive *mitzva* – especially one which helps you remember all the other *mitzvos* (Bamidbar 15:39)[114] – without due cause, then he has no respect or desire to do what the Ribono Shel Olam wants him to do. Why would such a person be interested in the זיו השכינה (Berachos 17a)[115] if he's not fulfilling such an easy *mitzva*? So too, there are certain *aveiros* which are harder and easier than others. For example, it's difficult not to eat all of Yom Kippur, so a person doesn't lose his Olam Haba for giving into his desire to eat – he is punished with *kares*, but doesn't lose his portion in Olam Haba. However, if a person puts himself into a difficult test for no reason by walking behind a woman in the river, that is a terrible *aveira*. Similarly, someone who speaks *lashon hara* is punished very severely and isn't מקבל פני השכינה (Sotah 42a)[116]. Why? There's no natural desire for a person to speak *lashon hara* as there is for eating delicious food. The desire for honor is a natural desire because you feel being honored might get you a job or a *shidduch*, but those who get together to speak *lashon hara* don't have a *yetzer hara* for it. So too, this person is putting himself in a difficult test by walking behind a woman in the river. However, Rav Moshe explains that since the patient who needs to swim for his health has no other alternative, it's similar to walking

---

זולתי על מי שיש לו בגד אשר לו ארבע כנפות ואם לו אין בגד כזה אינו חייב
לקנותו אף גם זאת (פי' כמו מכל מקום) אמרו רבותינו זכרונם לברכה כי ענוש
יענוש לעתות בצרה על דבר אשר לא חמד בלבבו יופי המצוה ושכרה לבעבור
סבב פני דברי חיובה עליו ולקחת לו בגד שיש לו ארבע כנפות לעשות בו ציצית
על כנפיו

[113] Pesachim (113b) - שבעה מנודין לשמים אלו הן יהודי שאין לו אשה
ושיש לו אשה ואין לו בנים ומי שיש לו בנים ואין מגדלן לתלמוד תורה ומי שאין
לו תפילין בראשו ותפילין בזרועו וציצית בבגדו ומזוזה בפתחו והמונע מנעלים
מרגליו

[114] Bamidbar (15:39) - וְהָיָה לָכֶם לְצִיצִת וּרְאִיתֶם אֹתוֹ וּזְכַרְתֶּם אֶת־כָּל־מִצְוֹת
ה' וַעֲשִׂיתֶם אֹתָם וְלֹא־תָתֻרוּ אַחֲרֵי לְבַבְכֶם וְאַחֲרֵי עֵינֵיכֶם אֲשֶׁר־אַתֶּם זֹנִים אַחֲרֵיהֶם

[115] Berachos (17a) - צדיקים יושבין ועטרותיהם בראשיהם ונהנים מזיו
השכינה שנאמר ויחזו את האלקים ויאכלו וישתו

[116] Sotah (42a) - א"ר ירמיה בר אבא ארבע כיתות אין מקבלות פני שכינה
כת ליצים וכת חניפים וכת שקרים וכת מספרי לשון הרע

in the street in America where women aren't dressed *tzinusdik*. It's permitted to walk in the streets of America since we're not walking around with the intention of seeing people who aren't *tznius*. The Gemara (Bava Basra 57b)[117] says if a person walks by a river where women are cleaning their laundry, then he's considered a *rasha*. Nonetheless, the Gemara says that if there was no alternative route - דליכא דרכא אחריתא - then it's permitted to walk by the river as long as the person doesn't have the intention of looking. There is a Gemara (Sanhedrin 75a)[118] which says there was a man who was in danger because he really wanted to marry a particular woman, but Chazal didn't want b'nos Yisroel to be considered *hefker* so they didn't let him. They said it was better for him to die than to make b'nos Yisroel *hefker*. However, the case of Rav Moshe is different because this person doesn't want to look at any women while he's swimming. Rather, he's just minding his own business and doesn't have any other option to improve his health without going to the beach. If another form of exercise would have been sufficient for the patient, then he would need to do that instead. If the patient could hardly see there are any women without his glasses on, then it would only be a question of *maras ayin*.

Q23. Are you allowed to accept experimental treatment?

A: (5755) Since there are a lot of cancer researchers trying new experiments around the United States, a lot of hospitals use the experimental procedures to see whether the treatment is actually

---

[117] Bava Basra (57b) - א"ר יוחנן משום ר' בנאה בכל שותפין מעכבין זה את זה חוץ מן הכביסה שאין דרכן של בנות ישראל להתבזות על הכביסה (ישעיהו לג:טו) ועוצם עיניו מראות ברע א"ר חייא בר אבא זה שאין מסתכל בנשים בשעה שעומדות על הכביסה היכי דמי אי דאיכא דרכא אחריתא רשע הוא אי דליכא דרכא אחריתא אנוס הוא לעולם דליכא דרכא אחריתא ואפ"ה מיבעי ליה למינס נפשיה

[118] Sanhedrin (75a) - אמר רב יהודה אמר רב מעשה באדם אחד שנתן עיניו באשה אחת והעלה לבו טינא ובאו ושאלו לרופאים ואמרו אין לו תקנה עד שתבעל אמרו חכמים ימות ואל תבעל לו תעמוד לפניו ערומה ימות ואל תעמוד לפניו ערומה תספר עמו מאחורי הגדר ימות ולא תספר עמו מאחורי הגדר פליגי בה ר' יעקב בר אידי ור' שמואל בר נחמני חד אמר אשת איש היתה וחד אמר פנויה היתה בשלמא למאן דאמר אשת איש היתה שפיר אלא למ"ד פנויה היתה מאי כולי האי

effective or not. The researchers first test their treatment on animals, and then test it on terminally ill patients. The United States government is the strictest government regarding allowing experimental treatment. In fact, they say that if aspirin was invented today then the United States government would have never permitted its use since it causes all kinds of problems like ulcers, blood hemorrhages, and the like, but since it's been in use for so long it's allowed. Aspirin was originally the trademark name Bayer's Aspirin, but its use became so widespread like Scotch Tape or Dupont Glue that eventually the company lost the rights to the name. Rav Moshe says that if there is a chance this experimental treatment will endanger the patient, then it is forbidden to accept the treatment. Very often these experimental treatments do endanger the patient, so the doctors tell the patient, "Look, our treatment is experimental and has a 3% success rate, but in a terminal situation where a person won't survive anyway then it's worth the risk." It's not that the treatment didn't work 97% of the time – it caused the death of the vast majority of the patients. Therefore, Rav Moshe says such an experimental treatment would be forbidden to accept upon oneself. The treatment might be very successful with treating lung cancer, but cause cancer somewhere else in the body which kills the patients. An *erhliche* doctor can give you the most accurate information to make an intelligent decision. Unless we know for sure that there is true success – not just a placebo effect – with this dangerous experimental treatment, it is not permitted to accept it.

Q24. Can a patient accept a risky surgery to live a normal life?

A: (5755) The Chachmas Adam (Binas Adam Sha'ar *Issur V'Heter* 73 [93])[119] brings a *shailah* where a patient has three

---

[119] Binas Adam Sha'ar Issur V'Heter 73 [93] - נראה לי דמותר ואף על גב דחיישינן לחיי שעה ולכן מפקחין עליו גל בשבת ואמרינן ביומא לא נצרכה אלא לחיי שעה כבר כתבו תוספות בעבודה זרה (כז:) הביא הט"ז (בסימן קנ"ה:ב) דלעולם חיישינן לטובתו ולכך בימי הש"ס שהיו העכו"ם חשודין על שפיכות דמים ואסור להתרפאות מהם אפילו בספק חי ספק מת אבל אם הוא ודאי מת מתרפאים מהם אף על גב שמא יקרב מיתתו קיימא לן דלחיי שעה לא חיישינן בהא כיון דאם לא כן ודאי ימות ואם כן הכי נמי עבדינן טובתו ולא חיישינן לחיי שעה

months left to live, but the doctors can perform an operation which will allow the person to live a normal life or die on the operating table. The Chachmas Adam says that the patient is allowed to accept the operation despite there being a chance that he'll die because there's also a chance that he'll live a normal life if the surgery is successful. Rav Moshe (Igros Moshe YD 2:58)[120] writes in one *teshuva* that if there is a 5% chance the patient will live, then he can undergo the surgery, but less than a 5% chance of survival would be forbidden to accept the surgery. In a *teshuva* written about 25 years later, Rav Moshe (Igros Moshe YD 3:36)[121] writes that if the doctors say there is a 40% chance the operation will be successful, then you are allowed to perform the operation – but you are not allowed to accept the procedure if it is successful less than 40% of the time. Rav Moshe's *talmidim* asked him how to answer the conflict in *teshuvos*. He explained that the first *teshuva* was saying the patient knows there is a 5% chance of survival, while the later *teshuva* says that if the doctors say there is a 40% chance of the operation being successful – which is really a 5% chance of survival – then you can accept the surgery. When doctors say an operation is successful, that doesn't mean the patient will survive. For instance, if the doctor performs a successful heart surgery on someone - but the patient then dies of something due to the operation - they will still say the operation was successful. They'll say that the patient just died from pneumonia or the flu due to his weakened state from the surgery. I'm really providing the general rules for these medical questions, but whenever it becomes a practical question you must discuss it with a Rav because the slightest differences in each case make significant changes to the *psak*.

---

[120] Igros Moshe YD (2:58) - דלכן היה מותר להם ליפול אל מחנה ארם אף שודאי יותר קרוב במלחמה שימיתום אלמא דלחיי שעה לא חיישינן אף כשהצלה הוא בספק רחוק ויותר קרוב שיהרגום תיכף

[121] Igros Moshe YD (3:36) - ויש גם קצת ראיה מהא דהקרא דילפינן מיניה דלחיי שעה לא חיישינן הוא מהא דאמרו לכו ונפלה אל מחנה ארם אם יחיונו נחיה ואם ימיתנו ומתנו דאפשר שהיה שם רק ספק השקול דטוב להם ליקח אותם יותר לעבדים ובע"כ נצטרך לומר כדכתבתי שאף בריפוי אצל רופאים עכו"ם שיליף שמותר ואין חוששין לחיי שעה הוא משום דנחשב לענין זה רק כספק השקול

Chapter 3: Patient's Perspective

Q25. Is one obligated to only use local anesthesia rather than the more dangerous anesthesia for a procedure?

A: (5755) No, you can accept general anesthesia for a necessary procedure because there are other issues with local anesthesia as well.

Q26. Must someone accept a life-saving operation if it will cause him to be handicapped for the rest of his life?

A: (5755) Let's say a person has gangrene in his feet. The doctors can amputate the gangrene to save the patient's life, but if they don't amputate his feet then the patient will die. The first question here is whether a person has the right to even decline a surgery if it will save his life. The second question is whether the doctor has an obligation to perform the operation against the patient's will. Rav Moshe Feinstein wrote a *kuntres* to Dr. Jacobovitz that a patient has no right to decline surgery if it will save his life (Igros Moshe CM 2:73:5)[122]. Just as every Jew has an obligation to save another Jew in danger (Shulchan Aruch CM 426:1)[123], we have an obligation to save ourselves as well – even if it means that the person will be handicapped. As far as the doctor is concerned, if the patient will become so mentally ill from you performing the surgery against his will, then you should not perform the surgery actively doing something which will make him a *choleh sheyesh bo sakana* since he'll become severely depressed. Moreover, if someone else in the family will become severely depressed with

---

[122] Igros Moshe (CM 2:73:5) - ובדבר כשהחולה אינו רוצה ליקה הרפואה תלוי אם הוא מחמת יאוש או מחמת שהוא צער לפניו ומתחשב רק עם שעה זו שאינו רוצה להצטער בה אף שמאמין להרופאים שהוא לטובתו שיתרפא בזה או שידעו מזה איך לרפאותו שהוא מעשה שטות ומעשה תינוקות צריכין לכפותו אם אפשר להם אבל אם הוא מחמת שאינו מאמין לרופאים אלו צריכין למצא רופא שמאמין בו

[123] Shulchan Aruch (CM 426:1) - הרואה את חבירו טובע בים או ליסטים באין עליו או חיה רעה באה עליו ויכול להצילו הוא בעצמו או שישכור אחרים להציל ולא הציל או ששמע עכו"ם או מוסרים מחשבים עליו רעה או טומנים לו פח ולא גילה אוזן חבירו והודיעו או שידע בעכו"ם או באנס שהו' בא על חבירו ויכול לפייסו בגלל חבירו ולהסיר מה שבלבו ולא פייסו וכיוצא בדברים אלו עובר על לא תעמוד על דם רעך

66

the surgery being done then the doctor should not perform the surgery. However, if the person won't be so terribly depressed with the doctor performing the surgery, then the doctor would need to perform the surgery to save the patient. Nonetheless, a doctor is not obligated to give up more than one-fifth (Rema 656:1)[124] of his assets by losing his practice after going to jail for performing the surgery against his patient's will. We don't heal people by giving them another sickness – especially since the first illness was not done through your hands and the second one is.

Q27. Can you perform an operation with the sole purpose being to relieve pain?

A: (5755) The question is based on the prohibition against injuring yourself unless done to heal a medical issue. Rav Moshe (Igros Moshe CM 2:73:9)[125] says that a person is allowed to have the operation done in order to alleviate his pain. Pain wears a person down and gradually takes away their will to live. Therefore, Rav Moshe says there is no doubt that alleviating the patient's pain will lengthen the person's life and would be permitted even in a case where you transgress an *aveira* in the process – like alleviating the pain caused from prostate cancer by removing the *beitzim* which is an issue of *sirus*.

---

124 Rema (656:1) - מִי שֶׁאֵין לוֹ אֶתְרוֹג אוֹ שְׁאָר מִצְוָה עוֹבֶרֶת אֵין צָרִיךְ לְבַזְבֵּז עָלֶיהָ הוֹן רַב וּכְמוֹ שֶׁאָמְרוּ הַמְבַזְבֵּז אַל יְבַזְבֵּז יוֹתֵר מֵחוֹמֶשׁ אפי' מִצְוָה עוֹבֶרֶת וְדַוְקָא מִצְוַת עֲשֵׂה אֲבָל לֹא תַעֲשֶׂה יִתֵּן כָּל מָמוֹנוֹ קוֹדֶם שֶׁיַּעֲבוֹר

125 Igros Moshe (CM 2:73:9) - הִנֵּה זֶה מוּתָּר שֶׁאַף בִּשְׁבִיל הֲסָרַת הַיִּסּוּרִין מוּתָּר לַעֲשׂוֹת נִיתּוּחַ בְּחוֹלָה דְּסַכָּנָה וְגַם מִסְתַּבֵּר שֶׁהוּא מַאֲרִיךְ חַיָּיו לְאֵיזוֹ שָׁעָה קְטַנָּה אַף שֶׁלֹּא יָדוּעַ זֶה גַם לָרוֹפְאִים דּוַדַּאי מִסְתַּבֵּר שֶׁשְּׁנֵי חוֹלִים מְסֻכָּנִים בְּמַחֲלָה אַחַת אֲבָל הָאֶחָד אֵין לוֹ יִסּוּרִין וְהָאֶחָד יֵשׁ לוֹ יִסּוּרִין שֶׁבְּדֶרֶךְ הַטֶּבַע מִי שֶׁאֵין לוֹ יִסּוּרִין יִחְיֶה יוֹתֵר מְעַט דְּהַיִּסּוּרִין גַּדוֹלִים נַמִּי מְקַצְּרִין הַחַיִּים וְלָכֵן וַדַּאי שָׁמּוּתָר אַף שֶׁעוֹשֶׂה סִירוּס שֶׁהוּא בְּלָאו כֵּיוָן שֶׁהוּא חוֹלֶה מְסֻכָּן יֵשׁ לַעֲשׂוֹת הַנִּיתּוּחַ הַזֶּה אַף שֶׁהוּא רַק לְהָקֵל יִסּוּרָיו

67

Chapter 4: Mothers in Halacha

Q1. If a woman asks a Jewish doctor to make an abortion, what should he do?

A: (5755) If the fetus is older than 40 days old, there isn't anything the Jewish doctor can do because it would be considered murder to abort the fetus which would be forbidden also by a Jew for various reasons. It doesn't matter whether the mother is Jewish or not since we can't murder a Jew or non-Jew. In fact, Rav Moshe (Igros Moshe CM 2:73:8)[126] says the Jewish doctor isn't allowed to refer the patient to another doctor whether the other doctor is Jewish or not since a non-Jew who kills a fetus is tantamount to murder. I think the doctor is allowed to say, "I can't do an abortion for you, but maybe if you go to another doctor then he'll be able to give you advice on what to do." In other words, you're allowed to recommend the mother to go a particular doctor who might give her a referral for where to get an abortion. *Lifnei iver* (Vayikra 19:14)[127] would only apply if you tell the mother to go to the other doctor for an abortion, but I don't think it would apply if you tell the mother to ask another doctor for advice. You're not telling the other doctor to do an abortion, rather you're just telling the mother that another doctor might be able to offer guidance on what to do. However, I'm not sure whether it's really not considered *lifnei iver* for the Jewish doctor. If that second doctor sends the mother to

---

[126] Igros Moshe (CM 2:73:8) - דלא נשים איכא בעוה"ר שבזה"ז הנשים מעליי ורוצות להפיל העובר שבמעיהן הנה זה הוא אסור מאיסור רציחה ואסור לסייע בזה לא רק לישראלית אלא אף לנכרית משום שבני נח נמי אסורין ברציחה גם בעובר ובני נח המורין בזה שגם נהרגין על רציחת עוברין שלכן אסור אף לסייע בזה וגם איכא משום לפני עור ואף כשאפשר לה להודיע מרופאים שעושין זה גם מאחריני אין לסייע בזה אף לא לנכרית אם אף היה בזה חשש איבה אבל בעצם ליכא חשש איבה כשיאמר שהוא אינו רוצה לעזור לדבר שהוא רציחת נפש שהרי יודעות אף הנשים הנכריות שאין זה דבר נכון לעשות שהרי גם כמה מדינות אוסרין זה משום רציחה ויכול הרופא יר"ש לומר שהוא אינו רוצה להתערב בדבר רציחת עובר כשאין זה לרפואה דסכנת האם

[127] Vayikra (19:14) - לֹא־תְקַלֵּל חֵרֵשׁ וְלִפְנֵי עִוֵּר לֹא תִתֵּן מִכְשֹׁל וְיָרֵאתָ מֵאֱלֹקֶיךָ אֲנִי ה

another doctor, then you only did a שְׁבוּת דִּשְׁבוּת by having one non-Jewish doctor send to another non-Jewish doctor (Shulchan Aruch 586:21)[128]. The Mishna Berura (307:20)[129] says that it's permitted in a pressing situation to tell a non-Jew to tell another non-Jew to do something forbidden for you on Shabbos.

Q2. Are abortions ever allowed halachically?

A: (5755) There are cases when you are allowed to perform an abortion from a halachic perspective, and there is a difference between the first 40 days of conception and after that time. Once the baby is 40 days old, you can no longer have an abortion unless the fetus is a threat to the mother's life. If the fetus is a threat to the mother's life for any reason – and this does happen often – then we look at the child as a *rodef* and remove the fetus from endangering the mother's life (Rambam Rotze'ach 1:9)[130]. If you see someone trying to kill someone else, you don't need to turn to Beis Din to decide what to do – these life-threatening situations require immediate action. In fact, the mother is not allowed to decide to take the chance of continuing the pregnancy since she's putting herself in danger. When the fetus is less than 40 days old, then there's more to speak about. Chazal say that the first 40 days a fetus is considered מיא בעלמא (Yevamos 69b)[131]. Meaning, the fetus is not in the stage of being considered a human being yet. In other words, a stillbirth after 40 days is *metameh b'ohel* like a regular *meis,* but before 40 days the fetus isn't considered anything. Nonetheless, aborting a fetus which is not yet 40 days old is still forbidden without any medical reason because there's an *issur* of *hashchasas zera*. This *zera* which could have been used

---

[128] Shulchan Aruch (OC 586:21) - וְעַל יְדֵי אֵינוֹ יְהוּדִי מֻתָּר דְּהָוֵי שְׁבוּת דִּשְׁבוּת פֵּרוּשׁ אָסוּר אֲמִירָה לְעַכּוּ"ם בְּאִסּוּר דְּאוֹרַיְתָא הוּא מִשּׁוּם שְׁבוּת שֶׁאָמְרוּ חֲכָמֵינוּ זִכְרוֹנָם לִבְרָכָה לְשַׁבָּת מֶזֶּה אֲמִירָה לְעַכּוּ"ם וּבְאָסּוּר דְּרַבָּנָן הוּא שְׁבוּת דִּשְׁבוּת

[129] Mishna Berura (307:20) - דכיון שהאיסור אינו אלא מדרבנן ואיסור אמירה לא"י הוא ג"כ רק מדרבנן והוי שבות דשבות לא גזרו באופנים אלו

[130] Rambam Rotze'ach (1:9) - הוֹרוּ חֲכָמִים שֶׁהָעֻבָּרָה שֶׁהִיא מַקְשָׁה לֵילֵד מֻתָּר לַחְתּךְ הָעֻבָּר בְּמֵעֶיהָ בֵּין בְּסַם בֵּין בְּיָד מִפְּנֵי שֶׁהוּא כְּרוֹדֵף אַחֲרֶיהָ לְהָרְגָהּ

[131] Yevamos (69b) - אמר רב חסדא טובלת ואוכלת עד ארבעים דאי לא מיעברא הא לא מיעברא ואי מיעברא עד ארבעים מיא בעלמא היא

to make a child is being destroyed (Chavos Yair 31). Nonetheless, non-Jews are not commanded against *hashchasas zera* and would be allowed to perform an abortion on a fetus younger than 40 days old. Nonetheless, telling a non-Jewish doctor to perform an abortion on a fetus younger than 40 days old is forbidden *mid'rabanan* for us. There are certain situations where you can be lenient for an *issur d'rabanan* – like if the mother will become sick or other issues. After 40 days from conception, then there is really no other leniency for abortion unless the mother's life is in danger. Let's say the mother is manic depressive and receives lithium to settle down her mood swings which she stops taking while pregnant because it's harmful for the baby. She shouldn't have become pregnant in the first place because someone who is manic depressive is considered a *choleh sheyesh bo sakana* in most cases. She can become so depressed that she doesn't have the energy or desire to save herself from a dangerous situation. Each case needs the opinion of a good psychiatrist or psychologist to decide whether the mother is in danger. We're very careful with what is considered a danger to the mother's health and might permit an abortion too.

(5779) If the mother is in danger due to the fetus not being aborted, then you are allowed to abort the child (Shulchan Aruch CM 425:2)[132]. As far as these *halachos* are concerned, I don't think there's a difference between Jewish and non-Jewish patients. Although non-Jews are commanded against aborting a fetus (Sanhedrin 57b)[133] while we're not – which can cause an issue of

---

[132] Shulchan Aruch CM 425:2 - לפיכך העוברת שהיא מקשה לילד מותר לחתוך העובר במעיה בין בסם בין ביד מפני שהוא כרודף אחריה להרגה ואם הוציא ראשו אין נוגעין בו שאין דוחין נפש מפני נפש וזהו טבעו של עולם

[133] Sanhedrin (57b) - אשכח ר' יעקב בר אחא דהוה כתיב בספר אגדתא דבי רב בן נח נהרג בדיין א' ובעד אחד שלא בהתראה מפי איש ולא מפי אשה ואפילו קרוב משום רבי ישמעאל אמרו אף על העוברין מנהני מילי אמר רב יהודה דאמר קרא (בראשית ט:ה) אך את דמכם לנפשותיכם אדרוש אפילו בדיין אחד (בראשית ט:ה) מיד כל חיה אפילו שלא בהתראה (בראשית ט:ה) אדרשנו ומיד האדם אפילו בעד אחד (בראשית ט:ה) מיד איש ולא מיד אשה אחיו אפילו קרוב משום רבי ישמעאל אמרו אף על העוברין מאי טעמיה דרבי ישמעאל דכתיב (בראשית ט:ו) שופך דם האדם באדם דמו ישפך איזהו אדם שהוא באדם הוי אומר זה עובר שבמעי אמו

lifnei iver if you ask a non-Jewish doctor to perform the abortion – you are allowed to ask a non-Jewish doctor to perform the abortion if it is a situation which permits an abortion. The Maharsha (Sanhedrin 57b)[134] writes that when Pharoah specifically told the Jewish midwives rather than the Egyptian midwives to kill all the males because non-Jews are commanded against killing a fetus. In former times, you could tell whether a male or female was about to be born because a boy would be born face down and a girl would be born face up (Sotah 11b)[135]. Pharoah was afraid the Egyptian midwives wouldn't listen to him because they knew they were commanded not to kill fetuses while the Jewish midwives weren't. Nonetheless, Pharoah made a mistake because he didn't know the Chavos Yair (31) who says that even though Jews aren't held accountable for murder by doing an abortion on a fetus, it's still forbidden because there's an *issur* of *mashchasas zera* - wasting seed.

Q3. May one perform an abortion if doctors say the child will be born sick?

A: (5755) Rav Moshe (Igros Moshe CM 2:69:3)[136] is stringent in not allowing an abortion to be done even if the fetus is younger than 40 days old if the doctors determined the child will not be 100% – like if it will be born with Tay-Sachs Disease. It's a very

---

[134] Maharsha Sanhedrin (57b) - בזה אמרתי ליישב בפ' שמות שדקדק הכתוב לאמר ויאמר מלך מצרים למילדות העבריות דודאי פרעה לא שאל מהם להרוג הזכרים בידים דבן נח מוזהר על שפיכות דמים ולכך לא אמר כן למילדות המצריות שהוזהרו על שפיכות דמים אפילו בעוברים אבל למילדות העבריות אמר שהותר לכם להרוג עובר במעי אמו וראיתם על האבנים קודם שיצא לאויר העולם אם בן הוא וגו' וכיון שאי אפשר בהם לפטור משפיכות דמים רק בתחילת יציאת הולד קודם שיצא ראשו או רובו הוצרך לתת להם סימנין כמו שכתוב בפרק קמא דסוטה וראיתם על האבנים סימן גדול מסר להם כו' יריכותיה מצטננות כו' וכן פניו למעלה

[135] Sotah (11b) - שמות א:טז) אם בן הוא והמתן אותו א"ר חנינא סימן גדול מסר להן בן פניו למטה בת פניה למעלה

[136] Igros Moshe (CM 2:69:3) – וברור ופשוט כדכתבתי הלכה הברורה ע"פ רבותינו הראשונים המפרשים והפוסקים ממש שאסור בדין רציחה ממש כל עובר בין כשר בין ממזר בין סתם עוברים ובין הידועים לחולי תיי-סקס שכולן אסורין מדינא ממש

traumatic period for the parents to have a baby with Tay-Sachs, and there has not been a child born with the disease which has survived. Parents who are prudent enough to perform the DNA tests through Dor Yesharim to find out whether they are both carriers for Tay-Sachs can avoid this painful situation (Igros Moshe EH 4:10)[137]. There are also alternative ways to have a healthy child even if both parents are carriers through IVF (in-vitro fertilization). IVF is done by taking the *zera* from the man, taking an egg from the mother - which isn't a carrier for Tay-Sachs since not every egg is a carrier - fertilizing them in a test tube, and then reinserting them back into the womb of the mother. There are a lot of problems involved with IVF since there is only a 10% chance that it will work and each attempt costs about $10,000. It's not something anyone wants to take upon themselves voluntarily and would be much better off avoiding the *shidduch* in the first place by going through Dor Yesharim. Moreover, there are many complex *shailos* involved with IVF like whether the child is truly the product of the mother and father. There are various occasions where the doctor donated his own *zera* for the IVF. The parents would need to tell the doctor performing the IVF that they will test the baby's DNA in a non-affiliated lab to make sure it is truly their child – and they should have the test done in order to know from a halachic perspective that the child is a product of the mother and father. Otherwise, they will need to reveal to potential *shidduchim* that their child is not necessarily their child with absolute certainty. You can always make such a DNA test later, but it's always better to do it sooner than later. Nonetheless, it is known that since doctors perform defensive medicine, they tend to exaggerate the problems which might occur in the child. They would much rather have the child aborted in order to be absolved of any blame. If the child doesn't turn out to be normal, then the parents will either blame the doctors for not telling them or say

---

[137] Igros Moshe (EH 4:10) - וזהו הנראה לע״ד כי אף שהוא מיעוט קטן ילדים נולדים כאלו ושייך לומר על זה הקרא דתמים תהיה עם ה' אלקיך וכפרש"י בחומש שם שכתב התהלך עמו בתמימות ותצפה לו ולא תחקור אחר העתידות מ״מ כיון שעתה נעשה זה באופן קל לבדוק יש לדון שאם אינו בודק את עצמו הוא כסגירת העינים לראות מה שאפשר לראות ומכיון שאם ח"ו אירע דבר כזה הוא להורי הילד צער גדול מאד מן הראוי למי שצריך לישא אשה לבדוק את עצמו ולכן טוב לפרסם הדבר ע״י עתונים ואופנים שידעו העולם שאיכא בדיקה כזו

the doctors didn't deliver him correctly. There is a very high rate of malpractice claims against obstetricians delivering babies. In fact, I believe obstetricians pay $84,000 a year for their malpractice insurance premiums. Part of what you're paying for in hospital care is the malpractice insurance since they need to get the money back somehow. The doctors can test the fetus using amniocentesis to see whether there is anything wrong with the fetus – but generally the test cannot be done until after 40 days of conception. Consequently, there isn't much you can do other than worry since you're not allowed to make an abortion at that point. There was a case I was involved with where a pregnant mother had a cyst on her ovary where the doctors said they must perform surgery to remove it. The doctor recommended she should abort the fetus because the anesthesia would affect the baby and might make the child be not normal. Her husband asked me whether they were allowed to do the abortion or not. I told them that they were not allowed to do the abortion since the baby was already a few months old and it wasn't a risk to the mother. The doctor then told the family, "Listen, I'm telling you that there is a great chance that this child will turn out not to be normal because of this operation, and I really think you must consider making an abortion because you're taking a big chance." The *yungerman* returned to me again to relay the doctor's strong suggestion, but I still said not to abort the baby. When they stood firm with the doctor, he told them, "You made the right choice. If it was my wife, I also wouldn't allow her to make an abortion either, but I needed to recommend that you abort the baby because I couldn't take any chances. Moreover, I couldn't just inform you of the risk since you could still return with a malpractice suit saying that I didn't impress upon you the importance of considering aborting the baby. Now I want to tell you that the chances of the anesthesia affecting the baby is very little and I think it's a terrible thing to do an abortion in such a situation." The doctor performed the procedure and the family later had a healthy, normal child. The doctors need to scare the parents in order to protect themselves. There was another time that the doctor took a sonogram and said the baby was dead since they couldn't detect any heartbeat. The doctor wanted to perform a DNC – cleaning out the uterus and remove the fetus – so the parents asked me if they should proceed. I told them that if the baby is certainly dead, then they are allowed to have the DNC performed, but also said there was no rush to do it since under normal circumstances the baby which was only a couple months old would come out by itself if it's dead. The husband told me the last time his wife had a DNC she had negative side effects, and she doesn't really want to have it done – so I said they really don't need to have a DNC. Then the mother told the doctor she didn't want a DNC. A couple weeks later, the doctor was getting nervous and really wanted to do the DNC, so he took another sonogram and lo and behold…there was no heartbeat. However, the baby had grown! The doctor couldn't figure out how the baby could grow if it was dead. They used another sonogram machine to see if they could detect a heartbeat, but they still weren't sure if there was a heartbeat. I'm just relating this story to show that just because a doctor is sure of something doesn't mean those are the facts 100%. However, if the doctors are confident with certainty that something will occur, then you must follow their medical advice.

Q4. Is it permitted to use an aborted fetus for scientific research?

A: (5755) There is no *din* of desecrating the dead for a fetus because *nivul hameis* only applies to someone who was considered an *adam* who lived at one time and makes the relatives become mourners (Shulchan Aruch YD 374:8)[138]. Nonetheless, the fetus or stillborn after 40 days is *metameh kohanim*. Additionally, the Noda B'Yehuda (Noda B'Yehuda YD 209)[139] says that anyone who is *metameh b'ohel* must be buried in order to prevent the *kohanim* from being *nichshol*. Rav Bina'ah marked the graves where the *tzadikim* died (Bava Basra 58a)[140] in order to ensure *kohanim* don't accidentally walk over their graves. The *mitzva* of burying someone only applies to an *adam*, but there is a

---

[138] Shulchan Aruch YD (374:8) - תינוק כל שלשים יום ויום שלשים בכלל אין מתאבלים עליו אפילו גמרו שערו וצפרניו ומשם ואילך מתאבל עליו אלא אם כן נודע שהוא בן ח' ואי קים ליה ביה שכלו לו חדשיו כגון שבעל ופירש ונולד חי לט' חדשים גמורי' אפי' מת ביום שנולד מתאבלים עליו

[139] Noda B'Yehuda (YD 209) - ומה שקוברין האברים הוא להציל מן הטומאה

[140] Bava Basra (58a) - ר' בנאה הוה קא מציין מערתא

second aspect to burial in preventing the *kohanim* from becoming *tameh*. Therefore, even though a fetus doesn't have a *mitzva* to bury it, we must still bury the fetus to ensure *kohanim* don't become *tameh*. If parents have a child which aborted itself or had to be aborted halachically for whatever reason, the doctors are allowed to use the fetus to figure out what issue occurred so that their future children won't suffer from the same issue. However, the doctors must either burn or bury the fetus afterwards – they cannot just throw it out.

Q5. May a non-Jewish doctor perform abortions?

A: (5755) It's a sad thing to think about, but the same people in the hospitals who help people live are the same people who murder others. Moreover, *b'nei Noach* are more commanded against abortions than Jews since *b'nei Noach* committing abortions receive the death penalty for murder (in former times) (Sanhedrin 57b)[141] while Jews who commit abortion transgress a negative commandment (Tosfos Sanhedrin 59a)[142]. Hospitals used to have the nursery next to the maternity ward where the mothers were staying. Nowadays the hospitals put the nursery much further away from the maternity ward since they say the mothers who had an abortion done shouldn't need to suffer hearing the babies crying realizing they don't have their own child even though they themselves elected to have the abortion done. The hospital is more worried about the mothers' feelings than killing the children because the mother is the one who pays the hospital bills.

---

[141] Sanhedrin (57b) - אשכח ר' יעקב בר אחא דהוה כתיב בספר אגדתא דבי רב בן נח נהרג בדיין א' ובעד אחד שלא בהתראה מפי איש ולא מפי אשה ואפילו קרוב משום רבי ישמעאל אמרו אף על העוברין מנהני מילי אמר רב יהודה דאמר קרא (בראשית ט:ה) אך את דמכם לנפשותיכם אדרוש אפילו בדיין אחד (בראשית ט:ה) מיד כל חיה אפילו שלא בהתראה (בראשית ט:ה) אדרשנו ומיד האדם אפילו בעד אחד (בראשית ט:ה) מיד איש ולא מיד אשה אחיו אפילו קרוב משום רבי ישמעאל אמרו אף על העוברין מאי טעמיה דרבי ישמעאל דכתיב (בראשית ט:ו) שופך דם האדם באדם דמו ישפך איזהו אדם שהוא באדם הוי אומר זה עובר שבמעי אמו

[142] Tosfos Sanhedrin (59a) - ועל העוברים דעובד כוכבים חייב וישראל פטור אע"ג דפטור מ"מ לא שרי and see Chavos Yair (31)

Chapter 4: Mothers in Halacha

Q6. Is there a leniency for *pikuach nefesh* when the danger only exists for the fetus and not the mother?

A: (5779) In general, we say any birth for a mother is considered *pikuach nefashos*. Consequently, you're allowed to desecrate Shabbos for a mother giving birth (Mishna Shabbos 18:3)[143]. Even though nowadays the incidence of a woman dying in childbirth is not very common, we don't follow the majority of cases when it comes to *pikuach nefashos* (Shulchan Aruch 329:2)[144] and do whatever is necessary for the mother even if she's not necessarily in danger right now. If it is considered *pikuach nefesh* for the fetus, then it is also *pikuach nefesh* for the mother. There's a *teshuva* from the Binyan Tzion who discusses a question by a *bris* where they cut the *orlah*, push back the *periya*, and then do *metzitza* by sucking out blood from the place where the incision was made in order to prevent infection or tetanus from occurring – I'm not sure which one they were concerned about and it doesn't matter. The Gemara then says if there's a *mohel* who doesn't perform *metzitza*, we terminate his right to be a *mohel* because he's putting children in danger (Shabbos 133b)[145]. The person asked the Binyan Tzion that since we are much more knowledgeable about infections nowadays, have sterilized medical equipment used for the *milah* - making sure the operation site is as clean as possible being washed with alcohol to remove 99% of the germs and the stainless-steel medical equipment is rarely affected by rust nowadays - the chance of infection or tetanus is very remote. Therefore, the person asked if we are still obligated to perform the *metzitza* (Binyan Tzion 24)[146]. This is particularly pertinent on Shabbos

---

[143] Mishna Shabbos (18:3) - וּמְיַלְּדִין אֶת הָאִשָּׁה בְּשַׁבָּת וְקוֹרִין לָהּ חֲכָמָה מִמָּקוֹם לְמָקוֹם וּמְחַלְּלִין עָלֶיהָ אֶת הַשַּׁבָּת וְקוֹשְׁרִין אֶת הַטַּבּוּר רַבִּי יוֹסֵי אוֹמֵר אַף חוֹתְכִין

[144] Shulchan Aruch (329:2) - אין הולכין בפיקוח נפש אחר הרוב

[145] Shabbos (133b) - אמר רב פפא האי אומנא דלא מייץ סכנה הוא ועברינן ליה

[146] Binyan Tzion (24) - ואם תאמרו הלא לא לחנם בטלנו המציצה רק באשר שראינו שנתהו' סכנה על ידה בשיש חולי בפה המוצץ וכי אפשר לבדוק בכל פעם את פיו כשמוצץ על זה אשיב הלא החזקה היא אחת מהיסודות אשר כל התורה נשענת עליהן וסוקלין ושורפין על החזקות ולמה נדאג שמי שהוא בחזקת בריא

76

since *metzitza* requires us to desecrate Shabbos by drawing out blood. Although you're allowed to draw out blood through *metzitza* on Shabbos when it protects the child from harm, it seems that if *metzitza* isn't necessary then it would be prohibited to draw out the blood on Shabbos (Shulchan Aruch 328:48)[147]. The Binyan Tzion replied, "How do you know there's no more danger nowadays for children who don't have *metzitza* done? There might still be one child who is put in danger by not doing *metzitza* today. Since we don't follow the majority of people when it comes to life-threatening situations, you are still obligated to do the *metzitza* even on Shabbos." So too, although the incidence of mothers dying in childbirth has significantly decreased over time, there are still occasions where mothers don't make it. The Gemara (Bava Basra 16a)[148] discusses a case where the child is too large to fit through its mother's pelvic canal, but nowadays doctors can measure the size of the baby using sonograms in order to prevent the mother from being put in danger. If the child is too large to fit through, then they induce the mother into labor earlier to ensure the child is born while it's still small enough to fit through the pelvic canal. There are other times where a mother wants to have a fully natural childbirth without speaking with medical doctors and puts her life in danger. It's not her right to risk her life by not speaking with a doctor. We don't take any chances with a mother's life and will deal with the fetus if it's putting the mother's life in danger.

Q7. Is it permitted for a pregnant mother to allow for her labor to be induced out of convenience?

וכשרות ע"י הבדיקה הראשונה שנתרע אח"כ ובפרט בדבר שאם נתרע אי אפשר להמוחזק שלא ידע ברייעותא שלו וכי בשופטני עסקינן שיסכנן נפשות על חנם ובדבר שעבידא לאגלויי דבלאי"ה לא משקרי בה אינשי

[147] Shulchan Aruch (328:48) - אסור להניח בגד על מכה שיוצ' ממנו דם מפני שהדם יצבע אותו ואסור להוציא דם מהמכה

[148] Bava Basra (16a) - חולל אילות תשמור אילה זו רחמה צר בשעה שכורעת ללדת אני מזמין לה דרקון שמכישה בבית הרחם ומתרפה ממולדה ואלמלי מקדים רגע אחד או מאחר רגע אחד מיד מתה בין רגע לרגע לא נתחלף לי בין איוב לאויב נתחלף לי

Chapter 4: Mothers in Halacha

A: (5755) Rav Moshe (Igros Moshe YD 2:74)[149] says it's forbidden to induce labor because a woman is not allowed to willingly put herself into a danger unless it is medically indicated. Women are allowed to put themselves in danger by accepting childbirth upon themselves because the Torah says there is a *mitzva* of פְּרוּ וּרְבוּ (Bereishis 1:28)[150], but for you to choose to put yourself in danger at an earlier time is not permitted. Childbirth is always considered a *sakana* as we are permitted to desecrate Shabbos even nowadays (Shulchan Aruch 330:1)[151]. Most of the time it's not a danger to the mother, but since it's possible the labor will become life-threatening we must take the mother to the hospital on Shabbos. I recently heard something fascinating from a doctor who told me that before World War I there was an infection which was common among mothers giving birth which seemed to stop after the war. Now it's starting to come back again, so it's something to be concerned about for childbirth. (See Igros Moshe OC 4:105:6)[152]

---

[149] Igros Moshe (YD 2:74) - ואין להקדים אף שהיא אותה סכנה טבעית
עצמה אם לא יאמרו הרופאים שיש סננה לחכות אבל לע״ד יש טעם יותר בדור
לאסור דלידה בזמנה כדרך הנשים לא נחשב לסכנה כלל דמאחר שכן ברא השי״ת
את העולם שיפרו וירבו ובודאי ברא שיהיה לברכה ולא לסכנה וגם הא ציוה
השי״ת בחיוב עשה להוליד בנים ולא מסתבר שיהיה הציווי ליכנס בסכנה בשביל
קיום עשה זו דפו״ר ובפרט שהנשים אין מחוייבות בהעשה דפו״ר שנצטרך לומר
שנתנה התורה להם רשות ליכנס בסכנה להוליד בנים אלא צריך לומר שאין בזה
סכנה כלל היינו שהבטיחה השי״ת שלא יהיה בזה סכנה לעולם ומה שאירע שמתות
בשעת לידתן הוא רק מחמת שמחוייבת עונש כדתנן בשבת דף ל״א על שלש
עבירות נשים מתות בשעת לידתן ולפ״ז הוא רק בלידה דבזמנה שעל זה איכא
הבטחת השי״ת בבריאתו ובציווי העשה דפו״ר שלא תסתכן דהעונש בשביל חטא
דעץ הדעת הוא רק יסורים דחבלי לידה ולא מיתה ח״ו אבל כשרוצין להקדים
הלידה שלא כפי שהיה צריך להיות ליכא ע״ז הבטחתו וממילא נכנסה לסכנה
דלידה שלולא הבטחת השי״ת הרי זה סכנה ולכן הוא דבר אסור לעשות תחבולות
להקדים לידה אם לא כשאיכא סכנה לחכות

[150] Bereishis (1:28) - וַיְבָרֶךְ אֹתָם אֱלֹקִים וַיֹּאמֶר לָהֶם אֱלֹקִים פְּרוּ וּרְבוּ וּמִלְאוּ
אֶת־הָאָרֶץ וְכִבְשֻׁהָ וּרְדוּ בִּדְגַת הַיָּם וּבְעוֹף הַשָּׁמַיִם וּבְכָל־חַיָּה הָרֹמֶשֶׂת עַל־הָאָרֶץ

[151] Shulchan Aruch (330:1) - יולדת היא כחולה שיש בו סכנה ומחללין
עליה השבת לכל מה שצריכה קוראין לה חכמה ממקום למקום ומילדין [אותה]
ומדליקין לה נר אפי' היא סומא

[152] Igros Moshe (OC 4:105:6) - לידה בזמנה כדרך הנשים לא נחשב לסכנה
כלל הוא אמת ברור היינו דמצד המציאות איכא בלידה סכנה אבל הוא הבטחה

Chapter 4: Mothers in Halacha

Q8. Is it permitted for a pregnant mother to allow doctors to induce her labor for medical reasons?

A: (5755) Yes, if the baby is getting too big and will force the doctors to perform a caesarian section since it won't fit through, then the Ribono Shel Olam is saying that the mother needs to be induced earlier. Similarly, if the doctors are concerned for any medical reason like a negative Rh factor problem or blood toxicity, then it would be permitted to induce the labor. There's another part of this shailah as the Gemara Shabbos (156a) explains the time a child is born has a *mazal* effect on him for the rest of his life. For instance, the Gemara[153] says someone born on a Sunday – "sun day" – will have no secrets as everyone will know what's happening with him so that if he tries to be a thief then he won't succeed. Others say the hour in which you are born is the main *mazal*, so those born under the sun hour would have difficulty protecting their secrets (Shabbos 156a)[154]. Someone born on Monday – "moon day" – will be more protected with keeping secrets and would be more successful if he chooses to steal[155]. Others say those born under the moon hour will have protection in keeping secrets[156]. There are also different *mazalos* depending on what time of the month you're born, and even

---

שלא יהיה בזה לעולם שום סכנה ואלו המתות בשעת לידתן הוא מחמת שמחוייבת עונש כדתנן בשבת דף ל"א ע"ב על שלש עבירות נשים מתות בשעת לידתן וטעם שנקבע זמן עונשן בשעת הלידה הוא מאחר שבעצם מצד הטבע יש בזה גם ענין סכנה כדאיתא שם בשבת דף ל"ב וכדאיתא גם בתנחומא והוא כמעט מפורש שם בתשובתי שלכן כתבתי שהוא רק בלידה בשעתה ממש אבל לא כשיקדים הלידה באיזה תחבולות דלא כפי שהיה צריך להיות שע"ז ליכא הבטחת השי"ת שלכן אסור לעשות תחבולות להקדים הלידה אם לא כשאיכא סכנה לחכות

[153] Shabbos (156a) - כתיב אפינקסיה דרבי יהושע בן לוי האי מאן דבחד בשבא יהי גבר ולא חדא ביה

[154] Shabbos (156a) - אמר להו רבי חנינא פוקו אמרו ליה לבר ליואי לא מזל יום גורם אלא מזל שעה גורם האי מאן דבחמה יהי גבר זיותן יהי אכיל מדיליה ושתי מדיליה ורזוהי גליין אם גניב לא מצלח

[155] Shabbos (156a) - האי מאן דבתרי בשבא יהי גבר רגזן מאי טעמא משום דאיפליגו ביה מיא

[156] Shabbos (156a) - האי מאן דבלבנה יהי גבר סביל מרעין בנאי וסתיר סתיר ובנאי אכיל דלא דיליה ושתי דלא דיליה ורזוהי כסיין אם גנב מצלח

79

different *mazalos* depending on the time of the day in which you are born. Therefore, when a person is born normally, the Ribono Shel Olam is deciding what the child's *mazal* should be. However, if you change that by inducing labor, you will be changing this child's *mazal* so that if he was supposed to be a millionaire you're causing him to be a pauper for the rest of his life. It's not so easy to know what the best thing is for each neshama, so we should let the Ribono Shel Olam decide on the *mazal* for each person. If you get involved by trying to help this child by having him born under the *mazal* which would make him a millionaire when he was supposed to struggle financially[157], you're going to make him unhappy. Some people don't have money but can cope with it and are happy people, while other people have money and are unhappy people. The Ribono Shel Olam decides what's best for each person based on the individual's strengths and talents. My Rosh Yeshiva Rav Aharon Kotler זכר צדיק לברכה had no money but was a happy person. All the money he received was given away. I remember someone asked him about depositing money in a bank account which is owned by a Jew since the money will accrue interest. The Jewish owned bank is essentially paying ribbis for the loan that you gave them (Shulchan Aruch YD 160:1)[158]. Rav Moshe (Igros Moshe YD 2:63)[159] has a *teshuva* saying that it's permitted to accept interest from a Jewish bank for your account because they pay based on their own assets rather than their personal liability. Nonetheless, my Rosh Yeshiva said, "It's forbidden for a Jew to put money into a Jewish owned bank account, and I never put money into a Jewish owned bank." Then after a few seconds he continued, "In my case, there was another reason why I didn't put money into a Jewish owned bank." We assume the reason was because the Rosh Yeshiva didn't have any

---

[157] Shabbos (156a) - האי מאן דבכוכב נוגה יהי גבר עתיר וזנאי

[158] Shulchan Aruch (YD 160:1) - צריך ליזהר ברבית וכמה לאוין נאמרו בו ואפי' הלוה הנותנו והערב והעדים עוברים

[159] Igros Moshe (YD 2:63) - אבל להלוות לקאמפאניעס כפי הסתם שבפה מדינתנו שאין הבעלים מחוייבין בעצמן לשלם ליכא איסור ריבית ואם גם בלאנדאן הוא כן תוכלו להלוות מקאמפאניע דאינשורענס שלכם לקאמפאניעס אחדים גם בסתם ואם בלאנדאן אינו כן בסתם הלואות אלא שאיכא חיוב גם על הבעלים בעצמן שלא כבכאן אמעריקא יש להתנות בפירוש בשטר הלואה שאין החיוב בתשלומין אלא על עסק הקאמפאניע ולא על הבעלים עצמן

money. You see that we have no right to meddle into the affairs of the Ribono Shel Olam since the Ribono Shel Olam knows what is good for each person – "פּוֹתֵחַ אֶת־יָדֶךָ וּמַשְׂבִּיעַ לְכָל־חַי רָצוֹן" (Tehillim 45:16). You can cause a lot of trouble by mixing in. On the other hand, there is an understanding that the *mazal* which the Ribono Shel Olam decreed for a person to be born under pulls out the child to be born during that *mazal*. In other words, each person is formed in his mother's womb with a specific *mazal* – not that he acquires the *mazal* at the time that he is born. If you understand the *mazalos* that way, then it doesn't matter when you induce labor since the *mazal* is pulling the child out at the time it's supposed to come out. Let's say the Gemara says someone born on Erev Shabbos has a leaning towards being a *tzadik*[160] since it is the *mazal* of Jupiter – *tzedek*[161]. Is the understanding that since he was born on Erev Shabbos he will be affected by the *mazal* to want to be a tzadik, or is the understanding that the Ribono Shel Olam decided this individual should have an inclination to be a tzadik and will therefore be pulled out on Erev Shabbos? Nonetheless, this doesn't have anything to do with the *teshuva* of Rav Moshe saying it's forbidden to put yourself in danger earlier through inducing unless medically indicated.

Q9. Seeing that the Gemara discusses the effects of *mazal* on one's time of birth (Shabbos 156a)[162], can a person schedule a c-section birth at a particular time?

---

[160] Shabbos (156a) - האי מאן דבמעלי שבתא יהי גבר חזרן אמר רב נחמן בר יצחק חזרן במצות

[161] Shabbos (156a) - האי מאן דבצדק יהי גבר צדקן אמר רב נחמן בר יצחק וצדקן במצות

[162] Shabbos (156a) - כתיב אפינקסיה דרבי יהושע בן לוי האי מאן דבחד בשבא יהי גבר ולא חדא ביה מאי [ולא חדא ביה] אילימא ולא חד לטיבו והאמר רב אשי אנא בחד בשבא הואי אלא לאו חדא לבישו והאמר רב אשי אנא ודימי בר קקוזתא הוויין בחד בשבא אנא מלך והוא ריש גנבי אלא אי כולי לטיבו אי כולי לבישו מאי טעמא דאיברו ביה אור וחושך האי מאן דבתרי בשבא יהי גבר רגזן מאי טעמא משום דאיפליגו ביה מיא האי מאן דבתלתא בשבא יהי גבר עתיר וזנאי יהא מאי טעמא משום דאיברו ביה עשבים האי מאן דבארבעה בשבא יהי גבר חכים ונהיר מאי טעמא משום דאיתלו ביה מאורות

A: (5779) It's true that if you have a c-section then you are causing the child to be born at the time of a different *mazal*. However, if it's medically indicated to have a c-section, then it's part of the child's *mazal*. If the doctor offers the mother multiple dates to have the c-section, that's also part of the child's *mazal*. On the other hand, if you decide to have a c-section because you want to schedule the birth before you go on vacation, then you are meddling around with the baby's *mazal*. Most of the time a c-section is done because the doctors are afraid of the child remaining in the mother for too long. Generally there is a medical reason why doctors want to have a c-section done – which is part of the child's *mazal*. The Arizal (Sha'ar HaGilgulim Introduction 23:8)[163] says that when parents give their child a name by the *bris*, Hashem gives the inspiration to the parents to name the child in accordance with his *shoresh haneshama*. Similarly, the Ribono Shel Olam puts the date and time of the c-section into the mind of the parents for him to have the proper *mazal* – assuming the c-section is required medically.

Q10. If one has to do a c-section, is there a specific day of the week they should do have the procedure done in order to get a better *mazal*?

A: (5779) The Gemara says that someone born under a certain *mazal* will be affected in different ways (Shabbos 156a)[164]. There

---

[163] Sha'ar HaGilgulim Introduction (23:8) - וכמו שנשמות הקדושות כל אחת ואחת יש לה שם ידוע כפי בחי' אבר שממנו חוצבה וכמו שארז"ל על פסוק אשר שם שמות בארץ אל תקרי שמות אלא שמות כך כל ניצוץ וניצוץ שבקליפה יש לה שם ידוע בפני עצמו ונמצא כי היצה"ר שבאיש הזה אינו כעין היצה"ר של האיש האחר ונמצא כי כאשר נולד האדם וקוראים לו אביו ואמו שם אחד העולה בדעתם אינו באקראי ובהזדמן כי אם הקב"ה משים בפיו השם ההוא המוכרח אל הנשמה ההיא כמש"ה אשר שם שמות בארץ כפי מקום האבר שבאדם העליון אשר ממנו חוצב והשם הזה נרשם למעלה בכסא הכבוד כנודע ולכן ארז"ל שמא גרים

[164] Shabbos (156a) - כתיב אפינקסיה דרבי יהושע בן לוי האי מאן דבחד בשבא יהי גבר ולא חדא ביה מאי [ולא חדא ביה] אילימא ולא חד לטיבו והאמר רב אשי אנא בחד בשבא הואי אלא לאו חדא לבישו והאמר רב אשי אנא ודימי בר קקוזתא הוויין בחד בשבא אנא מלך והוא ריש גנבי אלא אי כולי לטיבו אי כולי לבישו מאי טעמא דאיברו ביה אור וחושך האי מאן דבתרי בשבא יהי גבר

are twelve *mazalos* where each month has its own *mazal*. The month you were born in will affect you. Additionally, there is a different *mazal* for the week, the day, and the hour in which you were born. Each of the *mazalos* work together to affect each person. Even two twins who are born ten minutes apart can have different *mazalos* because one may have been born in an earlier *mazal* than the other one. They may share the same *mazal* of the day, week, and month, but they won't necessarily have the same *mazal* of the hour in which they were born. What does it mean that a person is born in a certain *mazal*? Does each person have an inherent *mazal* which pulls him out of his mother at that particular time, or is the understanding that we are originally *mazal-less* and whatever the *mazal* is at the time we're born will be what affects us? The answer to the question about inherent *mazalos* will answer this question about c-section. If a person has an inherent *mazal*, then it doesn't matter when the c-section is performed because he will retain his inherent *mazal* – and had the child been left to come out naturally (if possible) then he would be born in that *mazal*. However, if a child is originally *mazal-less*, and the *mazal* determined the time of birth – even though that from a halacha perspective a section isn't considered birth – his *mazal* would be determined by the time he came out of his mother. You could figure out your *mazal* based on the time and day in which you were born, but the time we use now is an artificially imposed time. The real time is calculated when the time of the sun above the horizon until sunset is 12 hours exactly and nighttime is 12 hours exactly. If the sun rises at 6:10 on a day when the night and day are both equally 12 hours, then you know our time is ten minutes off from what it's supposed to be. The *mazalos* don't follow *sha'os zmanios* – they follow regular hours. Consequently, 6:00AM is the beginning of the day for *mazalos* – whether it's daytime or nighttime. Also, each *mazal* has a weaker effect on you when it is near the end of its hour while the rising *mazal* is growing in strength. Now regarding the question of choosing the day for a c-section to receive a certain *mazal*, I would not mix into the *mazalos*. No one knows whether this "better" *mazal* will really be

---

רגזן מאי טעמא משום דאיפליגו ביה מיא האי מאן דבתלתא בשבא יהי גבר עתיר
וזנאי יהא מאי טעמא משום דאיברו ביה עשבים האי מאן דבארבעה בשבא יהי
גבר חכים ונהיר מאי טעמא משום דאיתלו ביה מאורות

beneficial for him. The Rema (YD 179:4)[165] says הַבּוֹטֵחַ בַּה חֶסֶד יְסוֹבְבֶנּוּ (Tehillim 32:10)[166] – don't worry about *mazalos*. The Gemara (Shabbos 156a)[167] says that a person born under the *mazal* of Madim - Mars - will be someone who spills blood. That might translate into being a murderer, a *mohel*, a *shochet*, or a doctor. You can choose to use your *mazal* to do *aveiros* like murder, *mitzvos* like *milah*, or a *reshus* like being a blood letter for health reasons. Just because you want your son to be a *mohel* is not a sufficient reason to make your child born with a c-section when the *mazal* of Madim is stronger – he might become a murderer. You don't know what's better for him. Your role as the parent of a child who needs a c-section is to have the procedure done when it's best for the doctor and the hospital – forget about the *mazal*. If you want to delay the c-section six hours to get a certain *mazal*, then you might get the doctor upset with you because you're ruining his golf game. You don't want your doctor angry with you. There are a lot of medical considerations which factor into when to perform the c-section, so we need to follow the medical advice to decide what time is best. It is true that America has the highest rate of c-sections in the world - and there are certainly unnecessary c-sections - but who are we to argue with the doctors? They are the experts, so if the medical professionals feel you need to have a c-section then you should listen to them because otherwise it may put the mother, child, or both at risk.

Q11. Doesn't the Gemara say that *mazal* doesn't apply to Jews (Shabbos 156a)[168]?

A: (5755) Have any of your friends ever become engaged? Did you say "*Mazal* Tov" to him? Evidently, you're wishing that he

---

[165] Rema YD (179:4) - וההולך בתום ובוטח בה' חסד יסובבנו

[166] Tehillim (32:10) - רַבִּים מַכְאוֹבִים לָרָשָׁע וְהַבּוֹטֵחַ בַּה חֶסֶד יְסוֹבְבֶנּוּ

[167] Shabbos (156a) - האי מאן דבצדק יהי גבר צדקן אמר רב נחמן בר יצחק וצדקן במצות האי מאן דבמאדים יהי גבר אשיד דמא אמר רב אשי אי אומנא אי גנבא אי טבחא אי מוהלא אמר רבה אנא במאדים הואי אמר אביי מר נמי עניש וקטיל

[168] Shabbos (156a) - אמר רבי יוחנן מניין שאין מזל לישראל שנאמר כה אמר ה' אל דרך הגוים אל תלמדו ומאותות השמים אל תחתו כי יחתו הגוים מהמה הם יחתו ולא ישראל

has good *mazal* for this *shidduch*. Tosfos (Shabbos 156a)[169] asks the same question about אין מזל לישראל given the fact that Chaldeans have the ability to identify each person's *mazal* (Shabbos 156b)[170], so Tosfos explains that it's possible for a *yid* to overcome his *mazal* through *davening*. However, that takes a lot of special merits. When Avraham Avinu was born in a *mazal* which didn't allow him to have children, the Ribono Shel Olam asked Avraham if he wanted to have the world destroyed in order to change his *mazal* to have children. Avraham was eventually taken out of his *mazal* וַיּוֹצֵא אֹתוֹ הַחוּצָה (Bereishis 15:5)[171] and had his name changed (Rashi Bereishis 15:5)[172]. We see with our own eyes the effects of *mazal* on each person as you can see some people are smarter than others. Why are they smarter? Some people are inherently smarter because they are born under the *mazal* on Tuesday or Wednesday[173]. At the same time, the Ribono Shel Olam demands more from a person who was given a greater intellect. We also see there are some people who turn everything they touch into nothing and others who turn everything they touch into gold. The automobile insurance policies increase a customer's insurance after the first accident. Why? There are certain people who are more accident prone even though the

---

[169] Tosfos Shabbos (156a) - (ושם. כח דף) והא דאמר רבא בשילהי מו"ק בני חיי ומזוני לאו בזכותא תליא מילתא אלא במזלא תליא מילתא מכל מקום על ידי זכות גדול משתנה אבל פעמים שאין המזל משתנה כדאמר ביבמות פרק החולץ (יבמות דף נ. ושם) זכה מוסיפין לו לא זכה פוחתין לו

[170] Shabbos (156b) - ומדרבי עקיבא נמי אין מזל לישראל דרבי עקיבא הויא ליה ברתא אמרי ליה כלדאי ההוא יומא דעיילה לבי גננא טריק לה חיויא ומיתא הוה דאיגא אמילתא טובא ההוא יומא שקלתה למכבנתא דצתא בגודא איתרמי איתיב בעיניה דחיויא לצפרא כי קא שקלה לה הוה קא סריך ואתי חיויא בתרה

[171] Bereishis (15:5) - וַיּוֹצֵא אֹתוֹ הַחוּצָה וַיֹּאמֶר הַבֶּט־נָא הַשָּׁמַיְמָה וּסְפֹר הַכּוֹכָבִים אִם־תּוּכַל לִסְפֹּר אֹתָם וַיֹּאמֶר לוֹ כֹּה יִהְיֶה זַרְעֶךָ

[172] Rashi Bereishis (15:5) - ולפי מדרשו אמר לו צא מאצטגנינות שלך שראית במזלות שאינך עתיד להעמיד בן, אברם אין לו בן, אבל אברהם יש לו בן וכן שרי לא תלד, אבל שרה תלד, אני קורא לכם שם אחר וישתנה המזל. דבר אחר הוציאו מחללו של עולם והגביהו למעלה מן הכוכבים, וזהו לשון הבטה מלמעלה למטה

[173] Shabbos (156a) - האי מאן דבכוכב יהי גבר נהיר וחכים משום דספרא האי מאן דבארבעה בשבא יהי גבר חכים ונהיר מאי טעמא משום and דחמה הוא דאיתלו ביה מאורות

accident wasn't their fault. Statistically Jews and non-Jews are the same for car accidents as it is all affected by *mazal*.

Q12. Is it permitted to undergo a hysterectomy?

A: (5755) The Shulchan Aruch (Shulchan Aruch EH 5:12)[174] says a woman is allowed to drink a *kos ikarin* if she has problems giving birth which is not considered normal in comparison to other women. The *kos ikarin* is a liquid made from the roots of plants which renders her unable to have children. Every woman has difficulty giving birth – it's part of the decree the Ribono Shel Olam put on women (Bereishis 3:16)[175] – but if a woman has unique problems during labor which other women don't have then she is allowed to drink a medicine which irreversibly prevents her from having any more children. It is not considered *hashchasas zera* being together with a woman who drank this *kos shel ikarin* because even when a woman is pregnant or past the age of being able to have children, it is also permitted for her to be with her husband and it is not considered *hashchasas zera* because if the *hotza'as zera* helps in his fulfilling the *mitzva* of *onah*, it is not considered going to waste (Mishna Berura 240:2)[176]. Similarly, if a woman takes a pill which prevents her from having a child, it is not considered *hashchasas zera* for the husband either. It is certainly not considered *sirus* especially with the pills today which allow the wife to have children later. However, even though there is no issue of *hashchasas zera* in this case of *kos shel ikarin*, there are two other issues. One issue is the *shibud* the wife has to her husband as part of the marriage contract which says she is obligated to give him children just as he is obligated to give her שאר, כסות, and עונה (Kesubos 47b)[177]. That is a monetary claim

---

[174] Shulchan Aruch (EH 5:12) - המשקה כוס של עקרין לאדם או לשאר בעלי חיים כדי לסרסו הרי זה אסור ואין לוקין עליו ואשה מתרת לשתות עקרין כדי לסרסה עד שלא תלד

[175] Bereishis (3:16) - אֶל־הָאִשָּׁה אָמַר הַרְבָּה אַרְבֶּה עִצְּבוֹנֵךְ וְהֵרֹנֵךְ בְּעֶצֶב תֵּלְדִי בָנִים

[176] Mishna Berura (240:2) - אלא בעונה וכו' - וצריך לקיים העונה גם כשהיא מעוברת או מניקה

[177] Kesubos (47b) - אמר רבא האי תנא סבר מזונות מדאורייתא דתניא (שמות כא:י) שארה אלו מזונות וכן הוא אומר (מיכה ג:ג) ואשר אכלו שאר עמי כסותה

which the husband is able to forgive. The second issue is the fact that the husband will not fulfill his *mitzva* of פריה ורביה (Rambam Ishus 15:2)[178] – and he has no right to forgive this *mitzva*. After he fulfills the *mitzva* by having a son and a daughter, then he still has *mitzva d'rabanan* to have more children (Rambam Ishus 15:16)[179]. There are certain *gedarim* mentioned in the *poskim* regarding the *mitzva d'rabanan* which may allow the husband to stop having more children. For instance, if a man marries a second wife and believes the children from his second wife won't get along with the children from his first wife, then he is allowed to marry a woman who can no longer have any children to avoid the issue (Rema EH 1:8)[180]. Rav Sternhell was a very big *posek* in Baltimore who had a situation with a *frum* woman whose husband was also initially *frum* but eventually no longer wanted to keep *taharas hamishpacha*. The woman asked Rav Sternhell what she could do – maybe she should do a hysterectomy in order to avoid becoming a *nidda* anymore, but that would also mean she would no longer have the ability to have more children. They didn't want to get divorced because divorce is always the last resort. The entire attitude towards divorce has changed over the last 30 years. I was once offered a job as a Rav in a *choshuv* town in Europe about 30 years ago and asked Rav Yaakov Kamenetsky whether I should take the job or not. He asked if I thought I could do a good job, so I said I thought I could do a good job but was afraid I wouldn't be good with being *mesader gittin*. Rav Yaakov started laughing, "In Europe, if a Rav had three *gittin* in his lifetime then that was considered a lot! If you need to write a *get*, you can just go to a neighboring Rav with more experience." Nowadays over 50% of *non-frum* people get divorced and it has boiled over into our community as well so that people don't think it's such a terrible

---

כמשמעו עונתה זו עונה האמורה בתורה וכן הוא אומר (בראשית לא:נ) אם תענה את בנותי

[178] Rambam Ishus (15:2) - האיש מצווה על פריה ורביה

[179] Rambam Ishus (15:16) - אַף עַל פִּי שֶׁקִּיֵּם אָדָם מִצְוַת פְּרִיָּה וּרְבִיָּה הֲרֵי הוּא מְצֻוֶּה מִדִּבְרֵי סוֹפְרִים שֶׁלֹּא יִבָּטֵל מִלִּפְרוֹת וְלִרְבּוֹת כָּל זְמַן שֶׁיֵּשׁ בּוֹ כֹּחַ שֶׁכָּל הַמּוֹסִיף נֶפֶשׁ אַחַת בְּיִשְׂרָאֵל כְּאִלּוּ בָּנָה עוֹלָם

[180] Rema (EH 1:8) - וכן אם יש לו בנים הרבה ומתיירא שאם ישא אשה בת בנים יבאו קטטות ומריבות בין הבנים ובין אשתו מותר לישא אשה שאינה בת בנים אבל אסור לישב בלא אשה משום חשש זו

thing. In Europe, when someone got divorced, they would be considered third grade citizens – not even second grade citizens. Clearly there is a fault in you for being incapable of getting along with your spouse. No matter how terrible the other person is, if you have any diplomacy and decency then you should be able to make it work. If they could not make it work, then it's a sign that there is something wrong. Not only are the husband and wife hurt by the divorce, but the children are scarred forever. They will never turn out the way they could have if you wouldn't have gotten divorced. They might become normal kids, but they would have been much better if they grew up in a close-knit family. Just because this woman's husband didn't keep Shabbos and ate at McDonalds wasn't her problem – that's his problem. At home she serves him kosher. However, *taharas hamishpacha* was her issue as much as it was his issue. Normally, a hysterectomy is not normally permitted because there is an issue of *sirus* that you cannot have an operation done which would prevent you from having children. Not only that, but a person who has a vasectomy done is not allowed to get married or be married to a *bas Yisroel* (Devarim 23:2)[181], although he is allowed to marry a convert (Rambam Isurei Biah 16:1)[182]. Recently the medical community has tried to develop a way of reversing the procedure, but they are currently only successful in one-third of the cases. If a doctor is able to reverse the effects of a vasectomy in a Jewish man, then it would seem that he could marry a bas Yisroel again. Preventing a man from having children is forbidden *m'doraysa* (Shulchan Aruch EH 5:11)[183] while preventing a woman from having children is forbidden *mid'rabanan* (Shulchan Aruch EH 5:11)[184] – and the Vilna Gaon says it's forbidden *m'doraysa* (Biur HaGra

---

[181] Devarim (23:2) – לֹא־יָבֹא פְצוּעַ־דַּכָּא וּכְרוּת שָׁפְכָה בִּקְהַל ה'

[182] Rambam Isurei Biah (16:1) - בַּת שֶׁנִּשְּׂאוּ שָׁפְכָה וּכְרוּת דַּכָּא פְצוּעַ יִשְׂרָאֵל וּבְעָלוּ לוֹקִין שֶׁנֶּאֱמַר (דברים כג:ב) לֹא יָבֹא פְצוּעַ דַּכָּא וּכְרוּת שָׁפְכָה בִּקְהַל ה' וּמֻתָּרִין לְשֵׂא גִּיֹּרֶת וּמְשֻׁחְרֶרֶת וַאֲפִלּוּ כֹהֵן שֶׁהוּא פְצוּעַ דַּכָּא מֻתָּר לְשֵׂא גִּיֹּרֶת וּמְשֻׁחְרֶרֶת לְפִי שֶׁאֵינוֹ בִּקְדֻשָּׁתוֹ

[183] Shulchan Aruch (EH 5:11) - אסור להפסיד אברי הזרע בין באדם בין בבהמה חיה ועוף א' טמאים וא' טהורים בין בא"י בין בח"ל וכל המסרס לוקה מן התורה בכל מקום ואפילו מסרס אחר מסרס לוקה

[184] Shulchan Aruch (EH 5:11) - והמסרס את הנקבה בין באדם בין בשאר מינים פטור אבל אסור

EH 5:25)[185]. Rav Sternhell allowed the woman asking this question to have a hysterectomy since it's *d'rabanan* according to many *poskim,* and having a non-Jew perform the procedure makes it a *shevus d'shevus* which is permitted in a pressing situation (Mishna Berura 307:77)[186] – and certainly in such a *tzorech* like this case. These are very serious *shailos* and you see how *poskim* tremble before answering such questions, so you need to ask a Rav who is knowledgeable in these *halachos*. One of the only times the Torah says that someone did ra b'einei Hashem was by *er v'onan* (Bereishis 38:10)[187] because they were *mashchis zera*. This entire story shows the mesiras nefesh this woman was willing to undergo this procedure in order not to be nichshol in *hilchos nidda*. I remember in Russia under the USSR, the government tried to dissuade women from going to the *mikva* by not providing heat for the building. That means the shower, bath, and *mikva* were cold – and in Russia the *mikva* would get so cold that it would freeze. One of the reasons the Jewish community in Russia brought me over there was to see if there was any way we could prevent the water from freezing despite the fact that the communist government didn't provide heat for their building. I told them that if they have two fans in the water propelling the water in different directions then it would prevent the water from freezing at 32 degrees. Although the water might remain liquid until it reaches zero degrees, how could you go into such freezing water? They told me, "We're not concerned about the temperature of the water. We're only concerned that the *mikva* might not be valid when it freezes." *Yidden* have an incredible sense of *mesiras nefesh* for keeping the Torah.

(5755) When a woman has a hysterectomy and it's a necessary procedure for whatever reason, then they also remove the reproductive system as well since there is a 5% chance that they will become cancerous if not removed. It is forbidden *m'doraysa*

---

[185] Biur HaGra (EH 5:25) - ת"כ שם מנין שאף הנקבות בסירוס ת"ל כי משחתם רי"א בהם ואין הנקבות בסירוס ופ' כת"ק אלא דאין בהם מלקות כיון דלא נכללו בל"ת דלא תעשו

[186] Mishna Berura (307:77) - וה"ה בכל דבר המוקצה דהו"ל שבות דשבות ואין מותר כ"א לצורך מצוה או קצת חולי

[187] Bereishis (38:10) - וַיֵּרַע בְּעֵינֵי ה' אֲשֶׁר עָשָׂה וַיָּמֶת גַּם־אֹתוֹ

to make a man unable to have children (Shulchan Aruch EH 5:11)[188], and it is forbidden *mid'rabanan* according to most *poskim* to make a woman unable to have children (Shulchan Aruch EH 5:11)[189]. The Gaon (Biur HaGra EH 5:25)[190] says it is forbidden *mid'oraysa* to make a woman unable to have children learned from a different *posuk* (Vayikra 22:25)[191]. However, if a person's life is at stake then it is permitted to have this procedure done. Nonetheless, there are other monetary *halachos* which apply for a married woman who has a responsibility to her husband. Rav Moshe (Igros Moshe CM 2:73:7)[192] writes that even if there wasn't a 5% chance that a woman's reproductive system would become cancerous, it would still be permitted for her to allow the doctors to remove the other parts of her reproductive system since אין סירוס אחר סירוס בנשים.

Q13. If a husband wants to have more children but his wife doesn't – and they already have a son and daughter – what should they do?

---

[188] Shulchan Aruch (EH 5:11) - אסור להפסיד אברי הזרע בין באדם בין בבהמה חיה ועוף א' טמאים וא' טהורים בין בא"י בין בח"ל וכל המסרס לוקה מן התורה בכל מקום ואפילו מסרס אחר מסרס לוקה

[189] Shulchan Aruch (EH 5:11) - והמסרס את הנקבה בין באדם בין בשאר מינים פטור אבל אסור

[190] Biur HaGra (EH 5:25) - ת"כ שם מנין שאף הנקבות בסירוס ת"ל כי משחתם רי"א בהם ואין הנקבות בסירוס ופ' כת"ק אלא דאין בהם מלקות כיון דלא נכללו בל"ת דלא תעשו

[191] Vayikra (22:25) - וּמִיַּד בֶּן־נֵכָר לֹא תַקְרִיבוּ אֶת־לֶחֶם אֱלֹהֵיכֶם מִכָּל־אֵלֶּה כִּי מָשְׁחָתָם בָּהֶם מוּם בָּם לֹא יֵרָצוּ לָכֶם

[192] Igros Moshe (CM 2:73:7) - וכ"ש דלרבנן שהאשה אינה מצווה על פו"ר דהאיסור סירוס באשה הוא רק איסור מדרבנן שודאי אין לאסור דבלא טעם לאסור ודאי לא יאסרו שלכן מאחר שמוכרחיו לחתוך את הרחם משום מחלתה ליכא שום איסור לנתח גם את השחלות ואת צנורות הרחם ואף להגר"א באה"ע סימן ה' ס"ק כ"ח שאיכא איסור דאורייתא גם בנקבה מקרא דמשחתם מסתברא דהשחתה שנאמר באברי הזרע ולא באברים אחרים הוא משום שנשחת עי"ז ענין הולדת בנים וכיון שנוטלין ממנה הרחם בשביל סכנה ליכא שום חשיבות ושם השחתה על מה שנשארו השחלות וצנורות הרחם והוי זה כצער וחבלה בשאר אבריה שלטובתה אין לאסור אף למ"ד אסור לחבול בעצמו

A: (5755) They should speak to a Rav to work out this *shalom bayis* issue. If the wife has a particular issue with having another child which a normal person could understand, then she may have a good claim. However, if she is just too tired and is no different than anyone else then she is technically *meshubad* to him (Teshuvos Chasam Sofer EH). That's only the halacha – in actual practice they should speak with a Rav.

Q14. Is IVF permitted?

A: (5779) Yes, IVF is permitted when necessary. A halachic authority should be consulted. Also, there may be a question if a boy is born on Shabbos whether his *bris* is *doche* Shabbos.

Q15. What is the halachic status of a surrogate mother?

A: (5779) This is a good question – sometimes a woman cannot carry a child herself. Some women can have a fertilized egg, but do not have the ability to carry the child to term. Nowadays, doctors are able to remove the eggs from one mother and put them into another woman who agrees to be a host mother for the egg to develop in her womb. Then, she gives birth to this child. The question now becomes who is the mother of this child – the one who the egg belongs to or the one who gave birth to it? It's a *machlokes haposkim* where there are proofs on both sides of the argument which I'm not going to get into now. I asked this question to Rav Elyashiv, and he told me that he was very upset that anyone would do something like this. He told me, "This is literally the sin of the generation of the Flood" (Bereishis 6:2)[193]. Then I asked him what the halacha is if someone actually did this. Rav Elyashiv answered that the child follows the egg of the mother. If the mother who gave the egg is Jewish, then the child is considered Jewish. If the egg comes from a non-Jewish woman but a Jewish mother gave birth to it, then child is considered non-Jewish. If the surrogate mother had given birth to another child before this one, then the second child would not be considered a firstborn regarding Taanis *Bechor*im. On the other hand, regarding

---

[193] Bereishis (6:2) - וַיִּרְאוּ בְנֵי־הָאֱלֹהִים אֶת־בְּנוֹת הָאָדָם כִּי טֹבֹת הֵנָּה וַיִּקְחוּ לָהֶם נָשִׁים מִכֹּל אֲשֶׁר בָּחָרוּ

inheritance we follow the father anyway, so it doesn't make any difference whether the son is a firstborn of the mother or not. Rav Elyashiv was against it because you shouldn't play around with these kinds of things.

(5777) I asked this question to Rav Elyashiv זכר צדיק לברכה, and this is a *machlokes* Achronim. Some bring a proof from Rebbi Akiva Eiger (YD 87:6) in Basar v'cholov that the mother who gave birth to the child is the halachic mother, though I don't know if it's such a big proof. Others say the one who conceived the child by giving her the egg is the halachic mother. A major question arises if the host mother is not Jewish, so I asked Rav Elyashiv. He was horrified by the question and said, "This is ממש the מעשה דור המבול – it's a terrible thing to be השחתת דרכם." So I asked what the halacha should be if it was already done, and he said, "Whichever mother donated the egg is considered the halachic mother."

Chapter 5: Mental Health

Q1. What is the status of mental health disorders in halacha?

A: (5755) Let's say someone is manic depressive, is very depressed, and has severe mood swings. The מנהג of the *poskim* is to consider such a person as a *choleh* in a life-threatening situation because when someone gets depressed and doesn't care about anything, then he won't try to save himself from a dangerous situation. For instance, if a car is coming down the road at 60 mph and honking the horn at this person telling him to move, someone who is severely depressed won't feel the need to move because he feels, "What's my life worth anyway?" Sometimes such people can become so upset that they put the lives of other in danger as well – especially children. Although such an individual is considered a *choleh sheyesh bo sakana*, he won't necessarily be allowed to eat on Yom Kippur unless eating on Yom Kippur will prevent him from becoming severely depressed or the medicine won't work well on an empty stomach. Moreover, if a pregnant mother needs to take a medication like lithium to treat her manic depression – but she won't take the medicine out of fear that it will hurt her fetus – then she may be allowed to abort the child since she is at risk of becoming severely depressed. A Rabbinic authority should be consulted. Also, if the person's doctor or psychiatrist says it's a possibility that he will have suicidal thoughts, then it's considered a question of *pikuach nefesh* – and if the person commits suicide then we would still give them a burial in a Jewish cemetery even though for anyone else who commits suicide out of embarrassment or not having money we don't bury them in the Jewish cemetery (Gilyon Maharsha 345:4)[194]. If someone makes a conscious - albeit emotional - decision to end his life as many people did when they jumped to their death in the market crash of 1929, then that person is held accountable for his decision. On the other hand, someone with a mental illness has an actual issue and doesn't have his full mental

---

[194] Gilyon Maharsha (345:4) - וירחיקו לקברו יותר משמונת אמות מקבר ישראל כשר

faculties to think properly like normal people. Rav Moshe (Igros Moshe EH 1:120)[195] had a *teshuva* about a person who thought he was *mashiach*. He used to take his clothing off, climb up into trees, and was completely whacked out. This person also happened to be married, so the question became whether he had the cognitive ability to give a *get*. If he's considered a *shoteh*, then he's not able to give a *get* (Shulchan Aruch EH 121:1)[196]. Rav Moshe *poskined* that the person was considered normal and able to give a *get*. He might do a lot of crazy things, but it all stems from one mistake: he thinks he's *mashiach*. He thinks clothing is only for simple people, while *mashiach* doesn't need clothing. Just because someone does crazy things doesn't mean they are considered *halachically* crazy. However, if the person has a מרה שחורה (Rambam Avos 2:11)[197], then it's considered an illness and potentially life-threatening depending on the severity.

Q2. Is hypnotherapy permitted?

A: (5779) Yes, that is permitted. There is a *teshuva* from the Binyan Tzion (67)[198] about hypnosis whether it uses *kishuf* or not.

---

[195] Igros Moshe EH (1:120) - אך אף אם נימא שהמעשים שעשה אינם שייכים לשיטתו והם עניני שטות ובפרט אם נאמינו שלא היה יכול להתאפק מלעשות מעשיו השטותים שזהו סימן גדול לשטות כיון דאינו בעלים על מעשיו מ"מ הרי עבר זמן רב שאינו עושה מעשים ההם ולא ניכר בו שום שטות ונשאר רק מה שמחזיק עצמו בלבו למשיח שזה הא ודאי מסתבר שאינו עושה לשוטה רק דהיא שיטה סכלית שבא לו מצד גאותו היתירה כדלעיל וא"כ עכ"פ הוא עתה חלים ויכול לגרש

[196] Shulchan Aruch EH (121:1) - צריך שיהיה בדעתו בשעה שמצוה לכתבו לפיכך אם אחזו רוח רעה בשעה שמצוה לכתבו אין כותבין אותו אפילו לכשיבריא

[197] Rambam Avos (2:11) - אמר שחריצות לממון ורוב התאוה ורוע הנפש והוא חולי המרה השחורה שיביא האדם למאוס ראות עיניו וישנאהו וייטב לו חברת החיות והתבודדות במדברות וביערות ויבחר לו מקום שאינן מיושב וזה אצלם לא מצד פרישות רק לרוע תאותם וקנאתם בזולתם אלו ימיתו [האדם] בלא ורוח - and Rambam (Bechoros 7:5) - ספק כי יחלה גופו וימות טרם עתו קצרית מקרה מחמת מרה השחורה כגון הנקראים בלשון ערב ממלבנין ואמדמין שגברה עליהן המרה השחורה כל כך עד שנפסדו פעולות הגוף וכחותיו

[198] Binyan Tzion (67) - ולכן לענ"ד אפילו לו יהי' כן שאין למצוא מפתח כלל איך בדרך הטבע יהי' שינוי גדול בכל העניינים ע"י פעולת המגנטיזירען עם כל

He says that if the doctors say hypnotherapy is something which utilizes the nature of people, then you are allowed to use hypnotherapy.

Q3. Are you allowed to perform hypnosis on Shabbos as a *refuah*?

A: (5779) I don't think it's forbidden to do hypnosis on Shabbos because it's not the *derech* to do it with grinding anything. However, if you're doing hypnosis to remove pain, then I would think you wouldn't be allowed to do it on Shabbos because the same effect is also achieved through medicine which would have an issue of שחיקת סממנים – grinding spices (Shulchan Aruch 328:1)[199]. However, where regular medicine is permitted, hypnosis is definitely permitted too.

Q4. What should you do if the patient wants to die and doesn't want to eat?

A: (5755) If the patient doesn't want to eat the food, then Rav Moshe says the patient does not have the right not to eat. He is essentially committing passive suicide. Nonetheless, if his pain is so great that he wants to die, then it's not necessarily considered suicide because we find that Shaul HaMelech told his weapon carrier to kill him (Shmuel I 31:4)[200]. The *poskim* explain that the enemies of Shaul HaMelech would have tortured and eventually

---

זה אין אנו צריכים להרחיק ולחוש שמכחות הטומאה נעשה שהרי לפי המבואר בפוסקים ופסק בטוש"ע י"ד (סי' קנ"ה) מותר להתרפות ע"י לחש מעע"ז כשאינו בודאי שמזכיר שם ע"ז על הלחש וכשאינו כומר לע"ז דכומר ודאי מזכיר שם ע"ז אבל בספק שרי והרי בלחש ודאי אין מבוא לטבע שיפעל על החולי ואעפ"כ אין חוששין שמא מרפא ע"י כחות הטומאה אלא תלין שיש הרבה עניני טבע שנעלמו עדיין ממנו ולמה נחוש יותר בענין מאגניטיזירען שעכ"פ העוסקים בו מאמינים שנעשה ע"י הטבע ולא ע"י פעולות רוחניים

[199] Shulchan Aruch (328:1) - מי שיש לו מיחוש בעלמא והוא מתחזק והולך כבריא אסור לעשות לו שום רפואה ואפילו על ידי עכו"ם גזירה משום שחיקת סממנים

[200] Shmuel I (31:4) - וַיֹּאמֶר שָׁאוּל לְנֹשֵׂא כֵלָיו שְׁלֹף חַרְבְּךָ וְדָקְרֵנִי בָהּ פֶּן יָבוֹאוּ הָעֲרֵלִים הָאֵלֶּה וּדְקָרֻנִי וְהִתְעַלְּלוּ־בִי וְלֹא אָבָה נֹשֵׂא כֵלָיו כִּי יָרֵא מְאֹד וַיִּקַּח שָׁאוּל אֶת־הַחֶרֶב וַיִּפֹּל עָלֶיהָ

killed him, so he was allowed to commit suicide (Shulchan Aruch YD 345:3)[201]. Similarly, if a person is in so much pain that they no longer want to live or eat food, then it's not necessarily considered halachic suicide. Still, it's not a *midas chassidus* for a person to commit passive suicide because the pain itself is an atonement. Just a little bit of pain in this world can counter a lot of pain in the Next World. However, Rav Moshe (Igros Moshe CM 2:74:3)[202] says that if the patient doesn't want to eat then you are not allowed to force him to eat against his will because the strong emotions you may stir up within him may cause his death. If it's possible to trick him into eating in order that he should accept the food, then you are allowed to do that, but forcing him by strapping him down and inserting a tube which will make him upset is forbidden.

Q5. Should you force a patient to take his medicine?

A: (5755) Rav Moshe (Igros Moshe CM 2:74:5)[203] says that if the patient doesn't want to take his medicine, then you cannot force him to do so if it will upset him and eventually cause him to die. If the reason why he doesn't want to accept the medicine is

---

[201] Shulchan Aruch YD (345:3) – קטן המאבד עצמו לדעת חשוב כשלא לדעת וכן גדול המאבד עצמו לדעת והוא אנוס וכשאול המלך אין מונעין ממנו כל כשאול המלך - שהרג את עצמו לפי שראה שהפלשתים - and Shach 6 דבר יעשו בו כרצונם ויהרגוהו

[202] Igros Moshe CM (2:74:3) - שבזה אין להאכילו בע"כ אלא ע"פ רופא אפילו דברים הראוים לחולים כאלו בסתמא ודוקא בע"כ כזה שהחולה גדול ועושה זה ברצון אך לא מחמת שרוצה ממש אלא מחמת שאומרין לו וגוזרין עליו אבל בע"כ ממש שצריך להחזיקו בכח ולהאכילו אין לעשות כן לגדול בר דעת כשאינו רוצה לאכול וכ"ש כשסובר שלא טוב לפניו האכילה אף שהרופא אומר שצריך לאכול ושטוב לו משום זה שסובר שלא טוב לו האכילה הוא סכנה לחולה כשלא ישמעו לו

[203] Igros Moshe CM (2:74:5) - וכשאין החולה רוצה לסכן חיי שעה בשביל ספק שיתרפא מהניתוח כשגם הרופאים מסתפקין ודאי אין לחייב אבל רשות להחולה ליכנס בספק חיי שעה אבל בספק השקול כשאיכא רוב לחד צד הנה כשהרוב מתרפאין וחיים מזה הוא גם מחוייב ואם הרוב אין מתרפאין תליא דאם ודאי אין מגרעין הזמן שהיה חי בלא הניתוח היה נמי שייך לחייב אבל קשה לסמוך על אומדנות הרופאים שלכן מסתבר שתלוי בדעת החולה ומשפחתו שאם רוצין לעשות הניתוח רשאין אבל אם אין רוצין אין לחייבן

because of the potential negative side effects, then he has the right to refuse the medicine. For instance, if the patient doesn't want to take morphine to ease his pain because he's afraid the morphine will cause his heart to stop beating then he is allowed to reject the morphine. Rav Moshe says a patient is allowed to be concerned for the 5% of cases where the side effects of medicine might include death, and you cannot force the person to take the medicine even if the person will probably die without the medicine. Even if 95% of the people who take this medicine survive, a person has the right to be concerned for the 5% of those who die from side effects of the medication.

Q6. Why does suicide have the most severe punishment?

A: (5755) If a person desecrates Shabbos, engages in *avoda zara*, forbidden relationships, and other serious *aveiros*, he technically still has a portion in Olam Haba – but not if he commits murder (Rambam *Teshuva* 3:6)[204]. If a person murders someone else - or kills himself through committing suicide - then he no longer has a portion in the Next World (Aruch Hashulchan YD 116:1)[205]. Our bodies don't belong to us. The body contains the tools for you – your *neshama* – to fulfill the *mitzvos* here. When a baby is born, the Ribono Shel Olam gives it the bodily tools necessary to fulfill the *mitzvos*. We should wash our face, hands, and feet every day out of honor for the Ribono Shel Olam (Shabbos 50b)[206]. If you had a statue of the king, then you would make sure to keep it clean. So too, you were created in His image, so you should make sure to keep your body looking good. We don't own our bodies and have no right to give it away or damage it. You have an obligation

---

[204] Rambam Teshuva (3:6) - וְאֵלּוּ הֵן שֶׁאֵין לָהֶן חֵלֶק לָעוֹלָם הַבָּא אֶלָּא נִכְרָתִים וְאוֹבְדִין וְנִדּוֹנִין עַל גֹּדֶל רִשְׁעָם וְחַטָּאתָם לְעוֹלָם וּלְעוֹלְמֵי עוֹלָמִים הָאֶפִּיקוֹרוֹסִין וְהַכּוֹפְרִים בַּתּוֹרָה וְהַכּוֹפְרִים בִּתְחִיַּת הַמֵּתִים וּבְבִיאַת הַגּוֹאֵל הַמּוֹרְדִים וּמַחְטִיאֵי הָרַבִּים. וְהַפּוֹרְשִׁין מִדַּרְכֵי צִבּוּר וְהָעוֹשֶׂה עֲבֵרוֹת בְּיָד רָמָה בְּפַרְהֶסְיָא כִּיהוֹיָקִים וְהַמּוֹסְרִים וּמַטִּילֵי אֵימָה עַל הַצִּבּוּר שֶׁלֹּא לְשֵׁם שָׁמַיִם וְשׁוֹפְכֵי דָמִים וּבַעֲלֵי לָשׁוֹן הָרַע וְהַמּוֹשֵׁךְ עָרְלָתוֹ

[205] Aruch Hashulchan YD (116:1) - והרי כתיב ואך את דמכם לנפשתיכם אדרוש וכתיב ושמרתם לנפשתיכם וכל המאבד עצמו לדעת אין לו חלק לעוה"ב

[206] Shabbos (50b) - ואינהו כמאן סברוה כי הא דתניא רוחץ אדם פניו ידיו ורגליו בכל יום בשביל קונו משום שנאמר כל פעל ה' למענהו

to keep the body in a healthy state in order to perform the *mitzvos*. The Chasam Sofer says that the Mishna at the end of Yoma (8:8)[207] explains different kinds of punishments will release you from certain *aveiros*. Some *aveiros* require *teshuva* and Yom Kippur, more severe ones require *teshuva*, Yom Kippur, and death. This tells you that death is an atonement. Therefore, the Chasam Sofer says that if a person takes the atonement of death and turns it into an *aveira* through suicide, then he has forfeited all of the potential atonement. A murderer can still technically gain atonement through his own death, but the person who commits suicide turns his ultimate atonement into an *aveira* itself. We're not talking about someone who was so mentally ill that he committed suicide. Such a person would still have a portion in Olam Haba (Aruch Hashulchan YD 345:5)[208]. There were people who lost all their money and jumped off the Empire State Building. Those people don't have an Olam Haba and aren't buried next to normal people since אין קוברין רשע אצל צדיק (Shulchan Aruch YD 362:5)[209]. On the other hand, someone who had a nervous breakdown and committed suicide is still allowed to be buried in the cemetery because he didn't have his *da'as*. If someone had a history of mental illness and killed himself one day, then we assume the suicide was based on his mental instability. However, if he tells a couple people before killing himself then evidently he has planned it out (Aruch Hashulchan

---

[207] Yoma (8:8) - חַטָּאת וְאָשָׁם וַדַּאי מְכַפְּרִין מִיתָה וְיוֹם הַכִּפּוּרִים מְכַפְּרִין עִם הַתְּשׁוּבָה הַתְּשׁוּבָה מְכַפֶּרֶת עַל עֲבֵרוֹת קַלּוֹת עַל עֲשֵׂה וְעַל לֹא תַעֲשֶׂה וְעַל הַחֲמוּרוֹת הִיא תוֹלָה עַד שֶׁיָּבֹא יוֹם הַכִּפּוּרִים וִיכַפֵּר

[208] Aruch Hashulchan YD (345:5) - כללו של דבר במאבד עצמו לדעת תלינן בכל איזה תלייה כל שהוא כגון לתלות ביראה או בצער או שיצא מדעתו או שסבור היה שזה מצוה לבלי להכשל בעברות אחרות וכיוצא באלו הדברים מפני שזהו באמת דבר רחוק שאדם יעשה נבלה כזו בדעת צלולה צא ולמד משאול הצדיק שנפל על חרבו לבלי יתעללו בו הפלשתים וכיוצא בזה מקרי אנוס וכל שכן קטן המאבד עצמו לדעת דחשוב כשלא לדעת

[209] Shulchan Aruch YD (362:5) - אין קוברין רשע אצל צדיק אפילו רשע חמור אצל רשע קל וכן אין קוברין צדיק וכשר ובינוני אצל חסיד מופלג

YD 345:4)[210] and is considered normal enough not to be buried with *frum yidden* or have his relatives mourn for him.

Q7. Is there anything wrong with taking drugs like cocaine and heroin?

A: (5755) Rav Moshe has a *teshuva* (Igros Moshe YD 3:35)[211] discussing whether it's forbidden by the Torah to take drugs. This has nothing to do with smoking which the Surgeon General has already determined is bad for your health. We're talking about marijuana or cocaine where I don't know whether it's bad for your health or not. I spoke with a doctor who specializes in therapy for drug addiction who said that anyone who uses the hard drugs eventually dies from them. He said it's impossible for such a person not to die if the patient doesn't receive medical treatment. Why? These drugs are habit forming and make the patient become physically dependent on them. If he doesn't have the drug then his entire body starts shaking, he'll break out in a fever and the chills, and can even blackout. After a while, the drugs he takes will not be sufficient and he'll need more and more on a steady basis. Eventually, the drug dose will become so high that it will begin affecting the medulla – the area of the brain which controls automatic reflexes like breathing – which will eventually stop

---

[210] Aruch Hashulchan YD (345:4) - ולמדנו מזה דמאבד עצמו לדעת לא מקרי אלא כשאמר מקודם שבמיתה זו יאבד עצמו וגם ראינו שמיד עשה לעצמו מיתה זו

[211] Igros Moshe YD (3:35) - הנה בדבר אשר התחילו איזה בחורים מהישיבה לעשן חשיש (מעראוואנא) פשוט שהוא דבר אסור מכמה עיקרי דינים שבתורה חדא שהוא מקלקל ומכלה את הגוף ואף אם נמצאו אנשים בריאים שלא מזיק להם כל כך אבל מקלקל הוא את הדעת ואינם יכולים להבין דבר לאשורו שזה עוד יותר חמור שלבד שמונע עצמו מלמוד התורה כראוי הוא מניעה גם מתפלה וממצות התורה שעשיה בלא דעת הראוי הוא כלא קיימם ועוד שהוא גורם תאוה גדולה אשר הוא יותר מתאות אכילה וכדומה הצריכים להאדם לחיותו ויש שלא יוכלו לצמצם ולהעביר תאותם, והוא איסור החמור שנאמר בבן סורר ומורה על תאוה היותר גדולה שיש לו לאכילה אף שהוא לאכילת כשרות וכ"ש שאסור להביא עצמו לתאוה גדולה עוד יותר ולדבר שליכא שום צורך להאדם בזה שהוא אסור ואף שלמלקות נימא שאין עונשין מן הדין מ"מ לאיסורא ודאי עובר על לאו זה ואיכא גם הטעם דאיכא בבן סורר ומורה שסופו שילסטם את הבריות כדאיתא בסנהדרין בפ' בן סורר

breathing. That eventuality might take five years, it might take ten years, but he will eventually die for sure due to these drugs. I don't know if these facts were known when Rav Moshe wrote his *teshuva*. At this point it's essentially considered suicide. Nonetheless, Rav Moshe answers the question from a different angle. He says we find in the Torah that we kill a *ben sorer u'morer* (Devarim 21:21)[212] even though he didn't do a serious *aveira* yet. Since he doesn't listen to his parents, eats a lot of meat and drinks a lot of wine (Rambam Mamrim 7:2)[213], so he will eventually need to fill his desires by robbing people (Rashi Devarim 21:18)[214]. Therefore, it's better to kill him when he's still OK than when he starts making tragic decisions. Similarly, it's known that these drugs cause people to become addicted and thereby eventually need to steal and murder to satisfy their drug habits. In fact, the *ben sorer u'morer's* desire for meat and wine isn't as addicting as drugs, so it would certainly apply to drugs as well. I was speaking once with Rav Halpern in Yerushalayim who is the head of an organization which tries to figure out ways to use technology for halachically complex situations. For instance, the Chazon Ish (OC 38:4)[215] said that people cannot use the electricity in Eretz Yisroel on Shabbos because there might be a desecration of Shabbos by the Jewish workers at the facilities which produce

---

[212] Devarim (21:21) - וּרְגָמֻהוּ כָּל־אַנְשֵׁי עִירוֹ בָאֲבָנִים וָמֵת וּבִעַרְתָּ הָרָע מִקִּרְבֶּךָ וְכָל־יִשְׂרָאֵל יִשְׁמְעוּ וְיִרָאוּ

[213] Rambam Mamrim (7:2) - אֵינוֹ חַיָּב סְקִילָה עַד שֶׁיִּגְנֹב מִשֶּׁל אָבִיו וְיִקְנֶה בָּשָׂר בְּזוֹל וְיַיִן בְּזוֹל וְיֹאכַל וְיִשְׁתֶּה חוּץ מֵרְשׁוּת אָבִיו בַּחֲבוּרָה שֶׁכֻּלָּן רֵיקָנִין וּפְחוּתִין וְיֹאכַל הַבָּשָׂר חַי וְאֵינוֹ חַי מְבֻשָּׁל וְאֵינוֹ מְבֻשָּׁל כְּדֶרֶךְ שֶׁהַגַּנָּבִים אוֹכְלִים וְיִשְׁתֶּה הַיַּיִן מָזוּג כְּדֶרֶךְ שֶׁהַגַּרְגְּרָנִים שׁוֹתִים וְהוּא שֶׁיֹּאכַל מִשְׁקַל חֲמִשִּׁים דִּינָרִין מִבָּשָׂר זֶה בְּמָלוּגְמָא אַחַת וְיִשְׁתֶּה חֲצִי לוֹג מִיַּיִן זֶה בְּבַת אַחַת

[214] Rashi Devarim (21:18) - וּבֶן סוֹרֵר וּמוֹרֶה נֶהֱרַג עַל שֵׁם סוֹפוֹ הִגִּיעָה תּוֹרָה לְסוֹף דַּעְתּוֹ סוֹף שֶׁמְּכַלֶּה מָמוֹן אָבִיו וּמְבַקֵּשׁ לִמּוּדוֹ וְאֵינוֹ מוֹצֵא וְעוֹמֵד בְּפָרָשַׁת דְּרָכִים וּמְלַסְטֵם אֶת הַבְּרִיּוֹת אָמְרָה תּוֹרָה יָמוּת זַכַּאי וְאַל יָמוּת חַיָּב

[215] Chazon Ish OC (38:4) - אבל אם נעשה בתחנת החשמל בשבת ע״י ישראל שאינו משמר שבתו אסור ליהנות ממנו ואף אם הוא באופן שיש היתר בשימושו מן הדין אסור להשתמש בו מפני שיש בשימושו איסור חילול השם שאינו חס לכבוד שמים, כיון שהוא שימוש ציבורי והעובד בשבת הוא עושה במרד ר״ל והנהנה ממעשיו מעיד ח״ו שאין לבו כואב על חילול שבת ויהא רעוא שישיבו בתשובה שלימה במהרה

the energy. Other *poskim* (Minchas Shlomo 27:6)[216] were lenient saying that since the electricity is also being made for hospitals which require the electricity for *pikuach nefashos*, we are allowed to use the electricity as well. However, even though the Minchas Shlomo felt it may have been permitted according to the letter of the law, he felt in actual practice it was better not to. The Chazon Ish disagreed and held that even *m'ikar hadin* the electricity was forbidden to use because the hospitals can use their own generators. Nowadays the electric facilities use oil rather than coal, so it's possible to set everything up before Shabbos. Maybe they'll need someone available to maneuver the wattage or fix the machine if something goes wrong, so Rav Halpern created his organization of engineers, doctors, and *kollel yungeleit* who work together to figure out ways to make it work. For instance, they made a *grama* phone which doesn't call the person right away and other inventions – it's a great idea for these situations. Although there may be some positive uses of drugs for medicinal purposes, that doesn't give us a *heter* to use drugs if it's not medically indicated.

Q8. Are you allowed to smoke cigarettes?

A: (5755) Everyone agrees that smoking cigarettes is certainly not a good thing to do because it has been determined today that it isn't good for your health – and you have an obligation to take care of your health וְנִשְׁמַרְתֶּם מְאֹד לְנַפְשֹׁתֵיכֶם (Devarim 4:15)[217]. Now if you want to smoke one cigarette, that's not forbidden because that's not going to make or break you. You can rationalize that just as one cigarette isn't forbidden, the second one isn't forbidden, and then the third one too, but even though you might

---

[216] Minchas Shlomo (27:6) - אף שבארנו שאפשר שמעיקר הדין אין לאסור ליהנות מהחשמל בשבת אף אם נעשה ח"ו ע"י ישראל מ"מ יש לדעת שע"י השימוש שאנו משתמשים בשבת בחשמל הננו גורמים שיכופו שם את הפועלים לחלל שבת וכמה מכוער הוא להתענג בשבת באש אשר לא צוה ד' וכ"ש לכבד את מקדשי ד' אלו בתי כנסיות ומדרשות באורים שהם חשך ולא אור וחובה גדולה מוטלת על עיני העדה להאיר את ההולכים בחשך ללכת באור ד' והיה לנו לאור עולם

[217] Devarim (4:15) - וְנִשְׁמַרְתֶּם מְאֹד לְנַפְשֹׁתֵיכֶם כִּי לֹא רְאִיתֶם כָּל־תְּמוּנָה בְּיוֹם דִּבֶּר ה' אֲלֵיכֶם בְּחֹרֵב מִתּוֹךְ הָאֵשׁ

figure out a *lomdus* to make it permitted to smoke each cigarette, it's forbidden to make smoking into a habit where you smoke on a regular basis because that isn't good for your health.

Q9. Are you obligated to stop smoking if you are already addicted to cigarettes?

A: (5755) Rav Moshe (Igros Moshe YD 2:49)[218] says that anything people do which is considered a normal activity will receive protection from the Ribono Shel Olam. Even though smoking a cigarette isn't promoting your health, Rav Moshe (Igros Moshe CM 2:76)[219] says that you cannot say it's forbidden since there are people who smoke and live into their 90s at a ripe old age, while others don't smoke and die in their 60s. Therefore, smoking cigarettes doesn't automatically translate into dying. However, since it's not a healthy practice to smoke in general, it's not the right thing to smoke.

Q10. Do I have the right to tell someone else to stop smoking a cigarette in the room?

A: (5755) Even though Rav Moshe says that you can't necessarily forbid smoking, he also agrees that you have the right to tell someone smoking a cigarette not to damage you (Igros Moshe CM

---

[218] Igros Moshe YD (2:49) – הנה בדבר עישון סיגריות ודאי מכיון שיש חשש להתחלות מזה מן הראוי להזהר מזה אבל לומר שאסור מאיסור סכנתא מכיון שדשו בה רבים כבר איתא בגמ' בכה"ג שומר פתאים ה' בשבת דף קכ"ט ובנדה דף ל"א ובפרט שכמה גדולי תורה מדורות שעברו ובדורנו שמעשנין וממילא אף לאלו שמחמירין לחוש להסכנה ליכא איסור לפנ"ע בהושטת אש וגפרורים למי שמעשן

[219] Igros Moshe CM (2:76) - הנה ליתן כלל להא דאמרו שומר פתאים ה' בשבת (קכ"ט ע"ב) ובנדה (מ"ה ע"א) בשני דברים שאיכא בהם חשש סכנתא ולא זהירי בהו אף שודאי בסתם חשש סכנתא אסור לסמוך ע"ז אף אם יזדמן כה"ג בדבר שיש בו חשש סכנתא ולא זהירי בהו אינשי נראה פשוט דבדבר דאיכא הרבה שלא קשה להו לבריאותם כלום כגון הרבה מיני אוכלין שהאינשי נהנין מהם ביותר כבשרא שמנא ודברים חריפים ביותר אבל קשה זה לבריאותן של כמה אינשי ליכא בזה איסור מלאוכלן מצד חשש סכנה מאחר דהרוב אינשי לא מסתכנין מזה

2:18)[220]. Even if you are only uncomfortable with having the cigarette smoke in the room, you are allowed to tell him to stop smoking just like you can tell someone to close the window in the winter when it's too cold in the room (Chazon Ish CM Bava Basra 13:11)[221]. He has no right to cause you this discomfort, so if you have a right to be in the room too – like in the dormitory – then you have a Choshen Mishpat (Shulchan Aruch CM 155:39)[222] right to tell him to stop. There has been a strong effort from the American government to reduce the amount of smoking, and it has been very effective. I remember when I was a *bochur* in America about 40 years ago, most Yeshiva *bochurim* smoked here. Most people today who have *seichel* don't smoke.

Q11. Is it permitted for a medical professional to shake a patient's hand of the opposite gender?

A: If it is necessary for the *refuah* which the doctor needs to give to shake the patient's hand, then it is permitted (Igros Moshe EH

---

[220] Igros Moshe (CM 2:18) - והנה פשוט וברור שאפילו אם ליכא חשש סכנה וחשש חולי דנפילה למשכב אלא שקשה להם לסבול דמצטערין מזה אסור שם לעשן כי אף רק בגירי דידיה שהוא גרמא ממש כהא להעמיד סולם פחות מד' אמות משובך נחשב גירי דידיה שמודה גם ר' יוסי בב"ב סוף דף כ"ב משום דזמנין בהדי דמנח ליה יתבא בחור ותקפוץ הנמיה ויזיק משום דא"ר טובי בר מתנא גרמא בנזקין אסור

[221] Chazon Ish (CM Bava Basra 13:11) - אבל אם יטעון איני יכול לישן מקול הרחיים יצטרך לבטל הרחיים והוא דחולה יכול לעכב י"ל דכן הוא שרש נזקי שכנים דהראשון עושה כל מה שירצה ועל השני שלא להזיקן וכמו דהעושה אוצר מעכב על חברו לעשות נחתום וצבעין ה"נ עושה ביתו בית חולים ועל חברו שלא לעשות אומנות של פטיש וכיו"ב

[222] Shulchan Aruch (CM 155:39) - מי שהחזיק לעשות מלאכת דם או נבילות וכיוצא בהן במקומו ויכנסו העורבים וכיוצא בהן בגלל הדם ויאכלו והרי הם מצירים את חבירו בקולם ובצפצופם או בדם שברגליהם שהם יושבים על האילנות ומכלים פירותיהם אם היה קפדן או חולה שצפצוף הזה מזיקו או שפירות שלו נפסדים לו בדם לבטל אותה המלאכה או ירחיק עד שלא יבא לו נזק מחמתן שהיזק זה דומה לריח בית הכסא וכיוצא בו שאין לו חזקה וה"ה כל נזק גדול שאין אדם יכול לסובלו

1:56)[223]. If it's not necessary for the *refuah*, then I don't say yes and I don't say no.

Q12. What about a psychotherapist?

A: It might be that for a psychotherapist, shaking hands has to do with the *refuah*. However, if it has nothing to do with the *refuah*, then I don't say yes and I don't say no. My Rosh Yeshiva Rav Aharon Kotler זכר צדיק לברכה said, "You should try to get out of it." Rav Moshe Feinstein (Igros Moshe OC 1:113)[224] said that you can't do it. Since there were some *poskim* who were lenient, I don't say yes and I don't say no.

Q13. Does it make a difference whether the patient puts out their hand expecting you to shake it?

A: Maybe. If the person is going to be insulted, then maybe there is more of a reason to shake the person's hand. It doesn't change the *halacha*, but maybe there is more reason to rely on those who are lenient. The question essentially is when you shake someone's hand, is this a way of התקרבות – becoming closer to another person? It could be that shaking another's hand is a form of התקרבות since it shows that you want to have something to do with the person. If shaking hands is a matter of coming closer to the

---

[223] Igros Moshe EH (1:56) - ובדבר שראית שיש מקילין אף מיראי ה' ליתן יד לאשה כשהיא מושיטה אולי סוברין דאין זה דרך חבה ותאוה אבל למעשה קשה למסוך and Shach (195:20) - ומיהו אם החולה מסוכן ואין שם רופאים ע"ז משמע קצת מדברי תשובת הרמב"ן סימן קכ"ז דשרי מפני פיקוח נפש אלא די"ל דלטעמיה אזיל דסבירא ליה דנגיעת נדה אינו אלא מדרבנן אבל להרמב"ם דנגיעת ערוה אסורה מן התורה הכא אע"פ שיש פיקוח נפש אפשר דאסור משום אביזרא דג"ע וצ"ע עכ"ל ב"י ואין נראה דודאי אף להרמב"ם ליכא איסור דאורייתא אלא כשעושה כן דרך תאוה וחיבת ביאה כמש"ל סי' קנ"ז ס"ק י' מה שאין כן הכא וכן המנהג פשוט שרופאים ישראלים ממששים הדפק של אשה אפילו אשת איש או עובדת כוכבים אע"פ שיש רופאים אחרים עובדי כוכבים וכן עושים שאר מיני משמושים ע"פ דרכי הרפואה אלא הדבר פשוט כמ"ש וזה נראה דעת הרב דלעיל
[224] Igros Moshe OC (1:113) - ולהושיט יד לאשה כדרך הנותנים שלום בהפגשם פשוט שאסור אף לפנויה שהרי הן נדות וכ"ש לאשת איש

other person, then there is an issue of לא תקרבו לגלות ערוה (Vayikra 18:6)[225].

---

[225] Vayikra (18:6) - אִישׁ אִישׁ אֶל־כָּל־שְׁאֵר בְּשָׂרוֹ לֹא תִקְרְבוּ לְגַלּוֹת עֶרְוָה אֲנִי
ה

Chapter 6: Alternative Medicine

Q1. Is there anything wrong with using acupuncture or other alternative medicine?

A: (5779) For many years, acupuncture was accepted by the entire world except the United States – they were the last country to accept it. Now medical doctors have accepted acupuncture, so there is nothing wrong with using acupuncture if the doctor feels it would be beneficial for you. Other forms of alternative medicines which aren't accepted by the medical world are just wishful thinking and aren't things you want to get involved with – unless medical society has no other alternative to helping you. At that point you have nothing to lose and might as well try the alternative medicine as long as it isn't involved with practices of *avoda zara*. That's something you need to be very careful about.

Q2. If one has a choice, is it better to use alternative medicine or conventional medicine?

A: (5779) We follow the conventional forms of medicine before turning to alternative forms of medicine. I had a story with a woman who had Hodgkin's disease who wanted to take a medicine called Laetrile – it's made from the nut inside a peach's pit. They claimed Laetrile was good for cancer in general - especially Hodgkins - while medical doctors said it didn't help. The United States government eventually got involved and started displaying signs in post offices saying, "Don't use Laetrile because not only does it not help, but it'll hurt you." I don't think they meant to say Laetrile actually hurt people, but that it made patients worse because they weren't receiving the proper medical treatment for their diseases. Part of the lure of Laetrile was the fact that there were no negative side effects in contrast to the side effects from chemotherapy like losing your hair. Not having any side effects isn't such a *chiddush* because you could drink orange juice and not have any side effects either. Nonetheless, since other people were praising Laetrile, this woman really wanted to have it while her husband was pushing her to listen to the doctors. They eventually agreed to go to Rav Moshe Feinstein to ask for a *psak*.

Chapter 6: Alternative Medicine

Rav Moshe explained that although the Gemara Gittin (67b)[226] in Perek HaNizakin lists many *refuos* which are good for various illnesses, the Rambam (Rambam De'os 4:18)[227] doesn't mention any of them when speaking about how a person should take care of his health – and he was a doctor. Some of the things he writes are not accepted today either. For instance, the Rambam (Rambam De'os 4:11)[228] said fruit is not healthy, so you should only eat it in moderation like once a week, and mushrooms are terrible for your health so you shouldn't even eat them in moderation. There is a *shinui hateva* of the illnesses, cures, and other things being different, as we see people are living longer today than they used to. Similarly, people are taller today than they used to be since we still have the suits of armor used by the soldiers of the armies in former years - which don't shrink over time - and are about four feet tall. These were the strong people of that period who fought in battle. We certainly see things have changed over time (Magen Avraham 173:1)[229], and Rebbi Akiva Eiger (YD 336) writes we're not allowed to try using the remedies mentioned in the Gemara because someone might try them, see they don't work, and then

---

[226] Gittin (67b) - אמר אביי אמרה לי אם לשימשא בת יומא כוזא דמיא בת תרי יומי סיכורי בת תלתא יומי בשרא סומקא אגומרי וחמרא מרקא לשימשא עתיקתא ליתי תרנגולתא אוכמתי וליקרעה שתי וערב ולינלחיה למציעתא דרישיה ולותביה עילויה וננחיה עילויה עד דמיסרך

[227] Rambam De'os (4:18) - לֹא יַרְגִּיל אָדָם לְהַקִּיז דָּם תָּמִיד וְלֹא יַקִּיז אֶלָּא אִם יִהְיֶה צָרִיךְ לוֹ בְּיוֹתֵר

[228] Rambam De'os (4:11) - לְעוֹלָם יִמְנַע אָדָם עַצְמוֹ מִפֵּרוֹת הָאִילָנוֹת וְלֹא יַרְבֶּה מֵהֶן וַאֲפִלּוּ יְבֵשִׁין וְאֵין צָרִיךְ לוֹמַר רְטֻבִּים אֲבָל קֹדֶם שֶׁיִּתְבַּשְּׁלוּ כָּל צָרְכָּן הֲרֵי הֵן כַּחֲרָבוֹת לַגּוּף וְכֵן הַחֲרוּבִים רָעִים לְעוֹלָם וְכָל הַפֵּרוֹת הַחֲמוּצִין רָעִים וְאֵין אוֹכְלִין מֵהֶן אֶלָּא מְעַט בִּימוֹת הַחַמָּה וּבַמְּקוֹמוֹת הַחַמִּים וְהַתְּאֵנִים וְהָעֲנָבִים וְהַשְּׁקֵדִים לְעוֹלָם טוֹבִים בֵּין רְטֻבִּין בֵּין יְבֵשִׁין וְאוֹכֵל מֵהֶם כָּל צָרְכּוֹ וְלֹא יַתְמִיד אֲכִילָתָם אַף עַל פִּי שֶׁהֵן טוֹבִים מִכָּל פְּרִי הָאִילָנוֹת

[229] Rav Sherira Gaon - צריכין אנן למימר לכון דרבנן לאו אסותא אינון ומילין בעלמא דחזונין כבזמניהון וכחד חד קצירא אמורין ולאו דברי מצווה אינון הילכך לא תסמכון על אלין אסותא וליכא דעביד מינהון מידעם אלא בתר דמבדיק וידע בודאי מחמת רופאים בקיאים דההיא מילתא לא מעיקא לה וליכא דלייתי נפשיה and Magen Avraham (173:1) - ואפשר דבזמן הזה אין לידי סכנה סכנה כל כך דחזינן כמה דברים המוזכרים בגמ' שהם סכנה לרוח רעה ושאר דברים והאידנא אינו מזיק דנשתנו הטבעיות וגם הכל לפי טבע הארצות

become an *apikores* (Igros Moshe YD 3:36)[230]. Therefore, Rav Moshe says you must follow the doctors of your day. The woman accepted the *psak* of Rav Moshe, used the conventional methods of medicine the doctors proscribed, and lived another 30 years Baruch Hashem. That probably wouldn't have happened if she continued only taking Laetrile.

Q3. How should we view Rambam's diet and medicine?

A: (5779) A lot of the things the Rambam says about medicine make sense. For instance, the Rambam says a person should work and not sit around doing nothing (Rambam De'os 4:14)[231], just as doctors today say you should exercise. Additionally, the Rambam says you shouldn't overeat and only eat ¾ of your fill (Rambam De'os 4:2)[232], and doctors say similar ideas. If you follow the Rambam's diet, then that would be fine – just make sure you take your vitamins also. Our food is not the same food as they had in the times of the Gemara or the Rambam. When they make bread today, they remove the wheat germ which has a lot of nutrients in it. 95% of wheat germ in America is eaten by domesticated animals because they don't consider it food fit for people. Then they also take the bran out – you can get whole wheat bread, but that doesn't include the wheat germ. Also, there are different kinds of wheat like Emmer wheat and Einkorn wheat, so how do you know which one is the healthiest? Similarly, apples are filled with a chemical which they pour into the roots of the tree in order to make all the apples ripen at the same time. The natural way of the

---

[230] Igros Moshe YD (3:36) - בְּרִפוּאוֹת וַדַּאי מִשְׁתַּנִּים הַטְּבָעִים דְּהָא חֲזֵינָן שֶׁנִּשְׁתַּנּוּ טְבָעִים דִּרְפוּאוֹת דִּלְכֵן לֹא מְרַפְּאִין אוֹתָנוּ הַרְבֵּה רְפוּאוֹת שֶׁאִיתָא בַּגְּמ' כַּמְפֹרָשׁ בַּתּוֹס' מו"ק (וְעַיֵּין בְּחִדּוּשֵׁי רעק"א יו"ד סִימָן של"ו דמהרי"ל אָסַר לַעֲשׂוֹת רְפוּאוֹת שֶׁבַּגְּמ' דְּשֶׁמָּא לֹא יַעֲלוּ בְּיָדָם וִילַעֲגוּ עַל דִּבְרֵי חֲכָמִים שֶׁלְּכְאוֹרָה אֵיזֶה סָפֵק הָיָה למהרי"ל שֶׁלֹּא יַעֲלוּ אֲבָל הוּא מִשּׁוּם שֶׁנִּשְׁתַּנּוּ הַטְּבָעִים בְּהַרְבֵּה רְפוּאוֹת וְלָכֵן הֲרֵי יֵשׁ לְהִסְתַּפֵּק עַל כָּל רְפוּאָה שֶׁמָּא לֹא תּוֹעִיל בַּזְּמַן הַזֶּה וְהַרְבֵּה רְפוּאוֹת וַדַּאי אֵין מוֹעִילִין מִשּׁוּם דְּנִשְׁתַּנּוּ הַטְּבָעִים

[231] Rambam De'os (4:14) - וְעוֹד כְּלָל אַחֵר אָמְרוּ בִּבְרִיאוּת הַגּוּף כָּל זְמַן שֶׁאָדָם מִתְעַמֵּל וְיָגֵעַ הַרְבֵּה וְאֵינוֹ שָׂבֵעַ וּמֵעָיו רָפִין אֵין חֳלִי בָּא עָלָיו וְכֹחוֹ מִתְחַזֵּק אֲפִלּוּ אוֹכֵל מַאֲכָלוֹת הָרָעִים

[232] Rambam De'os (4:2) - לֹא יֹאכַל אָדָם עַד שֶׁתִּתְמַלֵּא כְּרֵסוֹ אֶלָּא יִפְחֹת כְּמוֹ רְבִיעַ מִשָּׂבְעָתוֹ

world is that in July some of the apples get ripe, then in August more apples get ripe, and October they are just about finished. Why do they want to make all the apples ripe at the same time? When you bring in your harvesting machine and workers to the take the apples from the tree, you want to bring them all in at one time. It all boils down to money. This isn't a kashrus question since this chemical is coming through the ground – just as the apples would still be kosher even if you buried a few non-kosher animals around the tree. However, this does affect the apple as well as the human being who eats the apple. This is aside from the petroleum which they spray on apples. They spray apples with a petroleum compound so that when someone pays for 3 pounds of apples then they remain 3 pounds throughout the shipping process. Since 85% of an apple is water, some moisture will evaporate through the skin of the fruit and only be 2.9 pounds. Then the farmers will have a lawsuit on their hands. In order to ensure no water vapor leaves through the skin, they spray the apples with this petroleum compound. How healthy is that? So if the Gemara says an apple is a *refuah* for a certain type of sickness, does that really refer to our apples? Our fruit might make things worse, and this apple is just one example. There's another case where they took a gene from a turkey and put it into a tomato to accelerate the ripening process as well as make it larger. Is that genetic modification healthy? Besides the fact that *nishtaneh hateva* in that people have changed, food has also changed over the years. If you've ever noticed companies write in unclear writing on the plastic containers holding the tomatoes, "Wash before eating." Why? You need to wash all the chemicals off of them. All fruit is sprayed in order to prevent them from losing weight.

Q4. Is magnetic therapy permitted (magnets are placed on the body in specific areas to increase blood flow)?

A: (5779) Maybe the magnetic therapy does increase blood flow, maybe it doesn't – I'm not sure about that. It depends on how much iron you have in the blood.

Q5. Is alternative medicine *doche* Shabbos?

Chapter 6: Alternative Medicine

A: (5779) You are able to hypnotize a person without desecrating Shabbos, but you should make sure you're not just alleviating the person's pain without addressing the underlying medical issue. If a person is only in pain without a fixable solution through conventional medicine, then hypnosis is one of the ways which you can alleviate the pain. There are some dentists who use hypnosis for patients who don't respond well to injections for pain while they having dental procedures done – which is especially helpful for children. Also, if acupuncture is done right then there shouldn't be any blood which comes out of the body – so there would be no chillul Shabbos either (Shulchan Aruch 328:48)[233]. However, there are also times when the acupuncture can cause a person to die by masking the underlying medical issue. I was once in St. Johns, New Brunswick – it's one of the five divisions of Canada. There was a fish establishment which required us to review it in order to receive a *hechsher*. The person picked me up at the airport and drove me about an hour to his fish location. As we were talking during ride, he told me that he was originally from China where he learned to be a doctor. Although he had a license to be a doctor in China, he needed to spend another four years in medical school after moving to America because his doctorate was not accepted here. (He ended up as a fisherman in Canada because he realized he would make more money as a fisherman.) He told me that it was very important that he became a medical doctor in both China and America. Why? If a patient comes to you with a pain in his stomach, then a doctor in China would give him acupuncture to remove the pain – and he might die two days later from appendicitis. If he would go to a doctor in America, then the doctor would figure out that the patient has a ruptured appendix but would be in pain until eventually getting admitted to the hospital. If you have medical knowledge from both China and America, then you can order for the appendix to be removed and

---

[233] Shulchan Aruch (328:48) - אסור להניח בגד על מכה שיוצ' ממנו דם and Mishna Berura (147) מפני שהדם יצבע שהדם אותו ואסור להוציא דם מהמכה שאסור לדחוק בידיו על המכה כדי להוציא דם או כשכורך איזה דבר על המכה - [אפילו בדבר דלית ביה משום צביעה] אסור להדקה כדי שיצא דם דהוא חובל והוי אב מלאכה ויש שסוברין דה"ה אם מניח על המכה דבר שמושך ליחה ודם [כגון צו"ק זאל"ב וכיו"ב] ג"כ הוי מלאכה דאורייתא כיון שנתכוין לזה ועכ"פ איסור בודאי יש

110

alleviate the patient's pain while he's waiting for the surgery. Most of the alternative forms of medicine don't involve chillul Shabbos, so it's up to the doctor to decide whether the alternative therapy would be helpful.

Q6. If someone is very sick on Shabbos, can you go to a *gadol* to ask him to pray for the patient?

A: (5779) This question is addressed in the *poskim* as the *beracha* of a *gadol* has a lot of potency. Some people wanted to know if you can send a telegram on Shabbos to the Rebbe to receive a *beracha* (HaElef Lecha Shlomo). The *poskim* say that you are not allowed to desecrate Shabbos using means which are beyond the *derech hateva* (Shailos U'Teshvos U'Vacharta BaChaim 87)[234]. You are only allowed to desecrate Shabbos for medical needs with medicine which works *b'derech hateva*. Similarly, you cannot write an amulet on Shabbos even if you are an expert. I am highly doubtful whether an amulet written on Shabbos would even work since the entire concept of an amulet is to harness the power of *kedusha* to have angels act on the patient's behalf. Nonetheless, you are allowed to wear an amulet on Shabbos (Shulchan Aruch 301:27)[235].

Q7. Does alternative therapy work?

A: (5779) It depends who you ask. Let me tell you a *klal gadol*. There may be many cases where alternative medicine does work, but there is such a concept as the placebo effect. Meaning, if a person thinks he's getting better, then he sometimes he does get better. It's a powerful nature which the Ribono Shel Olam put into people. Consequently, when researchers want to test whether a medicine works or not, they need to administer a placebo as well.

---

[234] Shailos U'Teshvos U'Vacharta BaChaim (87) - אפילו חלול דרבנן אסור and see She'arim Metzuyanim B'Halacha (92:5)

[235] Shulchan Aruch (301:27) - יוצאין בביצת החרגול ובשן של שועל ובמסמר הצלוב בין בחול בין בשבת ואין בו משום דרכי האמורי וכן בכל דבר שהוא משום רפואה אבל אם עושה מעשה ואין ניכר בו משום רפואה אסור משום דרכי האמורי אבל כל לחש מותר ולא אסור אלא באותם שבדקו ואינם מועלים ויש מי שחושש בכל קמיע שאינה מומחה משום דרכי האמורי

Chapter 6: Alternative Medicine

For example, if they are treating 50 patients with a particular medicine and 10 people get better, then it would seem that the medicine helps some people because there is a 20% success rate. That's not true. If you give 50 patients a placebo pill and 10 of them get better, then the medicine isn't necessarily helping. It could be that alternative therapy will be successful by way of people thinking it's helping them. You can't say alternative therapy doesn't work, and if a person is sick then he doesn't care why it works – he just cares if it helps him get better.

Q8. Is it stealing to charge for alternative therapy?

A: (5779) No, it's not stealing to charge for alternative therapy. If a person requests a service and received the service – whether it helped or not – then the one who administers the service can charge for it. As long as the doctor and patient thinks the alternative therapy works, then that's all you need to ensure the transaction isn't considered a *mekach ta'os* – regardless of whether it works or not. It's similar to paying for a flight simulator where you feel like you're actually flying a plane, but practically you are just sitting there in a seat. You might even get excited, scared, and all of the emotions as you feel like you're falling off a cliff and appear to be reaching closer to the ground, but know the whole time that nothing is really happening. Still, paying for the experience is fine because it's agreed upon beforehand. You can go into alternative therapy the same way telling yourself that you know it's really nothing, but you feel like it helps you get better. Therefore, it's permitted to charge for alternative therapy.

Q9. Is it forbidden to put on a white coat, tell people you're a doctor, and charge people for your services if you're not actually a doctor?

A: (5779) In Baltimore, there is a shock trauma center in the one of the prestigious Maryland Hospitals. They have a helicopter landing pad on top of their hospital building to rush their patients from all over to the emergency room. There was a person who was in charge of the shock trauma unit for five years who wasn't a doctor, yet he performed the surgeries. Some patients died while other patients didn't die, but after five years of enough patients not surviving under his care they investigated his credentials and found out that he wasn't a doctor. They immediately fired the person who hired him since he's the person who did the *avla* of hiring this individual since he should've asked whether he was a doctor or not. There was another doctor in this hospital who was in the middle of an operation and had to rush to the bank to deposit a check since otherwise he was afraid that his account would bounce because he didn't have enough money to cover the checks he wrote to other people. So in the middle of the operation, the doctor left the patient on the operating table for half an hour. Then he returned and finished the operation. He actually was a doctor, but the hospital gave him a hefty punishment. I'm telling you all of this to realize that even if you go through the conventional ways of medicine, you're not guaranteed that it will be better than alternative therapy. I believe most doctors are honest and know what they're doing, so these cases are more extraordinary – evidenced by the fact that they made the news. If it happened all the time then it wouldn't have made it into the newspaper.

Q10. Do any forms of alternative medicine involve *kishuf* or *avoda zara*?

A: (5779) That's a very big question. The general rule that I would say is that if you or the doctor have to do any weird movements or say any strange statements or prayers, then those are red flags that the alternative medicine might involve *kishuf* or *avoda zara*. If everything throughout the procedures is done in a way which is understandable that it would help, then you can assume it's permitted. It's true that some of these practices may have started out as *avoda zara*, but today if you don't have to do anything unusual then we assume it's not considered *avoda zara* anymore.

Q11. Is meditation with background music considered *avoda zara*?

A: (5779) I don't think that meditation is *avoda zara*. I think it's just a relaxation of the mind which has an effect on the body. It may have been *avoda zara* at one point in time, but I don't think it's *avoda zara* today anymore.

Chapter 6: Alternative Medicine

Q12. Is it permitted to go to a reiki master?

A: (5779) I don't know too much about it. Lines of energy running through the body is similar to the way acupuncture works. It is a type of Asian thinking which is not necessarily *avoda zara*. However, it's a red flag that they require you to have a form of *semicha* from a previous reiki master in order for it to work – that sounds questionable.

Q13. Is there a connection between *kabbalah refuos* and alternative medicine?

A: (5779) The only thing I can think of is that they both don't work. There is such a thing as an expert in making amulets versus those who cannot aren't considered *mumchim* (Shulchan Aruch 301:25)[236]. If the amulet is made through channels of *kedusha* – without any channels of *tum'ah* – and the person who wrote the amulet is an expert, then you're allowed to use it. Being an expert at writing amulets means that he wrote three successful amulets or he wrote one amulet which worked for three people (Shulchan Aruch 301:25)[237]. However, I don't think alternative medicine works beyond the natural world. I think it works through the *derech hateva*, like homeopathic remedies which work through nature. There may be other forms of alternative medicine which work without medicine which are suspected to be *avoda zara* because of strange statements or movements. For instance,

---

[236] Shulchan Aruch (301:25) - אין יוצאין בקמיע שאינו מומחה ואם הוא מומחה יוצאין בו לא שנא אתמחי גברא ולא קמיע כגון שכתב לחש אחד בשלש אגרות ורפאו שלשתם שלש בני אדם שאיתמחי גברא לאותו לחש בכל פעם שיכתבנו אבל לא לשאר לחשים וגם אין הקמיע מומחה אם יכתבנו אחר לא שנא איתמחי קמיע ולא גברא כגון שכתב לחש אחד באגרת וריפא בו ג' פעמים שאותה אגרת מומחה לכל אדם וכ"ש אי איתמחי גברא וקמיע כגון שכתב לחש אחד בג' אגרות וכל אחד הועילה לג' אנשים או לאדם אחד ג' פעמים איתמחי גברא ללחש זה בכל אגרת שיכתבנו ואתמחו אגרות הללו לכל אדם

[237] Shulchan Aruch (301:25) - אבל אם כתב שלשה קמעים לאדם אחד ורפאו שלשה פעמים לא איתמחי לא גברא ולא קמיע ומותר לצאת בקמיע מומחה ל"ש היא של כתב או של עיקרים בין בחולה שיש בו סכנה בין בחולה שאין בו סכנה ולא שננכפה כבר ותולהו לרפואה אלא אפי' לא אחזו החולי אלא שהוא ממשפחת נכפין ותולהו שלא יאחזנו שרי וקושרו ומתירו ברה"ר

114

someone asked me if using synergy is permitted, so he gave me a handbook to read which was about an inch-and-a-half thick. I read through the whole manual and told him not to pursue it because they required making a strange statement before performing the synergy procedure. Strange statements raise a red flag.

Q14. Is there any reference of alternative healing in Chazal or Shulchan Aruch?

A: (5779) Yes, amulets are alternative forms of healing and there is also a concept of לוֹחֵשׁ עַל הַמַּכָּה (Mishna Sanhedrin 10:1)[238]. The Shulchan Aruch explains that it refers to saying something on the wound (Shulchan Aruch YD 179:8)[239]. The Rambam says, "If you need to use this procedure for someone, then even though it doesn't help whatsoever you can still do it because it makes the person feel better (Rambam Avoda Zara 11:11)[240]. There was no *avoda zara* involved, but the Rambam said this form of לוֹחֵשׁ עַל הַמַּכָּה didn't help – and he was a doctor, so he would know better than we do. There are some people who write amulets in Eretz Yisroel still today, but you need to be careful to find someone who knows what he's doing. There is someone who charges $4,800 for each amulet, and I don't think that's honest.

Q15. Did Chazal know about alternative healing?

A: (5779) I was in the main Manhattan Public Library where they have a complete library devoted to Jewish books dating back to when printing starting in about 1492 when the Jews were thrown

---

[238] Mishna Sanhedrin (10:1) - כָּל יִשְׂרָאֵל יֵשׁ לָהֶם חֵלֶק לָעוֹלָם הַבָּא שֶׁנֶּאֱמַר (ישעיה ס) וְעַמֵּךְ כֻּלָּם צַדִּיקִים לְעוֹלָם יִירְשׁוּ אָרֶץ נֵצֶר מַטָּעַי מַעֲשֵׂה יָדַי לְהִתְפָּאֵר וְאֵלּוּ שֶׁאֵין לָהֶם חֵלֶק לָעוֹלָם הַבָּא הָאוֹמֵר אֵין תְּחִיַּת הַמֵּתִים מִן הַתּוֹרָה וְאֵין תּוֹרָה מִן הַשָּׁמָיִם וְאֶפִּיקוֹרֶס רַבִּי עֲקִיבָא אוֹמֵר אַף הַקּוֹרֵא בַּסְּפָרִים הַחִיצוֹנִים וְהַלּוֹחֵשׁ עַל הַמַּכָּה וְאוֹמֵר (שמות טו) כָּל הַמַּחֲלָה אֲשֶׁר שַׂמְתִּי בְמִצְרַיִם לֹא אָשִׂים עָלֶיךָ כִּי אֲנִי ה' רֹפְאֶךָ

[239] Shulchan Aruch YD (179:8) - הלוחש על המכה או על החולה ורוקק ואחר כך קורא פסוק מן התורה אין לו חלק לעוה"ב

[240] Rambam Avoda Zara (11:11) - מִי שֶׁנְּשָׁכוֹ עַקְרָב אוֹ נָחָשׁ מֻתָּר לִלְחֹשׁ עַל מְקוֹם הַנְּשִׁיכָה וַאֲפִלּוּ בְּשַׁבָּת כְּדֵי לְיַשֵּׁב דַּעְתּוֹ וּלְחַזֵּק לִבּוֹ אַף עַל פִּי שֶׁאֵין הַדָּבָר מוֹעִיל כְּלוּם הוֹאִיל וּמְסֻכָּן הוּא הִתִּירוּ לוֹ כְּדֵי שֶׁלֹּא תִּטָּרֵף דַּעְתּוֹ עָלָיו

out of Spain. They started printing Hebrew books in the early 1500s. The largest library of Hebrew books is at the Reform Hebrew Union College, but the one in Manhattan is impressive too. In addition to the library devoted to Jewish books in New York, they also have a library filled with Chinese books. It's three times as large as the Jewish library – which is based on the *posuk* וַתֵּרֶב חׇכְמַת שְׁלֹמֹה מֵחׇכְמַת כׇּל־בְּנֵי־קֶדֶם (Melachim I 5:10)[241] – Shlomo HaMelech's wisdom was so noteworthy that he even had more wisdom than the B'nei Kedem which refers to the Chinese. It is possible that they are offspring of Avraham Avinu since it says that he took Ketura later in life (Bereishis 25:1)[242]. Then he sent them to Kedem – to the East – along with great wisdom (Bereishis 25:6)[243]. The amount that they have printed is much larger than the collection of Jewish *seforim*. Back in those days, people wouldn't print works which weren't important since it was very expensive to publish material. Chazal probably knew about alternative healing, and they make reference to certain procedures which may have been considered alternative medicine in those days. For instance, the Gemara says if a person was bit by a rabid dog then the person should eat its liver (Yoma 84b)[244]. Is that going to help you? Yes, even today's medical knowledge will tell you that eating the liver of such a dog will contain weakened pathogens removed from the dog's bloodstream – similar to the way a vaccination is a weakened form of the disease which the body can overcome. A person who takes a little bit of a weakened measles virus into his body will overcome it and develop antibodies against this weakened form of measles – which can protect you against stronger forms of measles. It might sound a little strange to us at first thought to eat a rabid dog's liver if it bites you, but this could potentially save your life. Chazal knew what they were talking about.

---

[241] Melachim I (5:10) - וַתֵּרֶב חׇכְמַת שְׁלֹמֹה מֵחׇכְמַת כׇּל־בְּנֵי־קֶדֶם וּמִכֹּל חׇכְמַת מִצְרׇיִם

[242] Bereishis (25:1) - וַיֹּסֶף אַבְרָהָם וַיִּקַּח אִשָּׁה וּשְׁמָהּ קְטוּרָה

[243] Bereishis (25:6) - וְלִבְנֵי הַפִּילַגְשִׁים אֲשֶׁר לְאַבְרָהָם נָתַן אַבְרָהָם מַתָּנֹת וַיְשַׁלְּחֵם מֵעַל יִצְחָק בְּנוֹ בְּעוֹדֶנּוּ חַי קֵדְמָה אֶל־אֶרֶץ קֶדֶם

[244] Yoma (84b) - ומי שנשכו כלב שוטה מאכילין אותו מחצר כבד שלו

Chapter 6: Alternative Medicine

Q16. If a person is in a situation where they need to eat a dog's liver, should they *shecht* it first?

A: (5779) No (Rambam Avos HaTumah 2:1)[245].

Q17. Does alternative medicine have the halachic status as medicine regarding using it on Shabbos?

A: (5779) If it works more than a placebo, then you are allowed to do alternative medicine on Shabbos where regular medicine is permitted.

Q18. Can you put pigeons on someone's liver or stomach on Shabbos to help with Hepatitis?

A: (5779) No, they have medicine to treat Hepatitis, so I don't think you can do it on Shabbos. Nonetheless, there's no rush for Hepatitis as you can do the procedure on motzei Shabbos. They use this form of treatment in Eretz Yisroel and it still works. Although it doesn't cure the patient, it does remove the Hepatitis that he has right now.

Q19. Does the חד חד נחית בלע (Shabbos 67a)[246] remedy work today?

A: (5780) I used to live on 401 Yeshiva Lane and lived there for about 30 years. Another person who lived in the building was eating a fish one Shabbos and a bone got stuck in his throat. This was in the time before Hatzala, so they asked if they could call an ambulance to take him to the hospital. I took a bone from the fish, said this, and it worked right away. As soon as I finished, he coughed up the bone and was OK.

---

[245] Rambam Avos HaTumah (2:1) - בְּהֵמָה אוֹ חַיָּה טְמֵאָה שֶׁנִּשְׁחֲטָה אֵינָהּ מְטַמְּאָה מִשׁוּם נְבֵלָה כָּל זְמַן שֶׁהִיא מְפַרְכֶּסֶת עַד שֶׁיַּתִּיז אֶת רֹאשָׁהּ וַהֲרֵי הִיא כָּאֳכָלִין טְמֵאִין

[246] Shabbos (67a) - תני תנא בפרק אמוראי קמיה דרבי חייא בר אבין אמר ליה כולהו אית בהו משום דרכי האמורי לבר מהני מי שיש לו עצם בגרונו מביא מאותו המין ומניח ליה על קדקדו ולימא הכי חד חד נחית בלע בלע נחית חד חד אין בו משום דרכי האמורי

117

Chapter 6: Alternative Medicine

Q20. How should it be practically performed?

A: (5780) Follow what it says in the Gemara: take a bone from the same fish, put it on top of the person's head, and say חד חד נחית בלע בלע נחית חד חד, then it will come out.

Chapter 7: Refuah on Shabbos

(5780)

Q1. Is it מותר to put oil on chapped lips on Shabbos?

A: If people put oil on their lips even if their lips are not chapped – which I don't think they do – then it would be permitted (Shulchan Aruch 328:37)[247]. The Shulchan Aruch (327:2)[248] mentions smearing oil on one's skin since in former times after taking a bath in the bathhouse, they would smear oil all over the body. The main reason for this procedure was since they didn't have soap the dirt wouldn't easily come off as the water wouldn't mix well with the grimy oil. However, smearing oil on oneself would mix with the dirt and come off when scraped away altogether. In places where people put oil on their skin for the purpose of cleanliness, then it is permitted to put oil on oneself on Shabbos because it doesn't appear like *refuah*. However, in places where people don't ordinarily put oil on their skin then it would be recognizable that you are putting oil on your skin for medicinal purposes and would be forbidden.

Q2. Is it מותר to use a normal food for רפואה if it's clear his intentions are for רפואה and everyone present knows that's what he's taking it for?

A: This halacha doesn't depend on what everyone present knows, rather it depends on what people in general know (Shulchan Aruch 328:37)[249]. For instance, are you allowed to use a retainer on

---

[247] Shulchan Aruch (328:37) - כל אוכלים ומשקין שהם מאכל בריאים מותר לאכלן ולשתותן לרפואה אע"פ שהם קשים לקצת בריאים ומוכחא מילתא דלרפואה עביד אפילו הכי שרי וכל שאינו מאכל ומשקה בריאים אסור לאכלו ולשתותו לרפואה ודוק' מי שיש לו מיחוש בעלמ' והוא מתחזק והולך כבריא אבל אם אין לו שום מיחוש מותר

[248] Shulchan Aruch (327:2) - סכין וממשמשין להנאתו ע"י שינוי שסך וממשמש ביחד ולא ימשמש בכח אלא ברפיון ידים

[249] Shulchan Aruch (328:37) - כל אוכלים ומשקין שהם מאכל בריאים מותר לאכלן ולשתותן לרפואה אע"פ שהם קשים לקצת בריאים ומוכחא מילתא דלרפואה עביד אפילו הכי שרי וכל שאינו מאכל ומשקה בריאים אסור לאכלו

Shabbos? Straightening out your teeth in order to improve your bite should be considered a *refuah* as the Shulchan Aruch (328:30)[250] says you cannot put a dislocated arm back in its place, but it is permitted to pour cold water on it and if it helps then that is fine because people normally pour cold water on themselves and it wouldn't appear like medicine. However, if one is straightening out his teeth just for good looks, then it would not be considered *refuah*. Regarding wearing the retainer on Shabbos, it is permitted because it would be similar to an amulet worn around the neck and is written by a *mekubal* which helps a person get better. Wearing an amulet around one's neck on Shabbos is permitted if the person who wrote it successfully wrote three amulets or this amulet was successful three times with other people (Shulchan Aruch 301:25)[251]. Since retainers have successfully treated more than three people in straightening their teeth, then it is considered *battel* to the body and can be carried on Shabbos. As far as *refuah* is concerned, there are two reasons why a person wants their teeth straight: one is for *refuah* as the dentist says teeth which aren't straight may cause other teeth to fall out, and the other is just for the sake of appearance. If you are using a retainer for beauty purposes, then it isn't *refuah* and would be permitted, but if you are using it because not having straight teeth is bad for your health, then it would be considered a *refuah* and would be forbidden. Since it is not recognizable why you are wearing the retainer, it is permitted on Shabbos. Similarly, regarding putting oil on chapped lips on Shabbos, if people do this even without chapped lips then it is permitted on Shabbos, but if people don't generally do that – and I don't think most people do this – then it would be forbidden. People used to say that milk was

---

ולשתותו לרפואה ודוק' מי שיש לו מיחוש בעלמ' והוא מתחזק והולך כבריא אבל אם אין לו שום מיחוש מותר

[250] Shulchan Aruch (328:30) - לא מי שנשמט פרק ידו או רגלו ממקומו לא ישפשפנה הרבה בצונן שזהו רפואתו אלא רוחץ כדרכו ואם נתרפא נתרפא

[251] Shulchan Aruch (301:25) - אין יוצאין בקמיע שאינו מומחה ואם הוא מומחה יוצאין בו לא שנא אתמחי גברא ולא קמיע כגון שכתב אחד לחש בשלש אגרות ורפאו שלשתם שלש בני אדם שאיתמחי גברא לאותו לחש בכל פעם שיכתבנו אבל לא לשאר לחשים וגם אין הקמיע מומחה אם יכתבנו אחר לא שנא איתמחי קמיע ולא גברא כגון שכתב לחש אחד באגרת ורפא בו ג' פעמים שאותה אגרת מומחה לכל אדם

good for ulcers. Doctors used to say that drinking milk helped reduce the acidity in the stomach. However, doctors recently realized their mistake – they don't say they made a mistake but that they found something better which really works – that a bacteria causes ulcers and therefore they prescribe medicine which gets rid of that bacteria. In the times when they used to use milk for ulcers, it didn't matter that your wife and children knew you were drinking milk for *refuah* purposes since the whole question is whether the world would view your drinking milk as being done for *refuah* or just for drinking. Therefore, someone with an ulcer would be allowed to drink milk on Shabbos. Moreover, people with a toothache drink whiskey to burn out the nerve which removes the toothache. Although people would not be allowed to tilt their head to keep the whiskey on the spot of the toothache, they would be allowed to drink the whiskey and have it flow past the spot of the toothache since people normally do drink whiskey – even if you personally ordinarily don't drink whiskey (Shulchan Aruch 328:32)[252].

Q3. Do we say בטל טעם בטל תקנה regarding רפואה on Shabbos since we don't do טוחן for medications anymore?

A: This is a very weak *heter* because we don't say בטל טעם בטל תקנה. Rather, we say even though the reason for the *takana* no longer applies, the *takana* is not *battel*. The Vilna Gaon explains that even when the Chachamim made a *takana* and told us the reason for it, that is not necessarily the only reason for the *takana*. Very often there were multiple reasons why the Chachamim made a *takana*, but they only revealed one reason because that was a reason we could understand more easily. Some reasons are משום קבלה which people wouldn't understand. The Chachamim said that we should keep two days of Yom Tov because we initially didn't know when the messengers of Beis Din would come to Chutz La'aretz (Rambam Kiddush HaChodesh 5:4)[253]. In Eretz

---

[252] Shulchan Aruch (328:32) - החושש בשיניו לא יגמע בהן חומץ ויפלוט אבל מגמע ובולע או מטבל בו כדרכו החושש בגרונו לא יערענו בשמן אבל בולע הוא שמן ואם נתרפא נתרפא

[253] Rambam Kiddush HaChodesh (5:4) - כְּשֶׁהָיְתָה סַנְהֶדְרִין קַיֶּמֶת וְהֵן קוֹבְעִין עַל הָרְאִיָּה. הָיוּ בְּנֵי אֶרֶץ יִשְׂרָאֵל וְכָל הַמְּקוֹמוֹת שֶׁמַּגִּיעִין אֲלֵיהֶן שְׁלוּחֵי תִּשְׁרֵי

Yisroel when the Beis Din would establish the new *chodesh*, then on the first day they would light the fires on top of the mountains so that all of Klal Yisroel living there would know about it within a few hours (Rosh Hashana 23a)[254]. However, the non-Jews started to make a problem later as they tried confusing us by lighting fires on the mountains at times when Beis Din did not establish the new *chodesh*. Consequently, Beis Din would send messengers via horseback to spread the news, but there wasn't enough time to reach everyone outside Eretz Yisroel in time for a Yom Tov in the middle of the month like Pesach. Therefore, the Chachamim said those people living outside of Eretz Yisroel would need to keep two days of Yom Tov. Nonetheless, they needed to keep two days מספק מן התורה because the Torah says you can't eat chametz on Pesach (Rambam Kiddush HaChodesh 5:4)[255]. Those who are not sure which day Pesach fell out would need to avoid chametz by keeping an extra day מספק. The last Beis Din in Eretz Yisroel established the Roshei Chadashim in advance until Mashiach comes, and when Mashich comes I guess they'll use email or another form of communication which no one else can copy. If they would use radios to communicate the next Rosh Chodesh, others might have the ability to copy it, so perhaps if they use a special frequency which only they know then they can use that. We don't know exactly what they will do, but we won't have any problems with knowing which days will be Rosh Chodesh when Mashiach comes. Until then, we know which day is the first day of the month as the second day Rosh Chodesh is the first day of the new month. There's really no ספק nowadays, but since מנהג אבותינו בידינו and there might come a time that the *malchus* will make decrees forcing Klal Yisroel to forget the established Roshei Chadashim established by Rav Yehuda

---

עוֹשִׂין יָמִים טוֹבִים יוֹם אֶחָד בִּלְבָד. וּשְׁאָר הַמְּקוֹמוֹת הָרְחוֹקוֹת שֶׁאֵין שְׁלוּחֵי תִּשְׁרֵי מַגִּיעִין אֲלֵיהֶם הָיוּ עוֹשִׂים שְׁנֵי יָמִים מִסָּפֵק לְפִי שֶׁלֹּא הָיוּ יוֹדְעִין בּוֹ בְּנֵי אֶרֶץ יִשְׂרָאֵל אֶת הַחֹדֶשׁ

[254] Rosh Hashana (23a) - וּמֵאֵין הָיוּ מַשְׂאִין מַשִׂיאוֹת כו' וּמִבֵּית בַּלְתִין

[255] Rambam Kiddush HaChodesh (5:4) - כְּשֶׁהָיְתָה סַנְהֶדְרִין קַיֶּמֶת וְהֵן קוֹבְעִין עַל הָרְאִיָּה. הָיוּ בְּנֵי אֶרֶץ יִשְׂרָאֵל וְכָל הַמְּקוֹמוֹת שֶׁמַּגִּיעִין אֲלֵיהֶן שְׁלוּחֵי תִּשְׁרֵי עוֹשִׂין יָמִים טוֹבִים יוֹם אֶחָד בִּלְבָד. וּשְׁאָר הַמְּקוֹמוֹת הָרְחוֹקוֹת שֶׁאֵין שְׁלוּחֵי תִּשְׁרֵי מַגִּיעִין אֲלֵיהֶם הָיוּ עוֹשִׂים שְׁנֵי יָמִים מִסָּפֵק לְפִי שֶׁלֹּא הָיוּ יוֹדְעִין בּוֹ בְּנֵי אֶרֶץ יִשְׂרָאֵל אֶת הַחֹדֶשׁ

Chapter 7: Refuah on Shabbos

HaNasi, we keep two days even now. We've never had a case where a mistake was made between Bayis Sheni until now regarding keeping Rosh Chodesh, so what were the Chachamim thinking? They had *ruach hakodesh*! In truth, it's very important for us to have two days even today because there is a difference of opinion which day Shabbos occurs in Japan, Tazmania, and even Australia. It might be Shabbos in Japan is on Saturday, but the Chazon Ish (*Kuntres Yud Ches Sha'os*) says Shabbos occurs on Sunday. The question is when does the day begin and end? The Chazon Ish brings proofs from the Gemara (Rosh Hashanah 20b) that the day starts at 90 degrees to the east of Yerushalayim, since Shanghai is around the same latitude as Yerushalayim everything attached to the mainland follows after that time zone. The Kuzari (2:20) says that there is no such thing as having two neighboring cities where it is Shabbos in one place and motzei Shabbos in the other unless there is a natural boundary like an ocean between the two regions. The Sea of Japan serves as that natural boundary. If you take a plane from New York to Los Angeles, then you will lose three hours. As you move towards the west, the time becomes earlier and earlier and if you move towards the east then the time becomes later – like when it is late motzei Shabbos in Baltimore then it is Sunday morning in Eretz Yisroel. There are all kinds of questions which result in crossing the international dateline. So if they would only keep one day of Pesach in Japan, then they would be eating chametz on the day after the 7th day of Pesach according to the Chazon Ish. Although there were no Jews in Japan, Tazmania, or the Fiji Islands at the time that the Chachamim made this *takana*, they were worried something like this would occur. In fact, we have a mashgiach in the Fiji Islands supervising tuna fish for a Canadian company who is the only *yid* living there, so we make sure to have him return to the Jewish community after two months so that he's not influenced by the non-Jewish environment. When we noticed they made hundreds of thousands of cases of tuna fish but didn't sell any of them in New York, we asked them why they didn't sell in New York if the main customer is there. They said, "We don't need the tuna to be kosher because we want to sell it to Jewish people, rather we want it to be kosher for Passover because in Canada there is a special tax on tuna fish which comes from outside the country (about $3 for every case of tuna fish). However, if the tuna fish is kosher for Passover then you don't need to pay that tax." They might pay $10,000 for the *hechsher* but save themselves hundreds of thousands of dollars in tax exemptions.

Q4. Do we ever say בטל טעם בטל תקנה?

A: We don't say בטל טעם בטל תקנה. Sometimes when the Chachamim made a *takana*, if they say the reason no longer applies in certain situations then the *takana* doesn't apply. For medicine, the Chachamim said you are allowed to place a hot water bottle on your stomach on Shabbos (Shabbos 40b)[256]. The water bottles used to be made of steel and they would remove the pain when placed on one's stomach. Nowadays we have a heating pad which essentially accomplishes the same goal. The Shulchan Aruch (326:6)[257] says that someone is allowed to use a heating pad on Shabbos if he has a stomachache because it is not treated with medicine – it's treated with heat. Although we do treat stomachaches with medicine nowadays, since they didn't make a decree on the heating bottle then it's permitted. Additionally, the Chachamim said you are not allowed to massage a patient on Shabbos because the massage itself would heal the person and the healing was also accomplished with medicine (Shulchan Aruch 328:42)[258].

Q5. May one eat a regular food in an abnormal quantity or fashion for רפואה on Shabbos?

---

[256] Shabbos (40b) - תנו רבנן מיחם אדם אלונטית ומניחה על בני מעים בשבת ובלבד שלא יביא קומקומוס של מים חמין ויניחנו על בני מעים בשבת ודבר זה אפילו בחול אסור מפני הסכנה

[257] Shulchan Aruch (326:6) - אסור ליתן ע"ג בטנו כלי שיש בו מים חמין ואפילו בחול מפני הסכנה שפעמים שהם רותחים [אבל מותר להחם בגד וליתנו על בטנו] and Mishna Berura (326:19) - וכ"ש דאסור בשבת שמא ישפכו עליו ונמצא כרוחץ בשבת כ"כ רש"י והר"ן ולפ"ז אם החמין בכלי סגור [שקורין ווארם פלאש] שרי אבל לפירוש התוספות דהטעם משום דמינכר שהוא לרפואה וגזירה משום שחיקת סמנים גם בזה אסור ולצורך גדול יש להקל

[258] Shulchan Aruch (328:42) - אין מתעמלים דהיינו שדורס על הגוף בכח כדי שייגע ויזיע ואסור לדחוק כריסו של תינוק כדי להוציא הרעי

Chapter 7: Refuah on Shabbos

A: If people don't normally eat food in this particular way, then it becomes noticeable and forbidden on Shabbos. If the way you are eating or drinking the food is not noticeable that it is being done for *refuah*, then it would be permitted on Shabbos (Shulchan Aruch 328:37)[259].

Q6. Can a diabetic check his glucose levels on a smartphone on Shabbos?

A: Someone who suffers from diabetes could be a question of *choleh sheyesh bo sakana*. If someone has a type of diabetes with unpredictable sugar levels whether he eats or not, then such a person can be in danger if he doesn't know what his sugar levels are. Therefore, he can do whatever is necessary in order to figure out his level to know how much food or medicine he should take (Shulchan Aruch 328:11)[260]. I don't know if you need a smartphone to check your glucose levels because I believe people checked their glucose levels before smartphones were invented. Some people have a pretty concise and regular pattern - like after breakfast they need more or less medicine - in which case they don't need to monitor the diabetes as much, so why check it more if you don't have to? However, if there is any possible concern for someone's health, then he is obligated to check his glucose levels. Diabetics certainly are considered to have an affliction which affects the whole body and is therefore permitted to perform any *melacha d'oraysa* through a non-Jew and any *melacha d'rabanan* himself with a *shinui* (Shulchan Aruch 328:17)[261]. I don't know if

---

[259] Shulchan Aruch (328:37) - כל אוכלים ומשקין שהם מאכל בריאים מותר לאכלן ולשתותן לרפואה אע"פ שהם קשים לקצת בריאים ומוכחא מילתא דלרפואה עביד אפילו הכי שרי וכל שאינו מאכל ומשקה בריאים אסור לאכלו ולשתותו לרפואה ודוק' מי שיש לו מיחוש בעלמ' והוא מתחזק והולך כבריא אבל אם אין לו שום מיחוש מותר

[260] Shulchan Aruch (328:11) - חולה שיש בו סכנה שאמדוהו ביום שבת שצריך לעשות לו רפואה ידועה שיש לו מלאכת חילול שבת שמנה ימים אין אומרים נמתין עד הלילה ונמצ' שלא לחלל עליו אלא שבת אחת אלא יעשו מיד

[261] Shulchan Aruch (328:17) - חולה שנפל מחמת חליו למשכב ואין בו סכנה. הגה: או שיש לו מיחוש שמצטער וחלה ממנו כל גופו שאז אף על פי שהולך כנפל למשכב דמי אומרים לעכו"ם לעשות לו רפואה אבל אין מחללין עליו את השבת באיסור דאורייתא אפילו יש בו סכנת אבר and Chayei Adam (69:12)

125

they are able to do the *melachos d'rabanan* with a *shinui*, but perhaps if they leave the smartphone on before Shabbos and have the glucose reading taken on Shabbos displayed on the smartphone, then I think that writing is only *d'rabanan* because it goes off after a while on its own (Shulchan Aruch Harav 340:6)[262]. However, if it's a question of a *melacha d'oraysa* then he wouldn't be allowed to do it himself unless there is a question of *sakana* (Shulchan Aruch 328:2)[263].

Q7. Can one take melatonin or give it to his children on Shabbos to help them fall asleep?

A: I believe if someone cannot sleep, then he is a zombie during the day and it would be considered a *choleh kol gufo*. Therefore, he would be allowed to take the melatonin himself or give it to his children in order to fall asleep (Mishna Berura 328:1)[264]. However, I want you to know that melatonin only helps for a certain period of time since after a while it loses its effectiveness. They say after half a year the effectiveness of melatonin on your body wears off.

Q8. What רפואה is מותר for a ספק פיקוח נפש?

A: Any *refuah* is permitted as long as it is a *refuah* which is a known and accepted medicine which is accepted by the medical profession. There are alternative forms of medicine which are not accepted by the medical profession which one cannot be lenient

---

[262] Shulchan Aruch Harav (340:6) - וְלַעֲשׂוֹת יִשְׂרָאֵל דָּבָר שֶׁאֵינוֹ אֶלָּא מִדְּרַבָּנָן יֵשׁ מַתִּירִין אֲבָל לְדַעַת רוֹב הַפּוֹסְקִים דְּאָסוּר אֶלָּא יַעֲשֶׂנָּה עַל יְדֵי שִׁנּוּי וְכֵן נ"ל. וְאִם א"א עַל יְדֵי שִׁנּוּי וְלֹא עַל יְדֵי נָכְרִי מוּתָּר לַעֲשׂוֹת כְּדַרְכּוֹ כֵּן נ"ל

אֵינוֹ חַיָּב אֶלָּא כְּשֶׁכּוֹתֵב בְּדָבָר הַמִּתְקַיֵּם עַל גַּבֵּי דָבָר הַמִּתְקַיֵּם אֲבָל מִדִּבְרֵי סוֹפְרִים אָסוּר אֲפִלּוּ בְּדָבָר שֶׁאֵינוֹ מִתְקַיֵּם עַל גַּבֵּי דָבָר שֶׁאֵינוֹ מִתְקַיֵּם כְּגוֹן לִכְתּוֹב בְּמַשְׁקִין וּמֵי פֵרוֹת עַל גַּבֵּי עָלֵי יְרָקוֹת וְכַיוֹצֵא בָּהֶן

[263] Shulchan Aruch (328:2) - מִי שֶׁיֵּשׁ לוֹ חוֹלִי שֶׁל סַכָּנָה מִצְוָה לְחַלֵּל עָלָיו אֶת הַשַּׁבָּת וְהַזָּרִיז הֲרֵי זֶה מְשׁוּבָּח וְהַשּׁוֹאֵל הֲרֵי זֶה שׁוֹפֵךְ דָּמִים

[264] Mishna Berura (328:1) - דְּאָם כָּאִיב לֵיהּ טוּבָא וְחָלָה כָּל גּוּפוֹ עִי"ז אוֹ שֶׁנָּפַל לְמִשְׁכָּב אַף שֶׁאֵין בּוֹ סַכָּנָה מוּתָּר לַעֲשׂוֹת בִּשְׁבִילוֹ רְפוּאָה שֶׁאֵין בָּה מְלָאכָה וְכַהַהִיא דְסִימָן שכ"ז ס"א וכה"ג

with using on Shabbos – unless you take it during the week and know that it helps you.

Q9. How far do we take ספק פיקוח נפש to be mechalel Shabbos (i.e. a 1% chance)?

A: Would this person go to the hospital during the week if there is a 1% chance of פיקוח נפש? When a person crosses the street, there is a ספק פיקוח נפש since it might be dangerous *chas v'shalom*. Maybe you should stay on one side of the street for the rest of your life. There is a *teshuva* from the Binyan Tzion (24)[265] which discusses the question of *metzitza* on Shabbos. After the *periya* at a *bris*, the mohel sucks out blood from the place of the wound. The Gemara (Shabbos 133b)[266] says that even though without the *metzitza* it is still considered a *kosher bris*, such a mohel should be fired on the spot because he is putting the baby is danger. I believe it is talking about the concern of tetanus because the baby is being cut with a metal knife. Therefore, since the surface blood might be infected with tetanus, the mohel needs to remove the blood from the מקומות הרחוקים. Someone asked the Binyan Tzion that since the mohel ensures his instruments were autoclaved and disinfected to prevent these issues, and the site of the *milah* is bathed in alcohol to ensure there are no germs as much as we can accomplish – and it is very unusual to hear about a *bris* becoming infected – perhaps we do not need to perform the *metzitza* anymore. Moreover, perhaps *metzitza* should not be permitted on Shabbos since it is forbidden to remove blood on Shabbos (Shulchan Aruch 328:48)[267]. The only leniency is ספק פיקוח נפש,

---

[265] Binyan Tzion (24) - ואם תאמרו הלא לא לחנם בטלנו המציצה רק באשר שראינו שנתהו' סכנה על ידה בשיש חולי בפה המוצץ וכי אפשר לבדוק בכל פעם את פיו כשמוצץ על זה אשיב הלא החזקה היא אחת מהיסודות אשר כל התורה נשענת עליהן וסוקלין ושורפין על החזקות ולמה נדאג שמי שהוא בחזקת בריא וכשרות ע"י הבדיקה הראשונה שנתרע אח"כ ובפרט בדבר שאם נתרע אי אפשר להמוחזק שלא ידע בריעותא שלו וכי בשופטני עסקינן שיסכנו נפשות על חנם ובדבר שעבידא לאגלויי דבלא"ה לא משקרי בה אינשי

[266] Shabbos (133b) - אמר רב פפא האי אומנא דלא מייץ סכנה הוא ועברינן ליה

[267] Shulchan Aruch (328:48) - אסור להניח בגד על מכה שיוצ' ממנו דם מפני שהדם יצבע אותו ואסור להוציא דם מהמכה

127

but since that no longer applies today perhaps the mohel should stop performing the *metzitza*. The Binyan Tzion responded, "How do you know that there is no longer any danger nowadays?" Even if one in 1,000 children dies, the non-Jews don't view that as an issue from not having a *metzitza* after their circumcisions. They say it was a heart attack or something, so we cannot rely on their statistics to decide whether there is no longer a danger not to perform *metzitza* anymore. Since one in 1,000 is enough of a concern, we are allowed to remove blood on Shabbos even though removing blood on Shabbos is forbidden *m'doraysa*. Rav Moshe Feinstein (Igros Moshe OC 1:129)[268] has an interesting *teshuva* where he says a fever of 102 degrees is considered a danger, and maybe even 101 degrees. One of my children had a fever of 107 degrees when about 10 months old. We figured we should call the doctor, so in those days - about 55 years ago - the doctors would come directly to the house. The doctor saw the baby standing in the crib and said, "It's OK, forget about it. If the baby was so sick, he wouldn't be standing" and he left. Baruch Hashem he was right, and the fever didn't mean anything. Babies can get a very high fever and not be affected, while adults can get the same fever and already be considered a *goses*. Therefore, Rav Moshe said 102 degrees is considered a danger enough to be mechalel Shabbos. The truth is that most fatal diseases don't come with a very high temperature. For instance, leukemia and the other serious diseases can reach upwards of 102 degrees. Therefore, Rav Moshe says that since 102 degrees can become a serious question of danger, people can be mechalel Shabbos for that as long as they would be mechalel Shabbos during the week. Generally, people aren't driving to the emergency room for a fever of 102 degrees, so they wouldn't be allowed to be mechalel Shabbos by going to the emergency room for the same fever on Shabbos.

---

[268] Igros Moshe OC (1:129) - הנה אין בזה דבר ברור אבל אין צריך שיהיה
ברור שהוא סכנה דעל ספק נמי מחללין וכל שהאדם חושש לזה שמא הוא חם
ביותר מחללין ורק מה שתופס שהוא רק מעט חום בברור אין מחללין. וסתם בני
אדם חוששין כשהוא קרוב למדת מאה ושנים שהוא חם ביותר ולכן על מדה זו
מחללין ואין רשאין להחמיר ואם אחד חושש גם בקרוב למאה ואחד ורוצה
שיחללו עליו נמי מחללין דלא גרע ממכת של חלל שאם חלל החולה אמר
שצריך לחלול שמחללין

Chapter 7: Refuah on Shabbos

Q10. Is it מותר for someone who takes Ritalin regularly to take it on Shabbos?

A: Even though for some people Ritalin is like cough drops, I would think that you are not allowed to take it on Shabbos unless it would be considered a *choleh kol gufo*.

Q11. May you use spray-on sunscreen on Shabbos?

A: You are allowed to put a gauze pad on a wound on Shabbos because you are just protecting it from further damage. Similarly, I would think that sunscreen is not a *refuah* but is more of a protection and would therefore be permitted to spray on Shabbos.

Q12. May one take moisturizing eye drops on Shabbos for comfort?

A: If this eyedrop would only be taken for comfort and not for *refuah*, then it would be permitted on Shabbos. However, most people use eye drops for *refuah* purposes like dry eye. Therefore, it would be forbidden to use on Shabbos (Shulchan Aruch 328:20)[269].

Q13. May someone who is not feeling well make tea on Shabbos with a tea bag if he is usually מחמיר not to make tea on Shabbos?

A: I hope this person is stringent with not making tea on Shabbos with a teabag since that may be an issue *mid'oraysa* (Igros Moshe

---

[269] Shulchan Aruch (328:20) - אין נותנין יין לתוך העין וליתנו על גביו אם פותח וסוגר העין אסור ואם אינו פותח וסוגר מותר ורוק תפל אפילו על גביו אסור דמוכחא מלתא דלרפואה קעביד

OC 4:74:4[270]. The Mishna Berura (318:42)[271] says even if you put in the bag after pouring the water, the tealeaves are considered *kalei habishul* and would be forbidden in a *kli sheni* – and the Chasam Sofer (Teshuvos Chasam Sofer YD 95)[272] says there is no difference between a *kli sheni* and a *kli shelishi*. You cannot make tea on Shabbos with a teabag unless you cooked the teabag from before Shabbos and rely on *ain bishul achar bishul* (Mishna Berura 318:39)[273] in a *kli sheni*. This is not a *refuah* question, this is a *hilchos* Shabbos question.

---

[270] Igros Moshe OC (4:74:4) - לא שייך לידע מנהג בזה משום דמחמירין אנו בכלי שני בכל דבר משום דיש דברים שמתבשלים גם בכלי שני ולא ידוע לנו שלכן החלוק ביד נכוית לא מצוי שיהיה נוגע לנו לדינא וליד נכוית בכלי שלישי שהוא נוגע לכל הדברים נוהגין שאין מחלקין דבכל כלי שלישי מקילין. אבל אין ללמוד ממנהג זה להקל גם בכלי שני דאפשר אף להח"א ליכא איסור בכלי שלישי אף בנכוית ואולי ליכא כלל מציאות זה

[271] Mishna Berura (318:42) - הוסיף בזה דין אחר והטעם דסבירא ליה לדעה זו דיש דברים שמתבשלים אפילו בכלי שני מפני שהם רכים ואין אנו בקיאים וע"כ הוסיף לאסור ליתן פת האפוי דהוא רכיך אפילו בכלי שני וה"ה דלדעה זו יש להחמיר נמי בשאר דברים שלא ליתנם בכלי שני ועיין לקמן בס"ט אודות תבלין

[272] Teshuvos Chasam Sofer YD (95) - דע בעיקר הדין לא נפקא מיניה כולי האי דאנו רגילים להחמיר בכל הכלים אפילו כלי שלישי כ"ז שהיס"ב וכמ"ש פר"ח ס"סי ס"ח אם לא בהפ"מ

[273] Mishna Berura (318:39) - ועתה נבאר דין בישול עלי הטיי"א השייך בכמה ענינים לסעיף זה. הנה טיי"א בשבת פשוט בפוסקים דיש בו משום בישול ובמזיד יש בו איסור סקילה ובשוגג חיוב חטאת וע"כ יש ליזהר בו מאד ובעו"ה רבים נכשלים בו ומקילין לעצמן בקולות שאין בהם ממש וע"כ מוכרח אני לבאר אופני ההיתר והאיסור בזה בעזה"י. הנה לערות מכלי ראשון על עלי הטיי"א יש בזה בודאי חשש אב מלאכה דקי"ל דעירוי מבשל כדי קליפה כדלקמן בסעיף יו"ד וכ"ש אם יעמידנו אח"כ על התנור או בתוך הקאכלין עד שיהיה היד סולדת בו בודאי יבוא לכו"ע לידי איסור סקילה עי"ז ואפילו אם ירצה ליתן את עלי הטיי"א לתוך הכלי אחר שיערה החמין לתוכה כדי שיהיה על המים שם כלי שני ג"כ אסור כדקי"ל בסעיף זה דדבר שלא בא בחמין מלפני השבת אין שורין בשבת אפילו בכ"ש וכ"ש ולפי מה שמבואר בסעיף זה דיש דברים רכים קלי הבישול שמתבשלים אפילו מכלי שני בהדחה דיש אפשר דיש בהעלים ג"כ חשש איסור דאורייתא אפילו באופן זה וכו' והנה אופן זה שבארנו אף שאין למחות ביד הנוהגים בו מ"מ כתבו האחרונים עצה המובחרת מזה דהיינו שיתקן העסענס מע"ש לגמרי שלא יצטרך לערות לתוכו עוד רותחין למחר בשבת ולמחר כשיצטרך לשתות יתן העסענס הצונן לתוך הכוס ששותה בו אחר שעירו המים

Chapter 7: Refuah on Shabbos

Q14. May one use liquid bacitracin for a cut on Shabbos if it is first put on a Band-Aid?

A: No, unless it is considered a *choleh kol gufo* – which I don't think it would be since it is just a cut. Also, a cut normally is not a concern of a *sakana* depending on where it is. If the cut is in the eye, then someone can be mechalel Shabbos since that is considered a *sakana* (Shulchan Aruch 328:9)[274]. It doesn't make a difference whether you put the bacitracin on the Band-Aid first or not.

Q15. Is there a problem of צובע to put a Band-Aid on a bleeding cut (Shulchan Aruch Harav 328:48)[275]?

A: No, there is no problem of coloring since this is being done דרך לכלוך since coloring the white part of the band-aid makes you no longer use it (Shulchan Aruch 302:10)[276]. Similarly, if you dry your hands on a towel and make the towel black or grey then it is not considered coloring because it's דרך לכלוך (Mishna Berura 302:51)[277].

Q16. May one apply pressure to a cut on Shabbos to stop the bleeding? What about by children?

A: Yes, you are allowed to apply pressure to a cut on Shabbos to stop the bleeding since that *refuah* is not done with medicine

---

חמין לתוכו ונעשה כ"ש וה"ה שמותר לתת לתוך הכוס הזה שהוא כ"ש חלב
שנצטנן אבל אסור לערות עליהם מכ"ר וכדלעיל בס"ד וכשהעסעענס שלו אינו צונן
הוא בודאי טוב לצאת בזה ידי כל הדעות

[274] Shulchan Aruch (328:9) - החושש בעיניו או בעינו ויש בו ציר או שהיו
שותתות ממנו דמעות מחמת הכאב או שהיה שותת דם או שהיה בו רירא ותחלת
אוכלא (פי' תחילת חולי) מחללין עליו את השבת

[275] Shulchan Aruch Harav (328:48) - אָסוּר לְהַנִּיחַ בֶּגֶד עַל מַכָּה שֶׁיּוֹצֵא
מִמֶּנּוּ דָם מִפְּנֵי שֶׁהַדָּם יִצָּבַע אוֹתוֹ וְאָסוּר לְהוֹצִיא דָם מֵהַמַּכָּה

[276] Shulchan Aruch (302:10) - הרוחץ ידיו טוב לנגבם בכח זו בזו ולהסיר
מהם המים כפי יכלתו קודם שיקנחם במפה. הגה: ויש שכתבו דאין לחוש לזה דלא
אמרינן שריית בגד זהו כבוסו בכי האי גוונא דאין זה רק דרך לכלוך וכן נוהגין

[277] Mishna Berura (302:51) - שידיו מלוכלכות ומטנף בהם את המפה ודוקא
במפה וכיוצא בהן שאין דרך להקפיד על המים הטפוחים אבל לנגב בדבר שדרך
להקפיד בחול על מימיו הבלועים בו אסור מטעם שמא יבוא לידי סחיטה

131

(Shulchan Aruch 328:24)[278]. Besides that, if you need to apply pressure on the cut to stop the bleeding, it could be serious.

Q17. May one remove a splinter on Shabbos if it might bleed?

A: If we are not sure whether the skin will bleed, then it is permitted to remove the splinter on Shabbos since you are not *mechaven* for it (Mishna Brura 328:88)[279]. However, if you will remove the splinter in a way that the skin will certainly bleed then it would not be permitted on Shabbos, even though you are not *mechaven* for the bleeding. You don't need to worry about a normal splinter potentially causing an infection on Shabbos – the Ribono Shel Olam will help. Maybe if there is some known infectious material on the splinter then such a person should be concerned, but otherwise people don't need to be too concerned.

Q18. How sick must one feel to take medication on Shabbos?

A: If he doesn't feel well, then he is considered a *choleh kol gufo* (Aruch HaShulchan 328:19)[280].

Q19. May one take medication for hay-fever on Shabbos?

A: No, I don't think most people consider hay-fever to be a *choleh sheyesh bo sakana* or a *choleh kol gufo*. There are pills and capsules nowadays which can last up to 24 hours which you can take before Shabbos. There are certain capsules with little balls inside. As the stomach dissolves the medicine, some of the balls dissolve into the bloodstream immediately while other balls will

---

[278] Shulchan Aruch (328:24) - נותנים עלה על גב מכה בשבת שאינו אלא כמשמרת חוץ מעלי גפנים שהם לרפואה (ואין נותנין גמי על המכה שהוא מרפא)

[279] Mishna Brura (328:88) - מותר ליטול הקוץ במחט ובלבד שיזהר שלא יוציא דם דעביד חבורה ואף דהוא מקלקל מ"מ אסור הוא לכו"ע ואף דבשחין התירו איסור דרבנן משום צערא וכדלקמיה הכא כיון דאפשר להוציא הקוץ בלי הוצאת דם אין לעבור איסורא בכדי

[280] Aruch HaShulchan (328:19) - אך מי שיש לו מיחוש שעל ידי זה נחלש כל גופו ואף שמתחזק והולך אך הילוכו בכבידות ובחלישות ודינו כנפל למשכב בחולה שאין בו סכנה

dissolve eight hours later, sixteen hours later, and twenty-four hours later.

Q20. What are the potential problems with band-aids on Shabbos; peeling the back off, wrapping it etc.?

A: The first problem with band-aids is removing it from its wrapper. The old type of band-aids had a thin string inside which you would pull out to remove the band-aids, while the new ones might be glued a little at the end, but you can pull them apart. It would be permitted to pull those band-aids apart on Shabbos without any question because they are glued *l'chatchila* to be separated. If you need to tear the wrapper, then you should not be lenient on Shabbos – even though others may be lenient. Then, wrapping the band-aid around the area – even sticking the band-aid on itself – is permitted.

Q21. What is the היתר for Hatzala if most of their calls are not פיקוח נפש?

A: The *heter* for Hatzala responders to drive to the *choleh* is that it might be a concern of *pikuach nefesh* since people calling Hatzala are usually nervous about a patient who fell. Maybe it is a heart attack or the like, so it's the right thing for people to call Hatzala even though most of the time it isn't a case of *pikuach nefeshos* since we are concerned for a ספק. The question becomes how Hatzala responders can drive back home. This is not such a simple thing to allow. Some say they are allowed to return the ambulance because if they can only walk back home then it will take a while to respond to the next call if they need to walk to the ambulance (Igros Moshe OC 4:80)[281]. Also, people need to know

---

[281] Igros Moshe OC (4:80) - אבל עיקר מה שיש לדון הוא לענין החזרה לביתו ממקום החולה כשהוא במקום רחוק וא״א לילך רגלי ואף אם הוא אינו רחוק כל כך אבל הוא בלילה שיש לחוש לילך רגלי מצד הרוצחים שמצדו עתה ולהשאר שם כל השבת ואף רק זמן גדול כעד היום ואף באם כשיצטרך לשהות בזה זמן גדול יש לחוש שבני ביתו לא יניחוהו בפעם אחר וגם שהוא עצמו יתרשל אם יש להתיר לבא בחזרה בנסיעה ברכב. וזה פשוט שבמקום ריבוי האוכלוסיו שמצוי שאפשר ליארע לעוד אינשי שיש צורך גם למיכל כי לא הכינו עוד מיכל שיש צורך גדול להביא המיכל בחזרה ברכב אבל הנידון הוא כשיש עוד מיכל בהמקום

quickly where the ambulance is currently parked. Still, that is not such a clear *heter* because we don't know for sure that there will be another call on Shabbos even though a Shabbos might have upwards of 15 calls in Baltimore. Therefore, we have a non-Jew who can drive the ambulance and the responder back home, but if he is not available then the Hatzala responder can drive the ambulance back to where it normally stays itself.

Q22. May one take cough drops on Shabbos? Is there a difference if he would eat one regularly even without being sick?

A: When you go to the supermarket, in which aisle are the cough drops sold – the candy section or the medicine section? Some cough drops are sold in the candy section because the sugar is good for coating the membranes. Actually, the best *refuah* for a cough is to take some whiskey and sugar together. That was the old *refuah*. Now they have come up with all types of other *refuos* which cost more money, but the old way was cheaper. If these cough drops are sold in the candy section then it would be permitted to take them on Shabbos, but if they are sold in the pharmacy section then they would be forbidden to take on Shabbos. If you would take these cough drops regularly without being sick, then it would be permitted for you to take them on Shabbos.

Q23. If one sees someone doing something some פוסקים hold is אסור (i.e. Using antiperspirant deodorant) should he tell him?

A: If that which the person is doing is a *machlokes haposkim* whether it is permitted or not, then you don't need to tell him unless you know that he wouldn't want to do it if he knew it was a *shailah*. However, if you are not sure whether the person would be sensitive to that, then you do not need to tell him.

Q24. Is medicine *muktzah*? If yes, may a healthy person give medicine to a חולה שאין בו סכנה?

שנמצאים חברי אגודת הצלה זו וגם יש עוד חברים מאגודת הצלה זו שהוא רק
לענין איש זה אם רשאי לחזור בנסיעה ברכב בכלל וגם אם ליכא נכרי שאפשר
לסמוך עליו מצד חשש ההתרשלות

Chapter 7: Refuah on Shabbos

A: The Chazon Ish (OC 43:7)[282] says that any medicine you are not allowed to use on Shabbos is considered *muktzah* just like anything else which has no use on Shabbos. Everything must be prepared in your mind from before Shabbos – וְהָיָה בַּיּוֹם הַשִּׁשִּׁי וְהֵכִינוּ אֵת אֲשֶׁר־יָבִיאוּ (Shemos 16:5)[283] was said regarding the *mun*. The Chachamim extended this concept to include requiring everything else to be prepared in your mind before Shabbos in order to use it on Shabbos. That doesn't mean you can't use a spoon if you didn't mentally prepare to use before Shabbos since anything which has use for a person is not considered *muktzah* from his *daas*, while things which people don't really have a use for on Shabbos – like some lumber leftover from a building which has been sitting around for half a year which no one has used – is considered *muktzah* (Shulchan Aruch 308:20)[284]. If you have stones sitting outside, then they are considered *muktzah* unless you specifically chose one stone to hold your door open (Shulchan Aruch 308:22)[285]. If you have hay-fever medicine in your cabinet when

---

[282] Orchos Shabbos - Chut Shani OC (3:42) – וידענא דמרן החזו"א חשש לטלטל תרופות בשבת לאחר גמר השימוש בהם ונראה עפ"י מש"כ בחזו"א לבאר מה דאמרינן במס' ביצה שפוד שצלו בו בשר אסור לטלטלו ביו"ט ומשמע שם בגמ' דאפילו לצורך מקומו אסור הקשה בחזו"א הרי שפוד הוא דבר שמלאכתו להיתר ביו"ט דראוי לצלות בו עוד הפעם וכתב וז"ל ואפשר דבסתמא נמאס ואינו עומד להשקה [אחרי הצליה] והלכך אסור בטלטול ומיהא אי יהיב דעתו להסיקו שרי ולפי"ז אסור לצלות בו פעם אחרת כיון שאין ראוי להשקה...ולענין טלטול תרופות שאינם ראויים לאכילה לפי מש"כ בחזו"א י"ל דכיון דאין להם תורת כלי וגם אינם אוכלין אסור לטלטלן לאחר שגמר להשתמש בהם אף אם מותר לטלטל סכין של מילה לאחר המילה

[283] Shemos (16:5) - וְהָיָה בַּיּוֹם הַשִּׁשִּׁי וְהֵכִינוּ אֵת אֲשֶׁר־יָבִיאוּ וְהָיָה מִשְׁנֶה עַל אֲשֶׁר־יִלְקְטוּ יוֹם יוֹם

[284] Shulchan Aruch (308:20) - חריות (פירוש ענפים) של דקל שקצצם לשריפה מוקצים הם ואסור לטלטלם ישב עליהם מעט מבעוד יום מותר לישב עליהם בשבת וכל שכן אם קשרן לישב עליהם או אם חשב עליהם מבעוד יום לישב עליהם אפילו בחול however, see Shulchan Aruch (308:17) - לבנים שנשארו מהבנין מותר לטלטלם דמדעתה לא קיימי לבנין אלא למזגא [פירוש להסמך ולשבת עליהן] עלייהו ואם סדרם זה על זה גלי אדעתיה שהקצם לבנין ואסור לטלטלם

[285] Shulchan Aruch (308:22) - אסור לכסות פי חבית באבן או בבקעת או לסגור בהן את הדלת או להכות בהן בברזא (פירוש הקנה שמשימים בחבית להוציא היין ממנו) אף על פי שחשב עליה מבעוד יום אסור אלא אם כן יחדה לכך

it is not hay-fever season, then it is considered *muktzah* since no one plans to use it. The Gemara (Shabbos 125a)[286] says that if you have a piece of cloth which is 3 *tefachim* by 3 *tefachim*, which is about 12 in x 12 in., that is not *muktzah* because it has a use. A typical handkerchief was 3 x 3 *tefachim*. If you have a cloth which was 3 fingerbreadths by 3 fingerbreadths, which is about 3 x 3 inches, that is *muktzah* for a wealthy individual but not *muktzah* for a poor person because the latter will use the cloth to patch his clothing while a wealthy individual will not patch his clothing (Shulchan Aruch 308:13)[287]. The Chazon Ish (OC 43:7)[288] explains that *muktzah* is dependent on the owner of the object, so if the poor person owns this piece of cloth then a wealthy person can move it as well since the owner designated the cloth for use. However, if the owner of the cloth is wealthy, then the poor person cannot move it either. Similarly, if the owner of the medicine is allowed to take it on Shabbos for any of the permitted reasons discussed earlier like *choleh kol gufo*, then it is not considered

---

לעולם אבל יחדה לשבת זה בלבד לא והני מילי בדבר שאין דרכה ליחדה לכך כגון הני דאמרן אבל בכל מידי דאורחיה בהכי כגון לפצוע בה אגוזים ביחוד לשבת אחת סגי ויש מי שאומר דלא שנא ויש אומרים שצריך שיעשה בה שום מעשה של תיקון מבעוד יום

[286] Shabbos (125a) - אמר רבי זירא אמר רב שירי פרוזמיות אסור לטלטלן בשבת אמר אביי במטלניות שאין בהן שלש על שלש דלא חזיין לא לעניים ולא לעשירים

[287] Shulchan Aruch (308:13) - שירי מטלניות שבלו אם יש בהם ג' אצבעות על ג' אצבעות מותר לטלטלן ואם לאו אסור ויש מתירין אפילו אין להם ג' על ג' and Mishna Berura (308:52) - דיש ובלבד שלא יהיו טליתות של מצוה בזה קצת חשיבות דחזיין לעניים ועיין באחרונים שכתבו דלעשירים אסור לטלטלן דלהם לא חשיבי שירי מטלניות אא"כ יש בהם ג' טפחים על ג' טפחים לדעה זו

[288] Chut Shani OC (3:42) – וידענא דמרן החזו"א חשש לטלטל תרופות בשבת לאחר גמר השימוש בהם ונראה עפ"י מש"כ בחזו"א לבאר מה דאמרינן במס' ביצה שפוד שצלו בו בשר אסור לטלטלו ביו"ט ומשמע שם בגמ' דאפילו לצורך מקומו אסור הקשה בחזו"א הרי שפוד זה דבר שמלאכתו להיתר ביו"ט דראוי לצלות בו עוד הפעם וכתב וז"ל ואפשר דבסתמא נמאס ואינו עומד להשקה [אחרי הצליה] והלכך אסור בטלטול ומיהו אי יהיב דעתו להסיקו שרי ולפי"ז אסור לצלות בו פעם אחרת כיון שאין ראוי להשקה...ולענין טלטול תרופות שאינם ראויים לאכילה לפי מש"כ בחזו"א י"ל דכיון דאין להם תורת כלי וגם אינם אוכלין אסור לטלטלן לאחר שגמר להשתמש בהם אף אם מותר לטלטל סכין של מילה לאחר המילה

muktzah, but if the owner of this medicine is not allowed to use it on Shabbos then even the sick individual would not be permitted to move it either.

Q25. Is it אסור to use a non-electric exercise bike for enjoyment on Shabbos?

A: It is not forbidden to use an exercise bike for enjoyment on Shabbos if you normally use it for enjoyment since it is not considered *refuah*. However, if it is only used as exercise for those who need to exercise, then it would be forbidden on Shabbos because it would be considered *refuah* (Shulchan Aruch 301:2)[289].

Q26. May a woman who is/may be pregnant or nursing take prenatal vitamins on Shabbos?

A: If she is not sure whether she is pregnant or not, then it is not crucial for her to take any vitamins on Shabbos. Even if she is pregnant, I don't know if it's so important for her to take medicine on Shabbos. Women became pregnant before vitamins were available, and Baruch Hashem they had children. There are certain vitamins - like folic acid - which are helpful for pregnant women to take, but if she skips it once a week then she will be fine. However, if doctors know there is a problem then she is considered a *choleh kol gufo* and would be allowed to take vitamins on Shabbos.

Q27. If a child cannot sleep because of a mosquito bite or other itch, can you dab an anti-itch on it? Does it matter how old the child is?

A: If a child cannot sleep because of a mosquito bite, then he is considered a *choleh kol gufo* and you would be allowed to dab an anti-itch cream on the area regardless of how old the child is –

---

[289] Shulchan Aruch (301:2) - בחורים המתענגים בקפיצתם ומרוצתם מותר and Mishna Berura וכן לראות כל דבר שמתענגים בו (וכן מותר לטייל) אפילו אם כונתו להתעמל ולהתחמם משום רפואה מ"מ שרי כיון דלא - (301:7) מוכחא מילתא שעושה כן לרפואה אבל אסור לרוץ כדי שיתחמם לרפואה כיון דמוכחא מילתא ואסור משום שחיקת סממנין ויש מחמירין אפילו בטיול אם כונתו להתעמל לרפואה

even if the child is 45 years old it would be permitted because it is considered a *choleh kol gufo*. The same would apply if someone's allergies are preventing him from falling asleep.

Q28. If a doctor says to put a hot compress on the eye, what is the best way to heat it up on Shabbos?

A: When did the doctor say to put the hot compress on the eye? If the doctor said this before Shabbos, then the best way is to heat it up before Shabbos. If the doctor said to put the hot compress on the eye on Shabbos, then you need to decide what kind of *choleh* this is considered in order to answer the question.

Q29. Can you use rubbing alcohol for a mosquito bite on Shabbos?

A: What is rubbing alcohol used for? You can use it to remove stains, disinfect bacteria, and many other things. If you use the rubbing alcohol on your skin for a noticeable issue, then it should not be used on Shabbos. When people see you pouring rubbing alcohol on your arm, they don't think you are using the alcohol just because you enjoy pouring rubbing alcohol on your arm.

Q30. Can one take caffeine pills on Shabbos, as they are not fixing something like vitamins, rather are just providing an extra boost?

A: You are allowed to take caffeine pills to keep you awake on the first night of Shavuos, and the same is true for any other Yom Tov. It's a normal thing to be tired late at night, so if you take a caffeine pill to remain awake then that is not a *refuah* – that is going against what is considered normal. Taking a caffeine pill for an extra boost is permitted, just as drinking coffee is permitted since people drink coffee even when they are not sick. There is a Magen Avraham (Mishna Berura 328:120)[290] which says that if someone takes something לחזק מזגו – to strengthen his constitution – that is considered a *refuah* which is forbidden on Shabbos. My

---

[290] Mishna Berura (328:120) - דהיינו שאוכל ושותה לרעבונו ולצמאונו אבל אם הוא עושה לרפואה דהיינו כדי לחזק מזגו כתב המ"א דאפילו בבריא גמור אסור

Chapter 7: Refuah on Shabbos

Rosh Yeshiva Rav Aharon Kotler זכר צדיק לברכה said that if the person takes a vitamin on Shabbos because he feels weak, then that is considered a *choleh kol gufo* and it would be permitted on Shabbos. However, if he feels OK but is just taking the vitamin to make himself feel better, then that is what the Magen Avraham is referring to and would say it's forbidden. Rav Moshe Feinstein (Igros Moshe OC 3:54)[291] says that if you are taking the vitamin pills because you feel weak, then it is a *refuah* and it would be forbidden. However, if you feel OK and take the vitamin then there is no *refuah* taking place and it would be permitted. Either way you look at it, if someone feels weak then he can rely on my Rosh Yeshiva who says such a person is considered a *choleh kol gufo*, and if he doesn't feel weak then he can rely on Rav Moshe Feinstein who says it is not considered a *refuah*. You always have someone to rely on in either case, though there is also someone who says it is forbidden in either case too. Since it's an *issur d'rabanan* you can be lenient.

Q31. May one adjust his hearing aid on Shabbos?

A: Typically, hearing aids run on electricity with a battery. Those hearing aids you cannot adjust on Shabbos. (see footnote)[292]

Q32. If one sees someone else adjusting his hearing aid, must he speak up?

---

[291] Igros Moshe OC (3:54) - ואע"כ באלו הוויטאמינים שאינם מבריאים את האדם לשנותו מכפי שהוא מי שחלש בטבעו לחזק יותר אלא שעושין שלא יהיה עלול להתחלות בנקל יש להתיר לכו"ע אף להמג"א. ואם יש וויטאמינים שמשנים בריאותו שעושים מחלש בטבעו לחזק יותר פליגי בזה הב"י והמג"א שיש להחמיר ולאסור כהמגן אברהם. והנה ראיתי בדברי הגר"י לעבאוויץ שליט"א שג"כ מחלק כעין זה מסברתו שהאיסור להמג"א הוא רק בשע"י מה שאוכל יתחזק יותר מבפי שהוא עתה ולא באם הוא רק שלא יתחלש ויגרע מכפי שהוא עתה שזה גם להמג"א מותר. ולפ"מ שביארתי הוא מוכרח כדלעיל וגם מסתבר שדוקא כשעושה מחלש בטבעו לגוף בריא וחזק ולא כשעושה רק להתחזק מעט יותר

[292] See Toras Hacheresh (I:2:fn41) who quotes Shemiras Shabbos Kehilchasa (1:34:28) and Minchas Shlomo (1:9 p.74) to be lenient when increasing or decreasing volume, not necessarily turning on or off

139

Chapter 7: Refuah on Shabbos

A: If you speak up, then you are using the hearing aid. Rather, you shouldn't speak up. The person's Rav will eventually see this person adjusting his hearing aid and will decide whether or not he should tell him.

Q33. May one put a hot compress on his eye on Shabbos?

A: It depends what is wrong with his eye. The Gemara (Beitza 22a)[293] says that an eye injury is considered a *choleh sheyesh bo sakana*. It could be that it is permitted to put on a compress because it is a *sakana* (Shulchan Aruch 328:9)[294]. However, the hot compress usually is made using a hot liquid, so there are different questions here like squeezing out water (Shulchan Aruch 320:17)[295] or how you obtain the hot water (Igros Moshe YD 2:33)[296]. There might also be an issue of laundering by soaking

---

[293] Beitza (22a) - בעא מיניה רב אשי מאמימר מהו לכחול את העין ביו"ט היכא דאיכא סכנה כגון רירא דיצא דמא דמעתא וקדחתא ותחלת אוכלא לא מבעיא לי דאפי' בשבת שרי כי קמבעיא לי סוף אוכלא ופצוחי עינא מאי א"ל אסור and וכי מדידי הוא דמר שמואל היא ההיא אמתא דהואי בי מר - Avoda Zara 28b שמואל דקדחא לה עינא בשבתא צווחא וליכא דאשגח בה פקעא עינא למחר נפק מר שמואל ודרש עין שמרדה מותר לכוחלה בשבת מאי טעמא דשוריינא דעינא באובנתא דליבא תלו

[294] Shulchan Aruch (328:9) - החושש בעיניו או בעינו ויש בו ציר או שהיו שותתות ממנו דמעות מחמת הכאב או שהיה שותת דם או רירא בו שהיה בו תחלת אוכלא (פי' תחילת חולי) מחללין עליו את השבת

[295] Shulchan Aruch (320:17) - ספוג אין מקנחין בו אלא אם כן יש בו בית אחיזה גזירה שמא יסחוט

[296] Igros Moshe YD (2:33) - ובדבר המים חמים שבבתים שכמה שמוציא נכנסים מים קרים תחתיהם ומתבשלים פשוט שאסור להוציא בשבת דהוא כפסיק רישיה שאסור אף בלא מתכוין וגם אפשר יש להחשיב שהוא גם מתכוין שהרי אם לא היו נכנסים מים אחרים הקרים לא יהיה לו בעוד איזה שעות מים חמים כשיצטרך להם ולכן אין מקום להתיר ורק מי שיש לו בית לעצמו יכול לכבות את האש ע"י כשתי שעות קודם השבת שיפסקו מלהיות רותחין שיותר קרוב שלא יתחממו המים קרים הנכנסים לשם במדה דהיד סולדת ויהיה מותר או כשיוכל לתקן שלא יכנסו הקרים ביום השבת יהיה מותר אבל בסתם הבתים אסור ואיני יודע שום צד היתר

water into the fabric of the hot compress (Shulchan Aruch 302:1)[297].

Q34. Does it matter if he soaks a towel in hot water or fills a water bottle with warm water?

A: Yes, if you soak a towel in hot water then it would be considered laundering, while if you fill a water bottle for the compress then it is not an issue of laundering. The Gemara (Shabbos 40b)[298] says you are allowed to use a hot water bottle for a stomach pain (Mishna Berura 326:19)[299] because the Chachamim did not decree on any kind of *refuah* which is not usually done with spices or other things you need to grind. Based on that, if someone has a heating pad on a time clock which he wants to use on Shabbos, that would also be permitted if the person has a stomachache.

Q35. May one walk with a walker or cane in a place where there is no *eruv*?

---

[297] Shulchan Aruch (302:1) - המנער טלית חדשה שחורה מן הטל שעליה חייב שהניעור יפה לה כמו כיבוס והוא שמקפיד עליה שלא ללבשו בלא ניעור. הגה: וכל שכן שאסור לנער בגד שנשר במים או שירדו עליו גשמים ודוקא בבגד חדש שמקפיד עליו יש אומרים דאסור לנער בגד מן האבק שעליו אם מקפיד עליו וטוב לחוש לדבריו

[298] Shabbos (40b) - תנו רבנן מיחם אדם אלונטית ומניחה על בני מעים בשבת ובלבד שלא יביא קומקומוס של מים חמין ויניחנו על בני מעים בשבת ודבר זה אפילו בחול אסור מפני הסכנה

[299] Mishna Berura (326:19) - וכ"ש דאסור בשבת שמא ישפכו עליו ונמצא כרוחץ בשבת כ"כ רש"י והר"י ולפ"ז אם החמין בכלי סגור [שקורין ווארם פלאש] שרי אבל לפירוש התוספות דהטעם משום דמינכר שהוא לרפואה וגזירה משום שחיקת סמנים גם בזה אסור ולצורך גדול יש להקל

Chapter 7: Refuah on Shabbos

A: Tosfos (Shabbos 65b)[300] and the Shulchan Aruch (301:17)[301] say that if a person can walk without the cane and the only reason why he is using the cane is because he is not so steady on his feet and wants the added protection from falling over – or if it helps him walk but he can walk without the assistance – then he is not allowed to use it on Shabbos in a place where there is no *eruv* (Mishna Berura 301:65)[302]. The reason for this is because if a person can walk without this assistance, then we are concerned he might walk *daled amos* with the cane in his hand without using it – which is an issue of carrying it. On the other hand, if a person needs the support and without it he cannot walk, then he is allowed to walk with the cane or walker because it is considered like an artificial foot for such an individual. Therefore, it is permitted as part of the person's body.

Q36. May a non-Jew push them in a wheelchair?

A: If you want a non-Jew to push this individual in a wheelchair in a place without an *eruv*, then you are asking the non-Jew to

---

[300] Tosfos (Shabbos 65b) - ואומר ר"י דמיירי - הקיטע יוצא בקב שלו שנושא בידו מקל ועיקר הליכתו היא בסמיכת המקל והשתא אי נמי מיפסיק יוכל להלך מכאן יש להתיר למי . שכוותצו גידי שוקיו ללכת במקלו בשבת והרב פור"ת פי' דקיטע יש לו סמך שקושר בכרעו ומגיע לארץ והשוק כפופה לאחוריה ובראש השוק במקום הרגל עושה לו קב להראות כמו שיש לו רגל ובהא פליגי ר' יוסי סבר כיון שאינו נסמך עליו אלא תלוי באויר חיישינן דילמא נפיל ור"מ לא חייש ולפי זה אין ראיה להתיר לקיטע לצאת במקלו אמנם יש להתיר מסיפא דמתניתין דאינו אוסר אלא סמוכות שלו לפי ששוקיו תלויין באויר ודילמא נפיל ואתי לאתויי (אבל הכסא) והספסלים שבידו אינו אוסר ואינהו הוו דומיא דמקל וק"ק לפי זה אמאי מטמא ליה רבא משום מדרס כיון שאינו נסמך עליו ושמא כשהוא יושב פעמים הוא נסמך עליו ולכך עושה לו בית קבול כתיתין שלא יוזק בקשר העץ שהוא יושב

[301] Shulchan Aruch (301:17) - חיגר שאינו יכול לילך בלא מקל מותר לילך בו אפילו אינו קשור בו אבל אם אפשר לו לילך זולתו ואינו נוטלו אלא להחזיק עצמו אסור

[302] Mishna Berura (301:65) - וכשאדם הולך במקום שיש חשש שיש שיפול מחמת שירדו גשמים והמקום משופע או שהולך בחורף על המים הנגלדים [שקורין איי"ז] ומפחד שמא יפול מותר ג"כ לצאת במקל דדמי לחיגר ואליהו רבא כתב עליו דאין דבריו מוכרחים וגם בעוד אחרונים ראיתי שדעתם שאין להתיר בזה רק במקום שיש עירוב

142

perform an *issur d'rabanan* since the wheelchair is *battel* to the *guf* and we say חי נושא את עצמו (Yevamos 66b)[303] if it's possible for him to walk a little bit. However, this is only permitted for a *mitzva* or a *tzorech gadol*. Even if he cannot walk without the wheelchair at all, he can move the wheelchair himself by moving the wheels with his hands since that is like moving his own foot. On the other hand, if he cannot walk at all by himself then it would be forbidden for the non-Jew to push such a person without an *eruv* since it would be like carrying him and would be a *melacha m'doraysa* (Har Tzvi OC 1:170)[304]. It could be that it's not a *melacha d'oraysa* because we don't have a רשות הרבים בזמן הזה as some opinions hold you need 600,000 people walking in this place every day in order to make a *reshus harabim d'oraysa* (Rashi Eruvin 59a)[305]. However, the Mishna Berura 364:8)[306] says that

---

[303] Yevamos (66b) - עתי ואפילו בשבת למאי הלכתא אמר רב ששת לומר שאם היה חולה מרכיבו על כתפו כמאן דלא כרבי נתן דאי רבי נתן האמר חי נושא את עצמו אפילו תימא רבי נתן חלה שאני

[304] Har Tzvi OC (1:170) - אבל כאן בעגלה אין העגלה מסייעת לו בהליכתו כי הוא אינו הולך בעצמו כלל בין שלא בעגלה בין בעגלה א״כ אין סברא לומר דהעגלה נעשית כנעל דהא אין לו רגלים ואינו הולך ולא שייך כאן תשמיש של נעל וא״כ כמו שאיש אחר אסור להוליך את העגלה כן גם הוא עצמו אסור לו להוליך את העגלה שאין כאן דין נעל ואין על העגלה שם מלבוש על גופו but, אבל לע״ד יש טעם גדול להתיר שישב על see Igros Moshe OC (4:90) - כסא עם אופנים שיכול לגלגלה בעצמו דהוא כמנעל שלו ועדיף דבמנעל לא כל דבר שנועל על רגליו מותר לצאת בשבת כמנעל של עץ לרש״י שבת דף פ״ו ע״א אליבא דר׳ יוסי אלא הוא כבגד מאחר שיושב עליו ואף שאינו קשור להכסא הוא בגד שלו שמותר כשליכא חשש דמשתליף ואתי לאתויי וכמו בשבת לצאת קיטע בכסא וספסלים קטנים שבידו והספסלים אינם קשורים

[305] Rashi Eruvin (59a) – שלא היו נכנסין בה תמיד ס' רבוא של בני אדם and Shulchan Aruch (345:7) - ולא חשיבא רה״ר דלא דמיא לדגלי מדבר ויש אומרים שכל שאין ששים רבוא עוברים בו בכל יום אינו רשות הרבים

[306] Mishna Berura (364:8) - ובעיירות שלנו שמנהג העולם לתקן ע״י צורת הפתח אף שרחובותיה רחבין הרבה ומפולשין משער לשער וגם פעמים רבות הולך דרך המלך תוך העיר ומדינא הוי ר״ה גמור עי״ז וכדלעיל בסימן שמ״ה וע״כ דסומכין על הי״א שבסימן שמ״ה דר״ה לא הוי אא״כ ששים רבוא בוקעין בו וזה אין מצוי אמנם באמת הרבה ראשונים חולקין על הי״א הנ״ל כמו שכתבנו שם בסימן שמ״ה וע״כ אף דאין למחות לאחרים הנוהגין להקל ע״י צורת הפתח שכן נהגו מעולם ע״פ דעת הפוסקים המקילין בזה מ״מ כל בעל נפש יחמיר לעצמו שלא לטלטל ע״י צורת הפתח לבד

most of the *poskim* do not hold like this opinion, so it's not so simple to rely on that opinion. However, since *hotza'ah* through a non-Jew is at worst an *issur d'rabanan*, by an *issur d'rabanan* it seems that the Biur Halacha (364:2)[307] is more lenient to rely on the opinion that you need 600,000 people.

Q37. If one gets a bruise on Shabbos, can he put Arnicare ointment on it to prevent swelling?

A: I don't know anything about Arnicare ointment for preventing swelling. You certainly cannot smear the ointment on the body because of the *issur d'oraysa* of smoothing (Mishna Berura 328:81)[308]. Moreover, this is also an issue of *refuah* on Shabbos (Shulchan Aruch 327:1)[309] which would require us to know whether the person is a *choleh kol gufo* or not. Nonetheless, what would be so terrible if the bruise swells? The Aruch Hashulchan (328:19)[310] says that if a person feels the need to go to bed – even if he doesn't actually go to bed – he is considered a *choleh kol gufo*. Therefore, if a person hurts his fingernail on Shabbos in a way which is so painful that he cannot get the pain out of his mind, then that is considered a *choleh kol gufo* if you see that he is not acting as he normally does.

Q38. What types of deodorant may one use on Shabbos?

---

[307] Biur Halacha (364:2) - והנכון דסומכין על שיטת הרמב"ם דפסק כר"א דלא אתו רבים ומבטלי מחיצתא ולדידיה בודאי מן התורה סגי בצוה"פ ולא נשאר לנו כ"א איסור דרבנן דיש גם לר"א בלא דלתות וכדמוכח מהרמב"ם ובזה אפשר דיש לסמוך אדעה דאין ר"ה אלא בששים ריבוא

[308] Mishna Berura (328:81) - שמא ימרח על גבה להחליק הגומות שיש בה ומירוח רטיה מלאכה דאורייתא היא משום שהוא בכלל ממחק אבל משום שחיקת סממנים ליכא למיגזר כיון דהיו מאתמול עלויה

[309] Shulchan Aruch (327:1) - החושש במתניו לא יסוך שמן וחומץ אבל סך הוא שמן לבדו אבל לא בשמן ורד משום דמוכחא מלתא דלרפואה קא עביד ואם הוא מקום שמצוי בו שמן ורד ודרך בני אדם לסוכו אפילו בלא רפואה מותר. הגה: ובמקום שאין נוהגין לסוך בשמן כי אם לרפואה בכל שמן אסור

[310] Aruch HaShulchan (328:19) - אך מי שיש לו מיחוש שעל ידי זה זה נחלש כל גופו ואף שמתחזק והולך אך הילוכו בכבידות ובחלישות ודינו כנפל למשכב בחולה שאין בו סכנה

Chapter 7: Refuah on Shabbos

A: You may use spray deodorant on Shabbos, though you cannot use it on Yom Kippur because that may be a form of *rechitza* (Shulchan Aruch 614:1)[311]. You may also use a powdered deodorant on Shabbos. However, you may not use a gel or cream deodorant because it is forbidden *mid'oraysa* (Shulchan Aruch 314:11)[312]. Antiperspirant deodorants are not allowed for a different reason. The Shulchan Aruch seems to have a סתירה since in *hilchos hotza'ah* (Shulchan Aruch 303:15)[313] it says someone is allowed to walk outside on Shabbos with a sweet-smelling gum in his mouth which is being used to sweeten his breath. In that case, the gum would be considered *battel* to the *guf* and would be permitted. On the other hand, the Shulchan Aruch writes in *hilchos refuah* (328:36)[314] that people may not put a certain sweet smelling sap in their mouth on Shabbos for medicinal purposes, but if it is being used to take away the bad odor then it is permitted (Mishna Berura 328:116)[315]. In *hilchos refuah*, the Shulchan Aruch says you can have something in your mouth for ריח הפה, but in *hilchos hotza'ah* it is not permitted unless used to sweeten your breath. The Achronim[316] explain that there are two ways to make one's breath smell good. The first way is to cover up the bad smell with a sweet gum, and that is permitted because it does not fix the problem of the bad breath. On the other hand, if you put rock salt

---

[311] Shulchan Aruch (614:1) - אסור לסוך אפילו מקצת גופו ואפילו אינו אלא להעביר הזוהמא

[312] Shulchan Aruch (314:11) - אסור ליתן שעוה או שמן עב בנקב החבית לסתמו מפני שהוא ממרח (פירש הערוך סיכה משיחה טיחה מריחה ענין שמא ימרח על גבה להחליק) - and Mishna Berura (328:81) אחד הוא הגומות שיש בה ומירוח רטיה מלאכה דאורייתא היא משום שהוא בכלל ממחק (אבל משום שחיקת סממנים ליכא למיגזר כיון דהיו מאתמול עלויה)

[313] Shulchan Aruch (303:15) - יוצאת וכו' ובפלפל ובגרגיר מלח ובכל בשם ושתתן לתוך פיה ובלבד שלא תתנם לכתחילה בשבת ואם נפל לא תחזיר and ובפלפל ובגרגיר מלח - פלפל לריח הפה ומלח - Mishna Berura (303:47) שלא תתנם וכו' - דבכל - לחולי השינים and Mishna Berura (303:49) רפואה גזרו משום שחיקת סממנים א"נ משום דמחזי כאלו מערמת להוציא משא"כ במוך הנ"ל מוכחא מילתא דצריכה לכך ולא מתחזי כמערמת להוציא

[314] Shulchan Aruch (328:36) - אין לועסין מצטכי (עסי' רי"ו סי"ג פירושו) ולא שפין בו השינים לרפואה ואם משום ריח הפה מותר

[315] Mishna Berura (328:116) - מותר - דמפני ריח לא מקרי רפואה

[316] Bris Olam Hilchos Refuah (59 and 71)

or pepper in your mouth to take care of the bad breath by burning out whatever is causing the odor, that is problematic on Shabbos because it is considered *refuah*. Similarly," we need to figure out what the deodorant is doing. If the deodorant is merely covering over the bad smell, then it would not be a problem on Shabbos. However, if the deodorant removes the cause of the odor by acting as an anti-perspirant, then that is considered *refuah* and is forbidden *mid'rabanan*.

Q39. May one use hand soap on Shabbos?

A: If the hand soap is thick enough that it smoothens the skin on your hand when it is used, then it is forbidden. It would only be permitted if the soap is diluted with water or you dilute it in water so that the soap does not make the skin smooth (Aruch Hashulchan 326:11)[317]. Rav Moshe Feinstein (Igros Moshe OC 1:113)[318] has a *teshuva* saying that you cannot use any liquid soap regardless of how thin the soap is. I think Rav Moshe believes the issue is because of the bubbles made by the soap. However, the מנהג העולם is not to be *makpid* for liquid soap if it pours easily. However, if the liquid soap comes out in blobs like honey, then you may not use it on Shabbos either. If the soap emerges as a steady stream, then it is thin enough to be permitted for use on Shabbos. I conducted an experiment to find out the permitted thickness of soap (600 cP or less), but since it required a knowledge of liquid viscosity and a viscometer it was of no practical use.

---

[317] Aruch Hashulchan (326:11) - אך יש שמכינים מערב שבת בורית שניתך שקורין מוליענע"ס ומותר בזה לנקות הידים, וכן מותר לנקות בעפר מן לבינה כתישה ויש שמתיר לסוך בבורית ודברים תמוהים הם ופשיטא שאסור and Kaf HaChaim 326:43 - והרוצין לרחוץ במי בורית בשבת ממחק הבורית במים מע"ש עד ונעשה כולו מים ואז רוחצין באותו מים בשבת

[318] Igros Moshe OC (1:113) - ובדבר להתרחץ עם בורית בשבת ויו"ט הנה פשוט שאמור משום ממחק ואף בבורית שהוא לח כמים אף שהרבה נוהגין להתיר אין ברור לי כ"כב ההיתר מכיון שנעשה מזה המוליענס ומתפשט הרבה יותר מכפי שהוא ע"י הרחיצה וא"כ ניכד שעדיין יש מה קצת ממחק לא כשאר דברים לחים כמים ושמן אף שאפשר שבדבר לח ליכא איסור ממחק ולכן אין נוהגין בביתי היתר זה וכן ראוי להחמיר

Chapter 7: Refuah on Shabbos

Q40. If one is told that his child needs stitches on Shabbos, and if he waits until afterwards there will be a scar, may he drive or have a non-Jew bring him to the hospital on Shabbos?

A: A Jew certainly may not drive on Shabbos for a scar, but he may have a non-Jew drive on Shabbos. Nowadays, everyone is crazy about things which people weren't concerned about in former times. If the individual who needs the stitches is a boy, then it's fine to have a scar – unless maybe he is a *kohen* and might be invalid for the *avodah*. If the person is a girl, then maybe it will affect her getting married if the stitches are needed for somewhere on her face and might be more serious. Nonetheless, just because a person gets stitches doesn't mean that he won't have a scar. In fact, very often the stitches themselves make a scar. Medical personnel like using butterfly bandages since they provide the least amount of scarring by keeping the skin together. However, if the cut is larger then the butterfly will not effectively keep the skin together. In that case, the issue might become more serious as it can become infected. Therefore, a non-Jew would be allowed to take the person to the hospital.

Q41. If a farther hospital is better at doing stitches and will not leave a scar, can he travel to the farther hospital?

A: If the non-Jew is driving to the hospital, then it is permitted to have him take the person to the hospital further away.

Q42. What vitamins may one take on Shabbos? (i.e. Omega-3, vitamin D, etc.)

A: I believe the American government says that no one needs to take any vitamins ever as long as people eat normal meals. All the vitamins should enter the body through a regular diet. When they found out that vitamin D was more necessary in the winter than the summer because during the summer people go outside in short sleeves and aren't dressed as warmly which allows more skin exposure to the sun to develop the vitamin D, people starting putting vitamin D in milk to fortify the body. However, Omega-3 is a more recent finding as people didn't know what Omega-3 was 25 years ago and we still lived. I read a report that someone who takes vitamins daily will have a 14% higher risk of dying that year than if he doesn't take any vitamins. Not that I put much faith in this report which was put out by Johns Hopkins since if people want to sell vitamins then they'll find a reason to sell vitamins, while if they want to sell an alternative remedy then they'll say you don't need vitamins anymore. It all depends on the business aspect of it. I previously mentioned a *machlokes* between Rav Aharon Kotler and Rav Moshe Feinstein about taking vitamins on Shabbos. However, the Magen Avraham says if you want to take something to strengthen your wellbeing on Shabbos, that is an issue of *refuah* and would be forbidden. That is only a problem if he is not considered a *choleh kol gufo*, but if the person doesn't feel well or feels sluggish then my Rosh Yeshiva considered such a person a *choleh kol gufo* and allowed to take vitamins. However, if the person is only taking the vitamin in order to avoid feeling bad in the future, then the reason for the vitamin is only to provide a *parnasa* for those who make the vitamins. That would not be considered a *choleh kol gufo* and would be forbidden. Rav Moshe Feinstein (Igros Moshe OC 3:54)[319] says that if the person feels OK, then the vitamin isn't acting as a *refuah* at all and it would be permitted to take it on Shabbos, but if he does need the vitamin then Rav Moshe says it would be considered *refuah* and would be forbidden on Shabbos. Therefore, if someone feels sluggish, he can rely on my Rosh Yeshiva that such an individual is considered a *choleh kol gufo* and can take the vitamin, and if he feels OK then he can rely on Rav Moshe.

Q43. Can you take Metamucil (fiber powder) on Shabbos?

A: If a person doesn't take Metamucil on Shabbos and becomes constipated, doesn't feel well, and gets headaches, then it is

---

[319] Igros Moshe OC (3:54) - ואכ"כ באלו הוויטאמינים שאינם מבריאים את האדם לשנותו מכפי שהוא שיהיה מי שחלש בטבעו לחזק יותר אלא שעושין שלא יהיה עלול להתחלות בנקל יש להתיר לכו"ע אף להמג"א. ואם יש וויטאמינים שמשנים בריאותו שעושים מחלש בטבעו לחזק יותר פליגי בזה הב"י והמג"א שיש להחמיר ולאסור כהמגן אברהם. והנה ראיתי בדברי הגר"י לעבאוויץ שליט"א שג"כ מחלק כעין זה מסברתו שהאיסור להמג"א הוא רק בשע"י מה שאוכל יתחזק יותר מבפי שהוא עתה ולא באם הוא רק שלא יתחלש ויגרע מכפי שהוא עתה שזה גם להמג"א מותר. ולפי"מ שבארתי הוא מוכרח כדלעיל וגם מסתבר שדוקא כשעושה מחלש בטבעו לגוף בריא וחזק ולא כשעושה רק להתחזק מעט יותר

considered a *choleh kol gufo*. Even though right now he feels OK, but in order to avoid becoming a *choleh kol gufo* it is permitted to take Metamucil.

Q44. Can one use Lactaid pills on Shabbos?

A: No. Lactaid pills are considered a *refuah* and would be forbidden to take on Shabbos. However, if you put the Lactaid pill into the milk in order to be able to drink it, that would be a different question. It seems from the *pashtus* of the Gemara (Shabbos 108a)[320] that putting the Lactaid pill into the food would be permitted. However, Rav Moshe Feinstein (Igros Moshe OC 2:86) has a different understanding of the Gemara and says that it is forbidden.

Q45. May one use a fluoride mouthwash on Shabbos?

A: Fluoride is used to prevent people from having cavities in their teeth. Even though the Gemara says that the teeth and the heart are connected (Avoda Zara 28a)[321], in general a cavity isn't considered a *choleh kol gufo* or *choleh sheyesh bo sakana*. I'm not sure if the fluoride helps at all, but if it does then you may not use it on Shabbos.

Q46. Is it permitted to use mouthwash on Shabbos?

A: Mouthwash is permitted to use on Shabbos because people use mouthwash even when they are not sick.

Q47. Is it permitted to use breath strips on Shabbos?

A: My understanding is the breath strips are only a cover up for the bad breath, so covering up the odor is permitted on Shabbos and is not considered a *refuah*.

---

[320] Shabbos (108a) - אמר מר עוקבא אמר שמואל שורה אדם קילורין מערב שבת ונותן על גב עיניו בשבת ואינו חושש

[321] Avoda Zara (28a) - אלמא כמכה של חלל דמיא אמר רב נחמן בר יצחק שאני צפדינא הואיל ומתחיל בפה וגומר בבני מעיים

Chapter 7: Refuah on Shabbos

Q48. May one place toothpaste in his mouth and swish it around to freshen his breath? What if his intention is to strengthen his teeth with the fluoride?

A: Yes, it is permitted to put toothpaste in your mouth and swish it around. Moreover, I don't think having the fluoride in the toothpaste once a week will make such a difference in preventing cavities from forming, so it would be permitted to put toothpaste in your mouth on Shabbos.

Q49. What if it is a Nano hydroxyapatite toothpaste which isn't standard in America but is more standard in Japan?

A: People say this is similar to Sensodyne which seems to be a regular toothpaste without the strong mint flavor of other toothpastes in order not to irritate the gums.

Q50. May one who has inserts in his shoes use them in a place with no *eruv*? Does it make a difference if they are half length or full length?

A: Yes, you may walk around with inserts in your shoes on Shabbos without an *eruv* because you are allowed to wear shoes on Shabbos without an *eruv*. It makes no difference whatsoever what kind of shoe insert it is for this question.

Q51. Can medicated baby powder be used on Shabbos? What about for an adult?

A: The question is what this medicated baby powder does. In former times, there were two types of Band-aids: regular Band-aids and Mercurochrome Band-aids. The Mercurochrome Band-aid had iodine to kill the germs. After selling this kind of Band-aid for about 50 years, they conducted some research which said that Mercurochrome Band-aids don't do anything. Therefore, they stopped making those Band-aids. Similarly, there are two types of medicated baby powder: cornstarch or talcum powder. I'm not sure whether the medication put into the baby powder accomplishes anything. It probably accomplishes the goal of getting more people to buy it, but I don't know if it will help with any *refuah*. Nonetheless, it is permitted on Shabbos for a baby since any ailment a baby has is considered a *choleh kol gufo* because when a baby cries his entire body is involved with his crying and it bothers him. On the other hand, an adult is not as bothered by a local pain as a baby is and would not be allowed to use baby powder if it helps medically. However, I have my doubts whether the baby powder accomplishes anything medically.

Q52. Can one use medicated baby powder on Shabbos for odorous or itchy feet?

A: My understanding is that the reason someone has itchy or odorous feet comes from perspiration. So when the baby powder soaks up the perspiration, it helps remove the odor. There are certain types of conditions for itchy feet like athlete's foot which only grow in wet areas. Consequently, the baby powder retards the growth of the fungus by making the area dry. The fact that the baby powder is medicated has nothing to do with removing the itch or smell from the feet since the baby powder is just removing the environment which encourages the growth of the fungus causing the itch or the smell (Shemiras Shabbos K'hilchasa 34:12).

Q53. May one use Invisalign on Shabbos?

A: If the Invisalign is used to straighten out the teeth, then it's the same question as using the retainer: is the person using Invisalign because the teeth don't look nice without it or will the unstraight teeth cause issues in the future? If the Invisalign is used to look nice, then it would not be considered a *refuah* and would be permitted on Shabbos. In fact, medical insurance will not pay for any procedures done to improve someone's looks – like straightening out a person's nose solely for the sake of appearance. Maybe the doctor can convince the insurance company saying that the person cannot breathe well with a crooked nose. Nonetheless, since the Invisalign is not recognizable whether it is being used for appearance or for *refuah* – like drinking milk for ulcers (Shulchan Aruch 328:37)[322] – it is permitted on Shabbos even if

---

[322] Shulchan Aruch (328:37) - כל אוכלים ומשקין שהם מאכל בריאים מותר לאכלן ולשתותן לרפואה אע"פ שהם קשים לקצת בריאים ומוכחא מילתא

the intention is that the Invisalign is being used to prevent the teeth from falling out in the future.

Q54. Can one ask a non-Jew on Shabbos to turn on the A/C to stop or prevent a migraine?

A: Someone who is prone to migraines – which is considered a *choleh kol gufo* – is allowed to ask a non-Jew to perform a *melacha d'oraysa*. If turning on or off the air conditioning will help prevent the migraine, then it is a permitted *refuah* to ask the non-Jew to perform.

Q55. If one cannot speak, can he use a device that translates brain waves onto an electronic display on Shabbos?

A: The question is if a person is allowed to think on Shabbos if it will cause an electronic display to activate. We say in the *zemiros*, "אסורים וגם לחשוב חשבונות הרהורים מותרים חפציך" – you are allowed to think on Shabbos since you are not doing an action. The Torah says (Shemos 20:10)[323] לֹא תַעֲשֶׂה כָל־מְלָאכָה, which the Gemara (Shabbos 120b)[324] says עשיה הוא דאסור אבל גרמא מותר – you are not allowed to do a forbidden action but may cause something to happen.

Q56. Can one walk for exercise on Shabbos?

A: Since people normally walk on Shabbos to get from one place to another without the intention of exercising, it is permitted to walk on Shabbos for exercise since it is not recognizable. However, if it is recognizable - like walking around a track - then it would be forbidden (Shulchan Aruch 328:42)[325].

דלרפואה עביד אפילו הכי שרי וכל שאינו מאכל ומשקה בריאים אסור לאכלו ולשתותו לרפואה ודוק' מי שיש לו מיחוש בעלמ' והוא מתחזק כבריא והולך אבל אם אין לו שום מיחוש מותר

[323] Shemos (20:10) - וְיוֹם הַשְּׁבִיעִי שַׁבָּת לַה' אֱלֹהֶיךָ לֹא־תַעֲשֶׂה כָל־מְלָאכָה אַתָּה וּבִנְךָ־וּבִתֶּךָ עַבְדְּךָ וַאֲמָתְךָ וּבְהֶמְתֶּךָ וְגֵרְךָ אֲשֶׁר בִּשְׁעָרֶיךָ

[324] Shabbos (120b) - אי הכי הכא נמי כתיב לא תעשה [כל] מלאכה עשייה הוא דאסור גרמא שרי מתוך שאדם בהול על ממונו אי שרית ליה אתי לכבויי

[325] Shulchan Aruch (328:42) - אין מתעמלים דהיינו שדורס על הגוף בכח כדי שייגע ויזיע

152

Chapter 8: End-of-Life Questions

Q1. Why don't people talk more about end of life issues?

A: (5755) Let me tell you about when I was in Russia during the communist regime and it was very difficult to be a *frum yid*. It was literally *mesiras nefesh* because if they caught you learning Torah or doing a *mitzva*, they would give you *tzaros tzeruros*. The first thing they would do was fire you from your job. The same thing was true for anyone who applied to leave the country– the government would fire you from your job. Not having a job wasn't the biggest deal in Russia since no one was able to make money there anyway. The issue was that it was illegal not to have a job in Russia. Anyone who didn't have a job for about 2 months would be sent to Siberia because they had plenty of backbreaking jobs out there with chopping down trees and making roads in the bitter cold winter where it reaches 40 below zero. There's also nothing there – you must find your own food. A lot of people in Siberia didn't make it because they just died from the cold. Therefore, when the communist government fired you from your job for keeping the Torah or applying for an exit visa to Israel, they would tell everyone not to give you a job. I know there was a civil engineer in Russia who applied for an exit visa to another country after becoming a *frum yid*, and they immediately fired him. I visited him at his home in Moscow, and he told me that he's in a very dangerous position since it's already been two months and they'll ship him off to Siberia any day now. The next day I returned to his home and he was completely *b'simcha* because he got a job. I asked him what his job was, and he replied, "I'm going to clean toilets." Then I asked him how he was able to get such a job, and he said, "I promised my boss a sizeable amount on an ongoing basis if he gets me a job, so he made me a janitor." Although the boss wasn't technically allowed to hire him, he could claim to the government that no one else was available for the janitorial job so he needed to hire him. How can these people live like this where they go to *shiurim* in secret places with the fear of the government over their heads? Although legally you are allowed to learn Torah after 18 years old, the people told me that's only the Torah *shebiksav* – but the Torah *sheba'al peh* is that learning Torah is forbidden forever as they'll make your life terrible. In fact, I gave *shiurim* there and wasn't worried about being sent to Siberia because I was an American – the most likely thing was that they'd put me on the next boat or plane out of the country, which they've done to plenty of other people. There are also some people who have been thrown into prison for a couple weeks which isn't very pleasant since they beat you there. So where did I give the *shiur*? You can't trust anyone in Russia because you need to suspect that everyone is an informer for the government. In fact, one-tenth of the population was informers. The *shiur* was given in the house of one the important members of the communist party. They paid him off a lot of money to allow it, but do you know what kind of risk they were running? There's a general rule in Russia for anyone, that you're not allowed to have ten people get together without a permit. So if you want to make a *minyan*, you need to have a permit. How could these people live day-to-day not knowing what's going to happen to them? There was another nine-month-old child whose mother brought him from over a thousand miles to Moscow to have a *milah* performed on him. It was forbidden to perform the *bris* in Russia, so the doctor, the mother, and the owners of the apartment were all putting themselves in danger. Then during the *bris*, there was a knock on the door and everyone turned completely white out of fear that they were caught. They decided they wouldn't answer the door and instead pretend no one was home. Then the knocks became louder and louder. At that point, the mother realized that the person might break down the door and they would be in even more trouble for suspicious activity, so she opened the door – it was a neighbor. However, no one knew if this neighbor was an informer or not. Thankfully the *bris* was taking place in another room, so the neighbor didn't see anything and eventually left, but you see what kind of fear people lived in while keeping the Torah. A friend of mine is an expert in all of the issues of living in Russia, and he said that people cannot live in fear their whole lifetime. It's not in our human nature – so these *yidden* eventually decide, "We're going to do what we need to do, and whatever happens happens." People get used to living the way they tell themselves they want to live – just like people tell themselves that they'll never die. The Chofetz Chaim says we believe people who die are part of a separate group which we don't belong to. Even though we know that's the natural way of the world, we're not comfortable thinking about life that way and don't want to take all the doctor's tests.

Q2. What is the Torah's perspective on quality of life?

A: (5755) Let's say you can save a patient's life after suffering from a stroke, but he won't know what's going on or be able to talk. Doctors might say it's not worth living a life like that and allow the stroke patient to die. A more extreme case is where someone is in a vegetative state, not knowing anything which is going on because he is brain-dead, and only has a heartbeat. He doesn't seem to have any quality of life, so perhaps we shouldn't save such a person. These are *shailos* which come up all the time, especially now that there are so many medical advances where things which were impossible a few years ago are now possible. When a person comes to the hospital today, the doctors are required by federal law to ask the patient what procedures he would like done to himself in case of a heart attack or the like – do you want to be saved or not? The doctor must offer the patient the opportunity to make the decision and sign a statement. The law doesn't say the patient is required to sign, but he must be offered the choice. While in many cases life is considered life where it's a *mitzva* to preserve it regardless of the quality, there are cases which quality of life makes a difference and a competent Rabbinic authority should be consulted.

Q3. What should one *daven* for if someone is diagnosed with terminal cancer?

A: (5755) When Rav Yaakov Kamenetsky was in his 60s and his first Rebbetzin developed cancer, he did not *daven* for her to live. He said that he holds it's a prayer made in vain since according to the *derech hateva* people with cancer cannot live, so he felt it was similar to the Gemara Berachos (54a)[326] which says that if you

---

[326] Berachos (54a) - והצועק לשעבר הרי זו תפלת שוא היתה אשתו מעוברת ואומר יהי רצון שתלד אשתי זכר הרי זו תפלת שוא היה בא בדרך ושמע קול צוחה בעיר ואומר יהי רצון שלא תהא בתוך ביתי הרי זו תפלת שוא

hear someone cry out in the city and ask Hakadosh Baruch Hu that the yell should not have come from your house, that is a תפלת שוא because how would the prayer help at all? Either the crying happened at your house or it didn't. Similarly, Rav Yaakov said not to pray for someone with terminal cancer to live just as you don't pray that someone should live forever. I once asked my Rosh Yeshiva Rav Aharon Kotler זכר צדיק לברכה a similar question about praying for someone who had cancer, and he said that we are allowed to pray for the patient – and it's not considered a prayer in vain because it's possible one of the many research institutions searching for a cure for cancer will find the *refuah*. Therefore, you can pray for them to find a cure. That's not considered an impossibility. Evidently there are over 3,000 labs right now working to find a cure for cancer across the country, so the government and other foundations funding this research feel there is a chance of finding a cure. Therefore, it's not considered praying for a miracle and you would be allowed to make a *mishaberach* for someone with cancer.

Q4. If it is permitted at times to pray for the *choleh* to die when he's in pain, what about the Gemara (Berachos 10a)[327] saying to never give up even if the sword is on your neck?

A: (5779) The Gemara is talking about a case where the person has a sword on his neck where the *derech hateva* is that he won't die. However, once the sword cuts through his neck then the way of the natural world is that he will die. Once they cut through his neck and he's in pain, we say the faster he dies the better it is for him. It's not natural to die just because a sword is sitting on your neck – but it is natural to die if someone has cancer of the pancreas for example, since statistically such an individual only has a few months to live. There may be those who are *yotzei min haklal* every now and then, but the normal thing is that such a patient doesn't really have any hope. You're not allowed to *daven* for a

---

[327] Berachos (10a) - אתמר נמי רבי יוחנן ורבי אליעזר דאמרי תרוייהו אפילו חרב חדה מונחת על צוארו של אדם אל ימנע עצמו מן הרחמים שנאמר הן יקטלני לו איחל

miracle (Rebbi Akiva Eiger 230:1)[328]. Even though Chazal say that a person can *daven* that a child should be a male or female, that is only within the first 40 days of conception when it's still possible to change the gender (Kaf HaChaim 270:2)[329]. Nonetheless, you may *daven* to the Ribono Shel Olam that we find a *refuah* for whatever illness is affecting the person. That's not praying for a miracle because they find cures for all sorts of illnesses. As a matter of fact, the Gemara says that Shlomo HaMelech wrote the Sefer Refuos which was the manual explaining to anyone who was sick what they should eat or do in order to become well (Rashi Pesachim 56a)[330]. That implies there is really a natural cure for every illness. There are a lot of diseases we have found the cures for already, and medical wisdom doubles its knowledge every five years. Just because the sick person didn't yet have a *refuah* available yesterday doesn't mean that he won't have a *refuah* available today. Especially in the last seventy-plus years, the strides we have made in medicine have been unbelievable. Diseases we thought had no hope seventy years ago are now not even a concern for us anymore.

Q5. How long must one be able to live to be called חיי שעה?

A: (5779) This time frame isn't clearly spelled out in the *poskim* as far as I know. It seems to me that חיי שעה – someone who won't live a regular life – which normally refers to living up to a year. The Gemara (Chullin 57b)[331] says a *treifa* can only live up to a year and is therefore considered to be in חיי שעה, so I would say the same thing applies here.

---

[328] Rebbi Akiva Eiger (230:1) - אל יתפלל אדם לבקש דבר שאינו כפי הטבע ואף שהיכולת ביד הקדוש ברוך הוא...אסור להתפלל שיעשה לו הקדוש ברוך הוא נס בשינוי עולם כגון שיוציא אילן זה פירות קודם זמנו

[329] Kaf HaChaim (270:2) - אבל תוך ארבעים יום יכולה תפלתו להועיל שעדיין לא נגמר יצירת הולד עד ארבעים יום לבוש והא דמועיל תפלה תוך ארבעים אם שניהם הזריעו בבת אחת אבל אם הזריע הוא תחלה יולדת נקבה ואין מועיל תפלתו ואם הזריעה היא תחלה יולדת זכר בלא תפלתו

[330] Rashi Pesachim (56a) - שגנז ספר רפואות לפי שלא היה לבם נכנע על חולים אלא מתרפאין מיד

[331] Chullin (57b) - אמר רב הונא סימן לטרפה י"ב חדש

Chapter 8: End-of-Life Questions

Q6. Can a חיי שעה undergo a risky procedure to save his life?

A: (5779) Yes, someone who is considered a חיי שעה is allowed to undergo risky procedures to try saving his life (Shulchan Aruch YD 155:1)[332]. There seems to be a conflict in the *teshuvos* of Rav Moshe regarding this question. In one place, Rav Moshe wrote if there is a 40% chance that the operation will be successful, then you are allowed to accept the operation on yourself (Igros Moshe YD 3:36)[333]. In another *teshuva*, he wrote that a person is allowed to accept an operation if there is a 5% chance that the operation will save his life (Igros Moshe YD 2:58)[334]. Rav Moshe's students asked him about the conflict in his *teshuvos*, and he said there was no conflict. In the first *teshuva* about the 40% success rate, that only means the surgery itself is 40% successful yet the person doesn't necessarily live afterwards. That is the same as the 5% chance that the person will live after the surgery. The surgery may have been fine, but the patient dies from complications afterwards – like after replacing a kidney. The procedure to give an individual a new kidney might be successful, but the body might reject the kidney. If the patient didn't take the right dose – whether too little or too much – of the anti-rejection medication, then he would likely die.

Q7. When is a person considered dead?

---

[332] Shulchan Aruch YD (155:1) - כל מכה וחולי שיש בהם סכנה שמחללים עליהם שבת אין מתרפאים מעובד כוכבים שאינו מומחה לרבים (וכל המקיזים דם הוו מומחים לענין הקזה) דחיישינן לשפיכת דמים ואפילו הוא ספק חי ספק מת אין מתרפאים ממנו אבל אם הוא ודאי מת מתרפאים ממנו דלחיי שעה לא חיישינן בהא

[333] Igros Moshe YD (3:36) - ויש גם קצת ראיה מהא דהקרא דהלפינן מיניה דלחיי שעה לא חיישינן הוא מהא דאמרו לכו ונפלה אל מחנה ארם אם יחיונו נחיה ואם ימיתנו ומתנו דאפשר שהיה שם רק ספק השקול דטוב להם ליקח אותם יותר לעבדים ובע"כ נצטרך לומר כדכתבתי שאף בריפוי אצל רופאים עכו"ם שיליף שמותר ואין חוששין לחיי שעה הוא משום דנחשב לענין זה רק כספק השקול

[334] Igros Moshe YD (2:58) - דלכן היה מותר להם ליפול אל מחנה ארם אף שודאי יותר קרוב במלחמה שימיתום אלמא דלחיי שעה לא חיישינן אף כשהצלה הוא בספק רחוק ויותר קרוב שיהרגום תיכף

158

Chapter 8: End-of-Life Questions

A: (5755) This has been a source of much controversy as Rav Moshe, Rav Elyashiv, Rav Shlomo Zalman, and many other Gedolei Yisroel have written about when a person is considered dead, yet we still don't have a conclusive *psak*. Today it's more of a problem because it's possible to keep people alive using artificial means like respirators for breathing or artificial hearts which pump the blood throughout the body. The brain is divided into three parts – one region is for thinking, one part is in charge of directing the muscles, and one area of the brain controls involuntary functions. We breathe without thinking, so that's part of the involuntary functions. The heart isn't regulated by the brain and continues to pump blood throughout the body even after the head is removed. However, if a person doesn't have a head anymore then even though his heart will continue to pump, his lungs will not continue to breathe. Consequently, there won't be any oxygen in the blood and the heart would no longer have the energy to pump anymore. Today, if you remove a person's head, the doctors can put the person on a respirator and he would continue living for many more years. This wasn't possible in former times where once a person stopped breathing, his heart would automatically stop. The *posuk* says כֹּל אֲשֶׁר נִשְׁמַת־רוּחַ חַיִּים בְּאַפָּיו מִכֹּל אֲשֶׁר בֶּחָרָבָה מֵתוּ (Bereishis 7:22) that once a person can no longer breathe then he is considered dead. Also, the Mishna in Yoma (83a)[335] says if a building collapses on someone on Shabbos, you can desecrate Shabbos to remove the rubble to check whether he's breathing through his nose. The P'nei Yehoshua was stuck under a beam in a collapsed building which protected him from dying, so he was *mekabel* on himself that if Hakadosh Baruch Hu would save him then he would write a *sefer* on *shas* which would enlighten the eyes of his *talmidim*. If it wouldn't have been for that incident, then we wouldn't have had a P'nei Yehoshua on *shas*. You see that people could remain alive in a collapsed building. The straightforward understanding of the Mishna shows you that once a person can no longer breathe, he is considered dead. Therefore, Rav Moshe (Igros Moshe YD

---

[335] Yoma (83a) - מי שנפלה עליו מפולת ספק הוא שם ספק אינו שם ספק חי ספק מת ספק כותי ספק ישראל מפקחין עליו את הגל מצאוהו חי מפקחין ואם מת יניחוהו

2:146)[336] proves from this that if a person can breathe under his own power, then he is considered alive, but if he cannot breathe naturally under his own power, then he is considered dead – whether or not his heart is beating. If the patient can only breathe through a respirator because the machine is pumping his lungs, that is not considered breathing enough to be considered alive. Others disagree saying that in the time of the Mishna and Gemara, if a person wasn't breathing then his heart wouldn't beat either, so maybe breathing is just a sign that a person's heart isn't beating (Chasam Sofer YD 338)[337]. They explain that when you remove all the debris from the collapsed building to check for signs of breathing, that is being done to know whether the person's heart is beating or not. Alternatively, it's very hard sometimes to see whether a person has a pulse. On the other hand, you can see if someone is breathing by putting a feather under a person's nose. In former times, there was a law that you were not allowed to bury a person until 48 hours after he was considered dead because there were too many cases where the person woke up during the funeral. Similarly, the Chochmas Adam (151:18)[338] writes that when a person dies, the Chevra Kadisha would wait an hour before doing anything because the person might still technically be alive – and it would be an issue of moving the body of a *goses*. The Gesher

---

[336] Igros Moshe YD (2:146) - אבל ברור ופשוט שאין החוטם האבר שהוא נותן החיות באדם וגם אינו מאברים שהנשמה תלויה בו כלל אלא דהמוח והלב הם אלו הנותנים חיות להאדם וגם שיהיה לו שייך לנשום ע"י חוטמו ורק הוא האבר שדרך שם נעשה מעשה הנשימה שבאין ע"י המוח והלב ואית לנו הסימן חיות רק ע"י החוטם אף שלא הוא הנותן ענין הנשימה משום שאין אנו מכירים היטב בלב ובטבור וכ"ש שאין מכירין במוח וכוונת הקרא דנשמת רוח חיים באפיו לא על עצם רוח החיים שזה ודאי ליכא בחוטם אלא הרוח חיים שאנו רואין איכא באפיו אף שלא נראה באברים הגדולים אברי התנועה וגם אחר שלא ניכר גם בדפיקת הלב ולא ניכר בטבור שלכן נמצא שלענין פקוח הגל בשבת תלוי רק בחוטם

[337] Chasam Sofer YD (338) - אבל כל שאחר שמוטל כאבן דומם ואין בו שום דפיקה ואם אח"כ בטל הנשימה אין לנו אלא דברי תורתינו הקדושה שהוא מת ולא ילינו אותו והמטמא לו אם הוא כהן אחר לוקה ההתראה and Chacham Tzvi 77

[338] Chochmas Adam (151:18) - לאחר שמת לא יזיזו אותו תיכף שמא נתעלף אלא ישהה מעט ונוהגין להניח אצל נחיריו נוצה ואם נשאר מונח שם בידוע שמת

Chapter 8: End-of-Life Questions

HaChaim (3:2:1) is lenient to allow the Chevra Kadisha to do what they need to do after 20 minutes of someone's death. It could be today that doctors have more sophisticated ways of seeing whether someone's heart is beating or not to allow us to wait even less time. However, it's not so easy even for a professional to know the time of death precisely.

Q8. Is brain dead considered dead?

A: (5755) There seems to be a conflict between the *teshuvos* of Rav Moshe where in one case he writes brain death is considered death but another *teshuva* he says it's not considered death. However, it's not a conflict – when Rav Moshe says brain death is not considered death refers to when the person's brain senses no feelings, thoughts, and cannot move any muscles. If that part of the brain dies, the person is still considered alive. On the other hand, if the brainstem is dead – the region of the brain which controls reflexes like the lungs breathing – then the person is considered dead. Today it's medically possible to put someone on a respirator to spread oxygen throughout the body even after the brainstem dies and can no longer control the lungs. Since the respirator continues to give oxygen to the body, the heart can continue pumping for years even after the person's brain is completely dead. A person could technically have his head removed yet continue living with the respirator spreading oxygen throughout the body. The Mishna (Ohalos 1:6)[339] says that if a person's head is severed, then he is *metameh* the room like a *meis*. Evidently, halachically a person is considered dead when he no longer has a head. Rav Moshe writes in a *teshuva* that when a patient cannot breathe on his own without the support of a respirator, then that is not considered breathing and the patient is considered dead. In fact, Rav Moshe says you can take the patient off of the respirator because that form of breathing isn't considered breathing. This question comes up all the time because there are many patients put on a respirator to assist their breathing

---

[339] Mishna Ohalos (1:6) - אָדָם אֵינוֹ מְטַמֵּא עַד שֶׁתֵּצֵא נַפְשׁוֹ וַאֲפִלּוּ מְגֻיָּד וַאֲפִלּוּ גוֹסֵס זוֹקֵק לְיִבּוּם וּפוֹטֵר מִן הַיִּבּוּם מַאֲכִיל בַּתְּרוּמָה וּפוֹסֵל בַּתְּרוּמָה וְכֵן בְּהֵמָה וְחַיָּה אֵינָן מְטַמְּאִין עַד שֶׁתֵּצֵא נַפְשָׁם הֻתְּזוּ רָאשֵׁיהֶם אַף עַל פִּי שֶׁמְּפַרְכְּסִים טְמֵאִים כְּגוֹן זָנָב שֶׁל לְטָאָה שֶׁהִיא מְפַרְכָּסֶת

– sometimes the patient gets worse and fully relies on the respirator and other times the patient gets better and no longer requires the support of a respirator.

Q9. How do you know when a person can no longer breathe on his own?

A: (5755) According to Rav Moshe, if the machine is the only thing allowing the patient to breathe then he is not considered alive. Although the medical machines do provide information regarding the patient's health, it's questionable if you can rely on that for cases of life and death. Therefore, we remove the respirator from the patient to see whether he can breathe on his own. He won't die immediately since there is still oxygen in his bloodstream. If you see that he's not breathing on his own, then you don't need to put him back on the respirator. Also, these machines typically must be cleaned every 12 hours or so because they get clogged with the mucus from a person's lungs. At that point when they clean the machine, they can test to see whether the patient can breathe on his own or not. If they see he is not breathing on his own and doctors have no hope *b'derech hateva* that he will be able to breathe on his own in the future, then Rav Moshe says the patient is considered dead.

Q10. Should you decide not to be put on a respirator in the first place?

A: (5755) Let's say that you're still considered alive when your heart is beating – not like Rav Moshe – then you can be on this machine for many years. You may no longer have a conscious life or exhibit any movements, but your body will still be warm and your heart will continue beating. Not following the understanding of Rav Moshe, you would still be considered alive even though you don't really have any life to speak of. If such a patient is considered alive at that point, then we are not allowed to kill him by doing anything which will cause his death. The Rema (Rema

YD 339:1)[340] says that if a *goses* is trying to die but someone is using a jackhammer outside and the noise is preventing the patient from dying – you need to relax when you die since it is difficulty to die in an agitated state – then you are allowed to stop the jackhammer's noise because it's preventing the death from happening. However, you cannot do anything which will cause the death – like moving a patient who has the status of a *goses* (Shulchan Aruch YD 339:1)[341] or removing the respirator which will eventually prevent the heart from beating if you don't follow the *psak* of Rav Moshe. You see these are very difficult *shailos* which occur all the time. Hospitals don't want to tie up their respirators with patients who are legally and clinically considered dead when the doctors really need these life-saving machines for other patients in life-threatening situations. Consequently, they don't necessarily want to put such people on respirators in the first place. The two *dinim* to consider regarding putting someone on a respirator are לֹא תַעֲמֹד עַל־דַּם רֵעֶךָ – don't stand by while your brother's blood is being spilled (Vayikra 19:16)[342] that you're not allowed to stand by idly if someone if someone is in trouble. If someone is drowning, then you must try to save him as long as it doesn't put your own life in danger (Shulchan Aruch CM 426:1)[343]. The second *din* is that you cannot cause another person

---

[340] Rema YD (339:1) - אבל אם יש שם דבר שגורם עכוב יציאת הנפש כגון
שיש סמוך לאותו בית קול דופק כגון חוטב עצים או שיש מלח על לשונו ואלו
מעכבים יציאת הנפש מותר להסירו משם דאין בזה מעשה כלל אלא שמסיר המונע

[341] Shulchan Aruch YD (339:1) - הגוסס הרי הוא כחי לכל דבריו אין
קושרין לחייו ואין סכין אותו ואין מדיחין אותו ואין פוקקין את נקביו ואין שומטין
הכר מתחתיו ואין נותנין אותו על גבי חול ולא על גבי חרסית ולא על גבי אדמה
ואין נותנין על כריסו לא קערה ולא מגריפה ולא צלוחית של מים ולא גרגיר של
מלח ואין משמיעין עליו עיירות ואין שוכרין חלילין ומקוננות ואין מעמצין עיניו
עד שתצא נפשו וכל המעמץ עם יציאת הנפש ה"ז שופך דמים ואין קורעין ולא
חולצין ולא מספידין עליו ולא מכניסין עמו ארון לבית עד שימות ואין פותחין עליו
בצדוק הדין עד שתצא עד שתצא נפשו

[342] Vayikra (19:16) - לֹא־תֵלֵךְ רָכִיל בְּעַמֶּיךָ לֹא תַעֲמֹד עַל־דַּם רֵעֶךָ אֲנִי ה׳

[343] Shulchan Aruch CM (426:1) - הרואה את חבירו טובע בים או ליסטים
באין עליו או חיה רעה באה עליו ויכול להצילו הוא בעצמו או שישכור אחרים
להציל ולא הציל או ששמע עכו"ם או מוסרים מחשבים עליו רעה או טומנין לו
פח ולא גילה אוזן חבירו והודיעו או שידע בעכו"ם או באנס שהו' בא על חבירו

to die. These are two separate *dinim* which are not dependent one on the other. In fact, לֹא תַעֲמֹד applies to *frum yidden* as opposed to the *din* of not killing someone else which applies to Jews and non-Jews alike. At the same time, there are some instances when you're not obligated to save a *frum* Jew which we learn from the Gemara Nedarim. The Gemara (Nedarim 40a)[344] says anyone who isn't *mevaker choleh*, then he won't pray for the patient to live or die. Based on this Gemara, the Rishonim say that one of the main aspects of *bikur cholim* is praying for the sick person. If you don't pray on behalf of the patient, then you did not completely fulfill the *mitzva* of *bikur cholim* (Rema YD 335:4)[345]. The other part of the *mitzva* of *bikur cholim* is seeing what the *choleh* needs – like Rebbi Akiva visited one of his students and cleaned up the room, removed the dirt, straightened things out, and the student lived (Nedarim 40a)[346]. The least part of the *mitzva* of *bikur cholim* is the fact that the person is happy to see others care about him and worry about him, but the main two parts of *bikur cholim* are praying for the person and seeing if the patient needs anything. Now what does the Gemara mean when it says you won't pray for the patient to live or die? The Ran (Nedarim 40a)[347] explains that

---

ויכול לפייסו בגלל חבירו ולהסיר מה שבלבו ולא פייסו ולא יוצא בדברים אלו עובר
על לא תעמוד על דם רעך

[344] Nedarim (40a) - כי אתא רב דימי אמר כל המבקר את החולה גורם לו
שיחיה וכל שאינו מבקר את החולה גורם לו שימות מאי גרמא אילימא כל המבקר
את החולה מבקש עליו רחמים שיחיה וכל שאין מבקר את החולה אין מבקש עליו
רחמים שימות שימות ס"ד אלא כל שאין מבקר חולה אין מבקש עליו רחמים לא
שיחיה ולא שימות

[345] Rema YD (335:4) - וכל שביקר ולא ביקש עליו רחמים לא קיים המצוה
(ב"י בשם הרמב"ן)

[346] Nedarim (40a) - רב חלבו באיש לא איכא דקא אתי אמר להו לא כך היה
מעשה בתלמיד אחד מתלמידי ר' עקיבא שחלה לא נכנסו חכמים לבקרו ונכנס ר'
עקיבא לבקרו ובשביל שכיבדו וריבצו לפניו חיה א"ל רבי החייתני יצא ר' עקיבא
ודרש כל מי שאין מבקר חולים כאילו שופך דמים

[347] Ran Nedarim (40a) - - אין מבקש עליו רחמים לא שיחיה ולא שימות
נראה בעיני דה"ק פעמים שצריך לבקש רחמים על החולה שימות כגון שמצטער
החולה בחליו הרבה ואי אפשר לו שיחיה כדאמרינן בפרק הנושא (כתובות קד)
דכיון דחזאי אמתיה דרבי דעל כמה זימנין לבית הכסא ואנח תפילין וקא מצטער
אמרה יהי רצון שיכופו העליונים את התחתונים כלומר דלימות רבי ומש"ה קאמר
דהמבקר חולה מועילו בתפלתו אפי' לחיות מפני שהיא תפלה יותר מועלת ומי

there are times when it's a *mitzva* to pray for the sick person to die – like if he has a terminal illness which has no way *b'derech hateva* to recover from this illness and the patient is in pain. The Ran brings a proof from Rebbi's maid who was a big *talmid chacham* who knew a lot of things most other people didn't know since she was in the house of the Rosh Beis Din who was also *mesader* the Mishna. For instance, the Gemara testifies that there are words which the Tannaim didn't understand until they learned it from her (Rosh Hashana 24a)[348]. At the end of Rebbi's life, his maid saw he was in a lot of pain as he had difficulty putting on and taking off his *tefillin*. Therefore, his maid *davened* that the prayers of Klal Yisroel should be overpowered by angels in the upper Beis Din to allow Rebbi to die (Kesubos 104a)[349]. The Ran said that since Rebbi had a terminal illness and was in pain, the maid was allowed to pray for him to no longer be alive. Rav Moshe (Igros Moshe YD 2:174) says in a *teshuva* that it doesn't make any sense to say that there are times that we are allowed to pray for someone to die yet still have a *mitzva* of לֹא תַעֲמֹד to save such a person. Consequently, if someone has a form of terminal cancer which he will die from *rachmana litzlan* and he's in pain, then there is no *mitzva* to save him or prolong his life. It is possible for doctors to perform heroic measures to keep such a person alive another couple months with various treatments and medications, but there is no *inyan* to do so – you're not doing any favors for the patient and there's no *mitzva* of לֹא תַעֲמֹד either. However, we cannot cause the death of the patient - even if it would be better for him - because there is an *issur* of murder which always applies.

שאינו מבקרו אין צריך לומר שאינו מועילו לחיות אלא אפי' היכא דאיכא ליה הנאה במיתה אפי' אותה זוטרתי אינו מהנהו

[348] Rosh Hashana (24a) - וטאטאתיה (ישעיהו יד:כג) מאי רבנן ידעי הוו לא במטאטא השמד יומא חד שמעוה לאמתא דבי רבי דהוות אמרה לחבירתה שקולי טאטיתא וטאטי ביתא

[349] Kesubos (104a) - ובעו תעניתא רבנן גזרו דרבי נפשיה דנח יומא ההוא רחמי ואמרי כל מאן דאמר נח נפשיה דר' ידקר בחרב סליקא אמתיה דרבי לאיגרא אמרה עליוני' מבקשין את רבי והתחתוני' מבקשין את רבי יהי רצון שיכופו תחתונים את העליונים כיון דחזאי כמה זימני דעייל לבית הכסא וחלץ תפילין ומנח להו וקמצטער אמרה יהי רצון שיכופו עליונים את התחתונים ולא הוו שתקי רבנן מלמיבעי רחמי שקלה כוזא שדייא מאיגרא [לארעא] אישתיקו מרחמי ונח נפשיה דרבי

Q11. If someone cannot breathe under his own power but is connected to a respirator, are you allowed to remove him from the machine?

A: (5755) We are obligated to give every person food and air. If the patient is breathing somewhat on his own – but not enough to breathe without the respirator – then we cannot take out the respirator. It's an entire procedure to remove the respirator. However, if the patient completely cannot breathe without the respirator, then Rav Moshe says that he is considered dead and you can remove the respirator (Igros Moshe YD 3:132)[350]. According to other *poskim*, even if the patient cannot breathe under his own power you are not allowed to remove him from the respirator since they consider that as part of our obligation to provide him with air. However, this leads to the hospital not wanting to put such an individual on a respirator in the first place since they don't want to devote one of their machines for a patient who is considered clinically dead to them.

Q12. What should you do for a person who slips into a coma?

A: (5755) A person in a coma doesn't yell when he's in pain, so we don't know whether a person in a coma has pain or not. If the patient in a coma is a terminal case where the question is only a matter of prolonging his life, then Rav Moshe (Igros Moshe CM

---

[350] Igros Moshe YD (3:132) - הנה בדבר ידיעת מיתת האדם מפורש בגמ' בגמ'
יומא דף פ"ה ע"א בנפל מפולת על האדם שמפקחין את הגל אפילו בשבת ובודקין
עד חוטמו ואיפסק כן ברמב"ם פ"ב משבת הי"ט ובש"ע או"ח סימן שכ"ט סעי' ד'
שאם לא הרגישו שום חיות הוא בדין מת שהוא בבדיקת הנשימה שאף אם הנשימה
קלה מאד נמי הוא בדין חי שרואין זה ע"י נוצה ועי"י חתיכת נייר דקה שמשימין
אצל החוטם אם לא מתנדנד הוא בחזקת מת אבל צריך שיבדקו בזה איזה פעמים
כדבארתי באגרות משה ח"ב דיו"ד סימן קע"ד סימן קע"ד ענף ב' בבאור דברי הרמב"ם בפ"ד
אבל ה"ה שכתב ישהא מעט שמא נתעלף שהוא זמן דאי אפשר לחיות בלא נשימה
והוא דוקא כשהסתכלו כל זמן זה בלא היסח הדעת אף לרגע קטן וראו שלא נשם
כל העת אבל כיון שאי אפשר לאינשי להסתכל אף משך זמן קצר בלא היסח הדעת
שיש לחוש שמא נתחזק מעט ונשם איזה נשימות ונחלש עוד הפעם וחזר ונתחזק
אי אפשר לידע אלא שיבדקו איזה פעמים ואם יראו שאינו נושם זהו סימן המיתה
שיש לסמור על זה ואין להרהר

2:74:1)[351] says that if the patient would have been in pain from his sickness if he was awake, then we have the right to assume that the person is in pain. However, if the person is not a terminal case then we have a *mitzva* of לֹא תַעֲמֹד עַל־דַּם רֵעֶךָ to save him (Vayikra 19:16)[352]. Some people try to solve this kind of case by starving the patient to death saying, "We haven't touched the patient or done anything to him – we just haven't given the patient anything to eat." Similarly, if you tie someone up in a bed so that he cannot move and you just leave him there, is that considered killing him? Rav Moshe (Igros Moshe CM 2:74:3)[353] explains that food and air are two things which you must give a *choleh* since they are not considered medicines – they are normal needs of all people which cannot be withheld. Moreover, if you withhold a patient's food or air, then it is as if you killed the individual. However, that doesn't mean you need to put such a person on a respirator. Rather, you put such an individual on oxygen even if he's a terminal case and is in pain. Nonetheless, if the person develops a fever or infection, you are not obligated to treat that sickness if he's a terminal case

---

[351] Igros Moshe CM (2:74:1) – שאם אין יודעין הרופאים שום רפואה לא
רק לרפאותו אלא אף לא להקל היסורין אלא להאריך קצת חייו כמו שהן בהיסורין
אין להם ליתן רפואות כאלו שהרי בכה"ג חזינן מעובדא דרבי (כתובות ק"ד.)
שלא הועילו רבנן בתפלתם שיתרפא וגם לא לסלק יסוריו אלא שהועילה תפלתם
שלא ימות ויחיה בהיסורים כמו שהם כל זמן שמתפללין אמרה אמתיה דרבי
שהיתה חכמה בתורה יה"ר שיכופו העליונים את התחתונים וכשראתה שלא
הועילה תפלתם מחמת שלא פסקו רבנן מלמיבעי רחמי עשתה מעשה להשתיקם
מתפלתם בשבירת כוזא ונח נפשיה

[352] Vayikra (19:16) - לֹא־תֵלֵךְ רָכִיל בְּעַמֶּיךָ לֹא תַעֲמֹד עַל־דַּם רֵעֶךָ אֲנִי ה -

[353] Igros Moshe CM (2:74:3) - והנה בתשובתי להרופאים כתבתי שלחולה
מסוכן שאינו יכול לנשום צריך ליתן לו חמצן (אקסידזשען) אף שהוא באופן
שא"א לרפאותו שהרי הוא להקל מיסוריו דהיסורין ממה שא"א לנשום הם יסורים
גדולים והחמצן מסלקן וכפי זה שאל כתר"ה אם בחולים שאינם יכולין לאכול אם
צריכין ליתן להו אוכל דרך הורידין כשהוא מסוכן שהוא להאריך חייו כמו שהן
ביסורין כשנדמה לנו שאין לו יסורין ממה שאינו אוכל פשוט שצריך להאכילו
דברים שאין מזיקין ואין מקלקלין דודאי מחזיקין כחו מעט אף שהחולה בעצמו
אינו מרגיש ואף העומדין ומשמשין אותו אין מרגישין ול"ד כלל לעניני סמי רפואה
והטעם פשוט שהאכילה הוא דבר טבעי שמוכרחין לאכול להחזיק החיות ושכל
אדם ואף בע"ח בעלמא מוכרחת לזה ורק בחולה דחום גדול החום הוא גם מזונותיו

(Igros Moshe CM 2:74:2)[354]. He might live for another few months if you treat the infection with antibiotics, but you are not required to do so – and there is no *inyan* to treat the infection either. Now if the patient himself expresses his wish to endure the pain of further treatment, then he is allowed to do so and we continue treating him.

Q13. If someone has a terminal sickness where the doctors already agreed to let him go, but then develops a second illness which can be treated – must the doctors treat the second illness?

A: (5755) If the patient will be in pain after treating the second illness, then we say it's better for him to die than prolong his life with an operation on the second illness (Igros Moshe CM 2:73:1)[355]. However, if he won't be in pain but become handicapped, then Rav Moshe (Igros Moshe CM 2:74:5)[356] says

---

[354] Igros Moshe CM (2:74:2) - דהנה אם נזדמן שנעשה מסוכן במחלה שניה וכשיתרפא ממחלה השניה וישאר חי עדיין יהיה חולה במחלה הראשונה ובהיסורים שיש לו ממנה ודאי איכא חיוב לרפאותו ממחלה השניה שודאי כולהו אינשי אף כשהן חולין רוצים וצריכים להתרפאות ממחלות נוספות אף כשעדיין אין יודעין רפואה לראשונה ואף באופן שלית לו יסורין ממנה רוצים כל אדם להתרפאות וממילא אף כשאיניש זה אין רוצה להתרפאות אין שומעין לו כיון דרצונו הוא שלא כדרך האינשי אבל באופן שיש לו יסורין ואין ידוע רפואה אף לא להקל מהיסורין שעל כעין זה ניחא להו לאינשי יותר אף למות מלחיות חיי יסורין כאלו כדאיתא בגמ' בכתובות ל"ג ע"ב דדלמא מלקות חמור אפשר כדמסתבר לכאורה דאין מחוייבין לרפאות חולה כזה כשאינו רוצה בעניני רפואה כאלו שמאריכין חייו בחיי יסורין כאלו ואף בסתמא כשלא שייך לידע דעת החולה יש לתלות שאין החולה רוצה וליכא החיוב לרפאותו

[355] Igros Moshe CM (2:73:1) - ובאינשי כה"ג שהרופאים מכירין שא"א לו להתרפאות ולחיות ואף לא שיחיה כמו שהוא חולה בלא יסורין אבל אפשר ליתן לו סמי רפואה להאריך ימיו כמו שהוא נמצא עתה ביסורין אין ליתן לו מיני רפואות אלא יניחום כמו שהם כי ליתן להם סמי רפואה שימות עי"ז וכן לעשות איזה פעולה שיגרום לקצר אפילו לרגע אחת הוא בחשיבות שופך דמים אלא שיהיו בשב ואל תעשה אבל אם איכא סמי מרפא שיקילו היסורין ולא יקצרו אף רגע מחייו צריך לעשות כשעדיין אינו גוסס

[356] Igros Moshe CM (2:74:5) - ואם אחד אינו רוצה ניתוח שנשאר מזה בעל מום ולדברי הרופאים לא יוכל לחיות בלא הניתוח והוא באופן שאין לחוש לשמא יטרף דעתו כשלא ישמעו לו כגון שחשש המיתה מהחולי ברור וטריפת

he should have the operation done. Rav Moshe (Igros Moshe CM 2:73:5)[357] writes in a separate place that since all surgeries have a risk – even something considered as simple as appendicitis – where 2% of people don't make it through the procedure generally due to issues from the anesthesia, the patient in such a terminal case has the right to decline having the operation if he's concerned for the minority of people who die from complications in surgery. However, if he doesn't want to live in general, then that's not enough of a reason not to have the procedure performed if it's successful in general.

Q14. Should we provide food for a patient who cannot eat?

A: (5755) Some hospitals stop giving a person food so that they die. It might take a few weeks and force the patient into a coma, so they starve him to death. We're not allowed to do that even if he cannot eat anything through his mouth. We need to provide the patient with food intravenously. People who don't have food for long periods of time are in physical pain from when the brain senses the low nourishment level in the blood. Therefore, Rav Moshe (Igros Moshe CM 2:74:3)[358] *poskins* you must feed a

---

הדעת כשלא ישמעו לו הוא רק ספק וגם בלא זה זה הא מיתה גרוע מטריפת הדעת
וכ"ש כשאין הספקות שוות דאם לא יעשו לו הניתוח ימות ודאי וחשש טירוף
הדעת הוא רק ספק וגם אולי פחות מספק ממש מאחר שאמרו לו הרופאים
שיתרפא מהניתוח ודאי שרשאין ומצוה גדולה דחיי נפש יהיה כשיעשו לו בעל
כרחו אף בכפיה דקשירת גופו

[357] Igros Moshe CM (2:73:5) - ובאם יש בהרפואה עצמה איזו סכנה אבל
הרופאים נוהגין ליתן רפואה זו להחולה שיש לו מחלה מסוכנת שמדת סכנה של
הרפואה פחותה הרבה מסכנת המחלה אין ליתן בעל כרחיה בכל אופן

[358] Igros Moshe CM (2:74:3) - והנה בתשובתי להרופאים כתבתי שלחולה
מסוכן שאינו יכול לנשום צריך ליתן לו חמצן (אקסידושען) אף שהוא באופן
שא"א לרפאותו שהרי הוא להקל מיסוריו דהיסורין ממה שא"א לנשום הם יסורים
גדולים והחמצן מסלקן וכפי זה שאל כתר"ה אם בחולים שאינם יכולין לאכול אם
צריכין ליתן להו אוכל דרך הורידין כשהוא מסוכן שהוא להאריך חייו כמו שהן
ביסורין כשנדמה לנו שאין לו יסורין ממה שאינו אוכל פשוט שאינו צריך להאכילו
דברים שאין מזיקין ואין מקלקלין דודאי מחזיקין כחו מעט אף שהחולה בעצמו
אינו מרגיש ואף העומדין ומשמשין אותו אין מרגישין ול"ד כלל לעניני סמי רפואה
והטעם פשוט שהאכילה הוא דבר טבעי שמוכרחין לאכול להחזיק החיות ושכל
אדם ואף בע"ח בעלמא מוכרחת לזה ורק בחולה דחום גדול החום הוא גם מזונותיו

person intravenously because otherwise the person will be in tremendous pain. However, if the terminal patient doesn't want you to provide him with food, then you are not obligated to give him food because it might terribly upset him – and he has the right to accept the pain which comes from refusing the food. The pain we have in this world is an atonement for Olam Haba (Berachos 5a)[359], but we can't put someone else in pain on his own *cheshbon*. We can't hurt people saying it will give them more Olam Haba. On the other hand, if he enters into a coma then we must provide him with food because we assume he would want to be fed. We don't fully understand what takes place when a person is in a coma. Patients who are in what doctors call a "light coma" cannot respond, but they can hear and understand what you say to them. Sometimes someone in such a coma is able to squeeze your hand if you ask them to do so despite not being able to move most other parts of the body – though you wouldn't be allowed to touch the patient if he's a *goses*. Although some people survive coming out of a deep coma, it's not so simple to figure out whether the person is in pain because they don't remember their experience after waking up. It's similar to being drunk where the person knows and feels everything happening to him while drunk, but forgets everything afterwards. In fact, Rav Moshe (Igros Moshe CM 2:74:1)[360] says we should assume someone in a coma is suffering from pain if he also has an illness which causes pain.

---

[359] Berachos (5a) - אמר רבא אמר רב סחורה אמר רב הונא כל שהקדוש ברוך הוא חפץ בו מדכאו ביסורין שנאמר וה' חפץ דכאו החלי יכול אפילו לא קבלם מאהבה תלמוד לומר אם תשים נפשו אשם מה אשם לדעת אף יסורין לדעת ואם קבלם מה שכרו יראה זרע יאריך ימים ולא עוד אלא שתלמודו מתקיים בידו שנאמר וחפץ ה' בידו יצלח

[360] Igros Moshe CM (2:74:1) - יש לנו למילף לחולה שהרופאים אין יודעין שום רפואה לרפאותו ואף לא להקל היסורין רק שיודעין מרפואה להאריך קצת חייו בהיסורין כמו שהם עתה ליתן רפואות כאלו אבל פשוט שאם יועילו הרפואות עד שיוכלו להשיג רופא גדול מהנמצאים אצל החולה שאפשר שעי"ז שיתארכו חייו ישיגו רופא שאפשר שידע רפואה שלא מועילה להקל היסורין אלא להאריך חייו כמו שהן בהיסורין עד שיוכלו להביא הרופא ההוא. ואין צריכין לשאול להחולה ע"ז ואף אם החולה אינו רוצה אין לשמוע לו אבל יש להשתדל שירצה החולה שלהביא רופא בעל כרחו יש ג"כ חשש סכנה אבל אם אינו רוצה בשום אופן שיביאו רופא אין לשמוע לו

Q15. What is the definition of a *treifa*?

A: (5755) The Gemara (Chullin 42a)[361] says an animal with a hole in its lungs is considered a *treifa*. If a person has a hole in his lung then he should also be considered a *treifa* – וּמוֹתַר הָאָדָם מִן־הַבְּהֵמָה אָיִן (Koheles 3:19)[362]. The Gemara (Avoda Zara 5b)[363] says explicitly that animals and people are the same when it comes to *treifos* (Igros Moshe CM 2:73:4)[364]. However, there is one major difference between the two. When the Gemara says an animal was considered a *treifa*, that meant it would die within 12 months (Chullin 57b)[365]. Nowadays, a lot of things have changed – *nishtane hateva* – and people don't necessarily die due to these *treifos*. On the other hand, we say an animal with such an issue is considered a *treifa* since whatever was considered a *treifa* for animals in the times of Chazal will remain a *treifa* forever (Rambam Shechita 10:13)[366]. For people with medical issues which would make them a *treifa*, we follow the modern definition

---

[361] Chullin (42a) - ר"ש שחסרה או שניקבה אלו טרפות בבהמה...הריאה
אומר עד שתינקב לבית הסמפונות ניקבה הקבה ניקבה המרה ניקבו הדקין הכרס הפנימית שניקבה או שנקרע רוב החיצונה רבי יהודה אומר הגדולה טפח והקטנה ברובה המסס ובית הכוסות שניקבו לחוץ

[362] Koheles (3:19) - כִּי מִקְרֶה בְנֵי־הָאָדָם וּמִקְרֶה הַבְּהֵמָה וּמִקְרֶה אֶחָד לָהֶם
כְּמוֹת זֶה כֵּן מוֹת זֶה וְרוּחַ אֶחָד לַכֹּל וּמוֹתַר הָאָדָם מִן־הַבְּהֵמָה אָיִן כִּי הַכֹּל הָבֶל

[363] Avoda Zara (5b) - דא"ר אלעזר מנין למחוסר אבר דאסור לבני נח דכתיב
(בראשית ו:יט) ומכל החי מכל בשר שנים מכל וגו' אמרה תורה הבא בהמה שחיין ראשי אברים שלה האי מיבעי ליה למעוטי טריפה דלא טריפה מלחיות זרע נפקא הניחא למאן דאמר טריפה אינה יולדת אלא למ"ד טריפה יולדת מאי איכא למימר אמר קרא אתך בדומין לך ודלמא נח גופיה טריפה הוה תמים כתיב ביה

[364] Igros Moshe CM (2:73:4) - טרפה הוא שיש לו חסרון באברים
הפנימיים כגון שיש בריאה ולב ובני מעים נקב ממש ואף כשליכא נקב אבל הקרומים שלהם הם לקויים ושחותפים בין כשאיכא מוגלא בין בליכא מוגלא ואיכא אברים שלא נטרף אלא דוקא בחסר וביתר ויש דוקא בלקותא וכמבואר ביו"ד בטריפות דבהמה ולרוב האברים גם באדם הוא כן

[365] Chullin (57b) - אמר רב הונא סימן לטרפה י"ב חדש

[366] Rambam Shechita (10:13) - וְכֵן אֵלּוּ שֶׁמָּנוּ וְאָמְרוּ שֶׁהֵן טְרֵפָה אַף עַל פִּי
שֶׁיֵּרָאֶה בְּדַרְכֵי הָרְפוּאָה שֶׁבְּיָדֵינוּ שֶׁמִּקְצָתָן אֵינָן מְמִיתִין וְאֶפְשָׁר שֶׁתִּחְיֶה מֵהֶן אֵין לְךָ אֶלָּא מַה שֶּׁמָּנוּ חֲכָמִים שֶׁנֶּאֱמַר (דברים יז:יא) עַל פִּי הַתּוֹרָה אֲשֶׁר יוֹרוּךָ

(Igros Moshe CM 2:73:4)[367]. For instance, if someone has appendicitis and has his appendix removed, then he has a hole in his intestines. The Gemara (Chullin 42a)[368] says if someone has a hole in his intestines then he is considered a *treifa* since they wouldn't be able to live. Today people have their appendix taken out and they live for more than a year. Evidently the person isn't a *treifa*. If he would be a *treifa*, then he would be an invalid witness since there's no din of eidim zomemin by *treifos* (Sanhedrin 78a)[369]. We don't say people whose appendix were removed are not able to serve as witnesses at a kiddushin since they are able to live for more than 12 months.

Q16. Does high blood pressure make someone a *treifa* if not taking his medication would make him die within the year?

A: (5755) No, high blood pressure doesn't make someone a *treifa*. High blood pressure doesn't mean there is a hole in the body somewhere which would cause his death within the next 12 months. Rather high blood pressure is dependent on deposits in the arteries. If there is a hole in the artery or heart, then you would be considered a *treifa* unless the doctors are able to sew it up.

Q17. When do we consider someone a *goses*?

A: (5755) - When people used to die naturally, it was easier to define their status as a *goses*. Meaning, at the end of one's life, people would develop a breathing problem and not have the

---

[367] Igros Moshe CM (2:73:4) - אבל בעצם איכא חלוק גדול לתנא בין טרפות דבהמה לאיסור אכילה למה שנוגע לדיני טרפות דאדם שהוא ליהרג עליו כדאבאר. דהרי כל עניני מחלות ורפואתן אינם דברים קבועים בכל ימות העולם דהרבה דברים טבעיים נתחלפו כמפורש בתוס' מו"ק דף י"א ע"א ד"ה כוורא וכמו כן שייך שישתנו גם במחלות ורפואות

[368] Chullin (42a) - אלו טרפות...הריאה שניקבה או שחסרה ר"ש אומר עד שתינקב לבית הסמפונות ניקבה הקבה הקבה ניקבה המרה ניקבו הדקין הכרס הפנימית שניקבה או שנקרע רוב החיצונה רבי יהודה אומר טפח והקטנה ברובה המסס ובית הכוסות שניקבו לחוץ

[369] Sanhedrin (78a) - ואמר רבא עדים שהעידו בטריפה והוזמו אין נהרגין עדי טריפה שהוזמו נהרגין רב אשי אמר אפילו עדי טריפה שהוזמו אין נהרגין לפי שאינן בזוממי זוממין

strength to cough out the phlegm in their lungs – coughing takes a lot of strength. At that point, people can hear the phlegm rattling back and forth in the bronchial tubes (Kitzur Shulchan Aruch 194:1)[370]. It's called the "death rattle" in English. Nowadays this doesn't occur too much because doctors administer antibiotics when a person develops an infection which would have otherwise produced the phlegm or the doctors pull the fluid out of the lungs. Therefore, the status of a *goses* is not so easily recognizable today.

(5779) - We don't really have the same concept of *goses* which they had in former times. *Goses* (Shulchan Aruch YD 339:1)[371] used to refer to an ill individual who lacked the strength to cough out the phlegm in his lungs (Kitzur Shulchan Aruch 194:1)[372]. You could hear a "death rattle" where every time the individual breathed in and out you could hear the phlegm in the bronchial tubes. That was a sign the person was near death – it could last a few days or just a couple hours. Once one's breathing is compromised, his life is in mortal danger. If he cannot breathe then he is not considered alive. Nowadays, Rav Moshe (Igros Moshe YD 3:132)[373] says that even though we can pump air into

---

[370] Kitzur Shulchan Aruch (194:1) - הַגּוֹסֵס פֵּרוּשׁ הַמַּעֲלֶה לֵחָה בִּגְרוֹנוֹ מִפְּנֵי צָרוּת הֶחָזֶה וְזֶה יִקְרֶה סָמוּךְ לַמִּיתָה וּלְשׁוֹן גּוֹסֵס הוּא מִלְשׁוֹן מֵגִיס בַּקְּדֵרָה שֶׁהַלֵּחָה מִתְהַפֶּכֶת בִּגְרוֹנוֹ כְּמוֹ הַמֵּגִיס בַּקְּדֵרָה

[371] Shulchan Aruch YD (339:1) - הגוסס הרי הוא כחי לכל לכל דבריו

[372] Shulchan Aruch (194:1) - הַגּוֹסֵס פֵּרוּשׁ הַמַּעֲלֶה לֵחָה בִּגְרוֹנוֹ מִפְּנֵי צָרוּת הֶחָזֶה וְזֶה יִקְרֶה סָמוּךְ לַמִּיתָה וּלְשׁוֹן גּוֹסֵס הוּא מִלְשׁוֹן מֵגִיס בַּקְּדֵרָה שֶׁהַלֵּחָה מִתְהַפֶּכֶת בִּגְרוֹנוֹ כְּמוֹ הַמֵּגִיס בַּקְּדֵרָה

[373] Igros Moshe YD (3:132) - הנה בדבר ידיעת מיתת האדם מפורש בגמ' יומא דף פ"ה ע"א בנפל מפולת על האדם שמפקחין את הגל אפילו בשבת ובודקין עד חוטמו ואיפסק כן ברמב"ם פ"ב משבת הי"ט ובש"ע או"ח סימן שכ"ט סעי' ד' שאם לא הרגישו שום חיות הוא בדין מת שהוא בבדיקת הנשימה שאף אם הנשימה קלה מאד נמי הוא בדין חי שרואין זה ע"י נוצה וע"י חתיכת נייר דקה שמשימין אצל החוטם אם לא מתנדנד הוא בחזקת מת אבל צריך שיבדקו בזה איזה פעמים כדבארתי באגרות משה ח"ב דיו"ד סימן קע"ד ענף ב' בבאור דברי הרמב"ם בפ"ד אבל ה"ה שכתב ישהא מעט שמא נתעלף שהוא זמן דאי אפשר לחיות בלא נשימה והוא דוקא כשהסתכלו כל זמן זה בלא היסח הדעת אף לרגע קטן וראו שלא נשם כל העת אבל כיון שאי אפשר לאינשי להסתכל אף משך זמן קצר בלא היסח הדעת שיש לחוש שמא נתחזק מעט ונשם איזה נשימות ונחלש עוד הפעם וחזר ונתחזק

his system, if a patient cannot breathe on his own - and there is no hope that he will be able to breathe on his own - then he is essentially dead. If the lungs cannot take in air to spread oxygen through the bloodstream, then the muscles won't have enough strength from the oxygenated blood to remove the phlegm in the lungs. However, nowadays we have the ability to suction out the phlegm from the lungs, so this situation isn't too common today. Since we're missing this *siman* for a *goses*, it's more difficult to define when a patient becomes a *goses*. Nonetheless, we would say anyone close to death would have the status of a *goses* – for instance when the doctor says the patient has an hour left to live. There was one occasion where I was with the doctor when he said a 14-year-old boy only had a few minutes left to live. I stayed there with the parents. After an hour the boy was still alive, but the doctor said, "Any minute now." After a few more hours, the doctor told the parents, "Tell your son that he has permission to die." They did that, and he died right away. The boy was using all of his strength to fight off death because he didn't want to upset his parents. Once they gave him permission to die, he was gone the next minute. Giving a person permission to die helps them move on. In fact, the Rema (YD 339:1)[374] says that if someone is about to die but is being kept alive by a loud noise - like a jackhammer working on the road outside - then you are allowed to tell the construction worker to turn off the jackhammer for a couple minutes and it's not considered murder. Rather, you're just removing what is preventing the person from dying. Yes, every minute counts, but we're talking about a case where he is going to die so there's no *mitzva* to prolong his life.

Q18. What is the practical definition of a *goses*?

A: (5755) Every movement for a *goses* is difficult for him – even blinking his eyes. The simple definition of a *goses* is someone who has difficulty coughing out the phlegm in his lungs which you can

---

אי אפשר לידע אלא שיבדקו איזה פעמים ואם יראו נושם זהו סימן המיתה שיש לסמור על זה ואין להרהר

[374] Rema YD (339:1) - אבל אם יש שם דבר שגורם עכוב יציאת הנפש כגון שיש סמוך לאותו בית קול דופק כגון חוטב עצים או שיש מלח על לשונו ואלו מעכבים יציאת הנפש מותר להסירו משם דאין בזה מעשה כלל אלא שמסיר המונע

hear going back and forth as he breathes (Kitzur Shulchan Aruch 194:1)[375]. A *goses* is someone who is very weak and his life is hanging by a thread.

Q19. Then should people not gather around a *goses* to *daven*?

A: (5779) Not every *goses* has to necessarily die (Kiddushin 71b)[376] since the Gemara only says most גוססים will die, but there are a minority of גוססים who will live as some cancers can go into remission and allow the person to live for twenty-plus years. Other cancers don't go into remission and grow very quickly. There are other diseases - like heart or kidney failure - which kill a person rather than cancer too, but I believe it's in the top three of causes of death nowadays. Very often at the end of a person's life, all of his systems start failing. At that point there is very little you can do.

Q20. Can you touch a *goses*?

A: (5755) Since a *goses* is holding close to death, we are concerned that the smallest movements – even moving a finger – might be too much for him to bear and cause his death. A person who moves a *goses* might even be considered a murderer (Shach YD 339:5)[377]. However, there is a difference between a *goses* and a *treifa*. A *treifa* is someone with a physical tear which will cause his death within the next 12 months (Chullin 57b)[378]. If someone kills a *treifa*, then he is not considered a murderer – it's forbidden to kill a *treifa*, but still not considered murder (Rambam Rotze'ach

---

[375] Kitzur Shulchan Aruch (194:1) - הַגּוֹסֵס פֵּרוּשׁ הַמַּעֲלֶה לֵחָה בִּגְרוֹנוֹ מִפְּנֵי צָרוּת הֶחָזֶה וְזֶה יִקְרֶה סָמוּךְ לְמִיתָה וּלְשׁוֹן גּוֹסֵס הוּא מִלְּשׁוֹן מֵגִיס בַּקְדֵרָה שֶׁהַלֵּחָה מִתְהַפֶּכֶת בִּגְרוֹנוֹ כְּמוֹ הַמֵּגִיס בַּקְדֵרָה

[376] Kiddushin (71b) - ומה בין חולין לגוססין רוב חולין לחיים רוב גוססים למיתה

[377] Shach (YD 339:5) - וכל המעמץ עם יציאת הנפש ה"ז שופך דמים. אלא ישהה מעט שמא נתעלף עכ"ל הרמב"ם. ובמס' שמחות מסיים וכל הנוגע בו ה"ז שופך דמים למה הדבר דומה לנר המטפטף שכיון שנוגע בו האדם מיד נכבה

[378] Chullin (57b) - אמר רב הונא סימן לטרפה י"ב חדש

2:8)[379]. On the other hand, if someone kills a *goses* then he is considered a murderer (Rambam Rotze'ach 2:7)[380]. The reason why killing a *treifa* doesn't receive capital punishment is because the *treifa* is already considered a dead person. For instance, if someone was stabbed in the heart and about to die, then someone else stabbed him as well, the second person is not considered a murderer since the person was already considered dead. On the other hand, a *goses* is on the verge of death but not yet considered dead. Therefore, even though there is an *inyan* to close the eyes of a *meis* – especially the firstborn son or any son as the *posuk* says by יוֹסֵף יָשִׁית יָדוֹ עַל־עֵינֶיךָ (Bereishis 46:4)[381] – the Shulchan Aruch says that if closing the eyes of the *goses* is done before death then it's considered murder. The patient's fragility may have allowed merely closing his eyes to cause his death. This *din* of not touching a *goses* applies to both Jews and non-Jews as they're commanded not to murder too (Rambam Melachim 9:1)[382].

Q21. Is it permitted to say *vidui* with a person is on his deathbed?

A: (5755) The patient realizes that he is in a dangerous situation, so either way it's a good thing to say *vidui* since he might live in the merit of saying *vidui* and getting rid of some of his *aveiros*

---

[379] Rambam Murder (2:8) - הַהוֹרֵג אֶת הַטְּרֵפָה אַף עַל פִּי שֶׁאוֹכֵל וְשׁוֹתֶה וּמְהַלֵּךְ בַּשּׁוּק הֲרֵי זֶה פָּטוּר מִדִּינֵי אָדָם וְכָל אָדָם בְּחֶזְקַת שָׁלֵם וְהַהוֹרְגוֹ נֶהֱרָג עַד שֶׁיִּוָּדַע בְּוַדַּאי שֶׁזֶּה טְרֵפָה וְיֹאמְרוּ הָרוֹפְאִים שֶׁמַּכָּה זוֹ אֵין לָהּ תְּעָלָה בָּאָדָם וּבָהּ יָמוּת אִם לֹא יְמִיתֶנּוּ דָּבָר אַחֵר

[380] Rambam Murder (2:7) - אֶחָד הַהוֹרֵג אֶת הַבָּרִיא אוֹ אֶת הַחוֹלֶה הַנּוֹטֶה לָמוּת וַאֲפִלּוּ הָרַג אֶת הַגּוֹסֵס נֶהֱרָג עָלָיו

[381] Bereishis (46:4) - אָנֹכִי אֵרֵד עִמְּךָ מִצְרַיְמָה וְאָנֹכִי אַעַלְךָ גַם־עָלֹה וְיוֹסֵף יָשִׁית יָדוֹ עַל־עֵינֶיךָ

[382] Rambam Melachim (9:1) - עַל שִׁשָּׁה דְּבָרִים נִצְטַוָּה אָדָם הָרִאשׁוֹן עַל עֲבוֹדָה זָרָה וְעַל בִּרְכַּת הַשֵּׁם וְעַל שְׁפִיכוּת דָּמִים וְעַל גִּלּוּי עֲרָיוֹת וְעַל הַגָּזֵל וְעַל הַדִּינִים אַף עַל פִּי שֶׁכֻּלָּן הֵן קַבָּלָה בְּיָדֵינוּ מִמֹּשֶׁה רַבֵּנוּ וְהַדַּעַת נוֹטָה לָהֶן מִכְּלַל דִּבְרֵי תוֹרָה יֵרָאֶה שֶׁעַל אֵלּוּ נִצְטַוָּה הוֹסִיף לְנֹחַ אֵבֶר מִן הַחַי שֶׁנֶּאֱמַר (בראשית ט:ד) אַךְ בָּשָׂר בְּנַפְשׁוֹ דָמוֹ לֹא תֹאכֵלוּ נִמְצְאוּ שֶׁבַע מִצְוֹת

(Shulchan Aruch YD 338:1)[383]. That's all included as part of the *vidui*. On the other hand, if he's going to die then it's definitely important to say *vidui*. We don't say that such a person will be shocked to death by saying *vidui* because he probably knows the situation isn't so simple. We're not obligated to save someone suffering from a terminal disease which will eventually cause him to die if the person is in pain – and we're not supposed to save him. *M'ikar hadin* the patient is not obligated to save himself either, although there is an *inyan* to do so. Rav Moshe (Igros Moshe CM 2:74:3)[384] explains that the reason we give such a terminal patient food is in order to alleviate the more painful experience of hunger rather than the lesser pain of the illness.

Q22. Do we need to use a feather to check for breathing of a patient who is considered dead according to the vital sign monitors?

A: (5755) Using the feather isn't an infallible method either because it could be that a faint breath isn't detectable using a feather. If the machines are as reliable as a feather, then you can rely on them. However, you must be very careful. I know a story of one of my distant relatives who was in the hospital where they pronounced him braindead. The doctors wanted to take him off the respirator, but the family said no. The doctors said they'll leave him on the respirator until another patient in the hospital needs it. In the meantime, the family was making funeral preparations and they left him on the respirator overnight. In the morning he awoke, eventually moved to Israel, and lived for another 20 years. The machine which said he was braindead probably wasn't working. There's another story of a student learning in Ner Yisroel. The Yeshiva made a deal with a kind Jewish doctor who would take

---

[383] Shulchan Aruch YD (338:1) - נטה למות אומרים לו התודה ואומרים לו הרבה התודו ולא מתו והרבה שלא התודו ומתו ובשכר שאתה מתודה אתה חי וכל המתודה יש לו חלק לעולם הבא

[384] Igros Moshe CM (2:74:3) - פשוט שצריך להאכילו דברים שאין מזיקין ואין מקלקלין דודאי מחזיקת כחו מעט אף שהחולה בעצמו אינו מרגיש ואף העומדין ומשמשין אותו אין מרגישין ול"ד כלל לעניני סמי רפואה, והטעם פשוט שהאכילה הוא דבר טבעי שמוכרחין לאכול להחזיק החיות ושכל אדם ואף בע"ח בעלמא מוכרחת לזה ורק בחולה דחום גדול החום הוא גם מזונותיו

care of those studying in the Yeshiva for a very affordable price of $3. One *yungerman* came to the doctor saying he wasn't feeling so well, so the doctor took an EKG of his heart. The doctor looked at the EKG and said, "You just had a heart attack – go home and stay in bed for two weeks." The *yungerman* was a young fellow in his 20s who had just gotten married. He and his wife were very upset, but he stayed in bed for two weeks and returned for another checkup. The doctor performed another EKG and said, "Baruch Hashem the EKG looks normal. I want you to know that a few other young patients came to me after you and also had heart attacks – the EKG was broken." Can you imagine how *ehrlich* this doctor was? Who would admit their medical machine wasn't working properly? They'll get sued for all the aggravation caused from the inaccurate machine, so I don't know how many doctors would be honest about that today. Sonograms are fairly accurate measures, so if the doctor says the sonogram is relaying that the person is no longer alive then we can rely on that.

Q23. Are autopsies ever allowed in halacha?

A: (5755) Performing an autopsy is a question of degrading the honor of the *meis*. There are times when it is very difficult to avoid an autopsy because if there is any suspicion that a person was murdered then the government will investigate the situation via autopsy. For example, if a person was relatively healthy and died suddenly, then there is a concern that he might have been killed. In such a case, the government will utilize an autopsy to determine the cause of death. If it can't be avoided, then there's nothing you can do. Nonetheless, there are medical procedures which aren't forbidden to do to the *meis*. Rav Moshe (Igros Moshe YD 2:151)[385] says taking blood from a deceased person is not degrading since whatever procedures doctors perform on live people is not considered degrading when done to a *meis*. Maybe there's a question whether you need to bury the blood used for

---

[385] Igros Moshe YD (2:151) - אבל נראה לע"ד דאם לא יחתכו האברים ולא יפתחו צוארו ובטנו רק רוצים לתחוב נידעל להוציא ממנו איזה לחלוחית להודע מזה איזו דברים הנוגעים להמחלה שזה אין להחשיב לניוול שהרי דבר כזה מצוי טובא בזמננו שעושים כן גם לחיים ויש להתיר בפשיטות וכן להוציא מעט דם לבדוק וכדומה ע"י נידעל אינו ניוול ויש להתיר

such an autopsy (Shailos U'Teshuvos Maharsham 162)[386], but Rav Moshe says it's not considered degrading the *meis*. Moreover, you should request the hospital return the organs to the *meis* which were checked during the autopsy. Usually the people performing the autopsy dissect every single part of the body so that the murderer doesn't later claim in court, "The guy looked like he was dying already, so I shot him out of mercy." The murderer would get off of the criminal charges because there is no way to prove that he wasn't killing the person out of mercy unless the autopsy shows that the *meis* was healthy. After the autopsy is complete, the Chevra Kadisha needs to bring the *meis* back together to bury him. This could delay the burial many days because the medical examiner doesn't work on the weekend, Lincoln's Birthday, New Year's Day, and other legal holidays. This keeps the family in a state of *aninus* for as long as they are waiting for the burial to take place (Shulchan Aruch YD 341:1)[387]. The Noda B'Yehuda (Noda B'Yehuda YD 210)[388] writes in a *teshuva* that there are times when autopsies are permitted. For instance, if investigating the *meis* will allow you to save other people with the same sickness, then he allows performing an autopsy for life-threatening situations. However, this leniency only applies if there are people sick with that disease right now – not if investigating the *meis* might allow for medical advancement for an issue in the future.

---

[386] Shailos U'Teshuvos Maharsham (162) - וכיון שהמנהג לקבור גם הבגדים שיש בהם דם משום שיש להסתפק בדם הנפש ובפרט אם ידוע שיצא דם אחר מיתה הרי דמו כבשרו בזה

[387] Shulchan Aruch (YD 341:1) - מי שמת לו מת שהוא חייב להתאבל עליו קודם קבורה וכו

[388] Noda B'Yehuda (YD 210) - אבל בנדון דידן אין כאן שום חולה הצריך לזה רק שרוצים ללמוד חכמה זו אולי יזדמן חולה שיהיה צריך לזה ודאי דלא דחינן משום חששא קלה זו שום איסור תורה או אפילו איסור דרבנן שאם אתה קורא לחששא זו ספק נפשות א"כ יהיה כל מלאכת הרפואות שחיקת ובישול סמנים והכנת כלי איזמל להקזה מותר בשבת שמא יזדמן היום או בלילה חולה שיהיה צורך לזה ולחלק בין חששא לזמן קרוב לחששא לזמן רחוק קשה לחלק. וחלילה להתיר דבר זה ואפילו רופאי האומות אינם עושים נסיון בחכמת הניתוח ע"י שום מת כי אם בהרוגים ע"פ משפט או במי שהסכים בעצמו בחייו לכך ואם אנו ח"ו מקילים בדבר זה א"כ ינתחו כל המתים כדי ללמוד סידור אברים הפנימים ומהותן כדי שידעו לעשות רפואות להחיים

Otherwise they'll perform autopsies on everyone for potential medical diseases.

Q24. Can doctors perform an autopsy on a *meis*?

A: (5755) You cannot perform an autopsy on a Jewish *meis* unless there is a person in front of us who might be saved from us examining this *meis* (Noda B'Yehuda YD 210)[389]. There are some hospitals which are affiliated with teaching schools like Hopkins and Sinai which train doctors and need cadavers to practice on, so they pressure as many people as possible to allow their deceased to be used for medical teaching purposes. Sometimes the doctors will tell you that they want to investigate the cause of death so that they can find out how to help other family members in the future who suffer from similar heart issues or the like. However, most of the time they know the cause of death and just want you to allow for the autopsy to take place to teach the doctors, so it's not permitted to allow them to take the *meis*. If you're a Jewish doctor, then you can tell the Jewish patient that he should discuss with his Rabbi to get himself off the hook. Even if the Rabbi isn't Orthodox, the family will follow their Rabbi's opinion rather than making the Jewish doctor decide. On the other hand, it's permitted for non-Jews to have autopsies done since *nivul hameis* doesn't apply to non-Jews and a Jewish doctor would be allowed to follow the hospital's protocol by pushing for an autopsy.

Q25. What should you do if the medical examiner is pushing for more investigation?

A: (5779) In the state of Maryland, the vast majority of the time they're fine with not pushing for further autopsy investigations. If it is an extreme case where there is a real suspicion that the person was murdered, then there is very little you can do. We don't have much we can say at that point because the government has their

---

[389] Noda B'Yehuda (YD 210) - למה לכם כל הפלפול והלא זה הוא דין ערוך ומפורש שאפילו ספק דוחה שבת החמורה ומשנה מפורשת ביומא דף פ"ג וכל ספק נפשות דוחה שבת ושם דף פ"ד ע"ד ולא ספק שבת זו אלא אפילו ספק שבת אחרת ע"ש ואמנם כ"ז ביש ספק סכנת נפשות לפנינו כגון חולה או נפילת גל

laws in place. You can't bury anyone in America without a permit. You can't legally get married without a permit and you shouldn't be born without a certificate. You have to register your baby when it's born otherwise your child won't get social security benefits. Until recently, there was a law in China which forbade families from having more than one child. If someone had the *chutzpah* of having another child, the government considered it as if the second child didn't exist as far as they were concerned. This is particularly more difficult living in a communist country where you can't do anything if the government doesn't consider that you exist. You can't rent an apartment, you can't get a job, you're not even allowed to die. By implementing those policies, they cut their population in half. Now they need more workers since they have added so much business with America and are running out of manpower, so I think they started allowing more children.

Q26. Should we try to figure out who murdered a Jew through autopsy or just bury him?

A: (5779) The Gemara (Chullin 11b)[390] implies that you are not allowed to be *mevazeh* the *meis* even if it will give you a lead on who murdered him (Binyan Tzion 170)[391]. We do find that some *tzadikim* said to throw rocks on their coffin to be an atonement even though that normally constitutes a degradation of the *meis* as Rebbi Akiva Eiger wrote in his *tzava'ah* to have his *kever* stoned.

---

[390] Chullin (11b) - רב כהנא אמר אתיא מהורג את הנפש דאמר רחמנא קטליה וליחוש דלמא טרפה הוה אלא לאו משום דאמרינן זיל בתר רובא וכי תימא דבדקינן ליה הא קא מינוול וכי תימא משום איבוד נשמה דהאי נינוליה וניחוש שמא במקום סייף נקב הוה

[391] Binyan Tzion (170) - רק דעדיין יש לדון בזה שהרי כלל גדול בתורה דאין לך דבר עומד בפני פקוח נפש ואין חילוק בין ודאי לספק פ"נ אבל נלענ"ד דגם מטעם זה אין להתיר כאן דכבר הוכחתי במ"א (סי' קס"ז) שדעת רש"י ע"פ גמרא דב"ק (דף ס') דאמרינן שם שאסור להציל עצמו בממון חבירו שאסור לאדם לגזול ממון חבירו למען הציל עצמו ממיתה ונגד דעת התוספ' והרא"ש שפירשו הסוגיא שם דוקא לענין דצריך לשלם אבל לא שיהי' אסור לכתחלה להציל והנה לדעת רש"י כיון שאסור להציל עצמו בממון חבירו כש"כ דאסור להציל עצמו בקלון חבירו דכבודו חביב לו מממונו כדאמרינן בב"ק פ' החובל בהאשה שבאת לפני ר"ע ע"ש וא"כ האיך נאמר דמשום פ"נ דהחולה יהי' מותר לבזות ולנוול המת דמסתמא לא מחל על בזיונו

Perhaps having something done as an atonement is different than mutilating the deceased's body.

Q27. Can a person be *mochel* on his own honor to allow more invasive autopsy or donating organs after death?

A: (5779) I don't think a person can be *mochel* on his body because we were created in the image of the Ribono Shel Olam (Bereishis 1:27)[392] – Hashem created us with a *tzelem elokim* which we cannot be *mochel* (Chasam Sofer YD 336)[393]. It's not considered an atonement for the *meis* having his organs removed because an *aveirah* does not serve as a *kapara*. However, Rav Moshe Feinstein (Igros Moshe YD 2:174) says that it is permitted for a person to will his organs to save other people's lives or to enhance the lives of others. It is only permitted to donate these organs if they will be removed according to the halacha, but not after he is considered legally dead.

Q28. Should one be *makpid* not to be buried next to a *rasha* (Shulchan Aruch YD 362:5)[394]?

A: (5755) My in-laws had a situation where they were buried in a Shomer Shabbos cemetery but later, the cemetery buried someone with some Italian-sounding name next to my mother-in-law. We suspected something was wrong and found out this woman married a non-Jew and took on his last name. So we complained to the cemetery that we specifically buried our in-laws in the Shomer Shabbos section yet they were putting someone who wasn't Shomer Shabbos next to them. We insisted that either they move the body somewhere else or permit us to put up a fence around my in-laws so that they would be considered in their own property. Even the people in charge of the cemetery were very

---

[392] Bereishis (1:27) - וַיִּבְרָא אֱלֹקִים אֶת־הָאָדָם בְּצַלְמוֹ בְּצֶלֶם אֱלֹקִים בָּרָא אֹתוֹ זָכָר וּנְקֵבָה בָּרָא אֹתָם

[393] Chasam Sofer YD (336) - אך בני ישראל מאמינים גם אדם כי ימות באהל עדיין במותו נקרא אדם פנימי ולא פגר (קערפער) כי גם בגופו שהיה נרתק לנשמה נשאר בו לחלוחי' קדושה ונוהגים בו כבוד

[394] Shulchan Aruch YD (362:5) - אין קוברין רשע אצל צדיק אפילו רשע חמור אצל רשע קל וכן אין קוברין צדיק וכשר ובינוני אצל חסיד מופלג

upset that this could happen since that area was designated for people who were Shomer Shabbos. We investigated the situation and found out that the reason she was buried next to my in-laws was because the plot really belonged to the Rav of a *shul* who gave up his spot when he saw the non-Jewish family didn't have any plans for a burial. Consequently, the people in charge of the cemetery realized we had a good claim and allowed us to put a wrought iron fence around our in-laws which is still there today (Igros Moshe YD 2:152)[395]. We immediately bought the plot next to my in-laws as well so that the mistake should not be made on the other side also.

---

[395] Igros Moshe YD (2:152) - ואם ציוה יש לקיים מצותו אבל אם הוא מפורסם למחלל שבת משום שהוא מחלל השבת בפהרהסיא אין צורך לקבלת עדות בפניו ובפני ב"ד ואסור לקוברו אצל סתם אנשים שנחשבים לכשרים וצריך להרחיק מלקבור אדם כשר ממנו שמנה אמות של תורה שהם לענין זה חמשה יארד במדת מדינתנו ורק כשידוע שאחד רצה שיקבדוהו אצל קרוביו אף שהיו מחללי שבת רשאין לקוברו וכ"ש כשציוה שיקברוהו שם ואם אי אפשר להרחיק האדם כשר מהמחלל שבת בפרהסיא מצד דוחק המקום וכדומה יצטרכו לעשות גדר גבוה עשרה טפחים ביניהם

Chapter 9: Halachic Will

Q1. What is a *halachic* will?

A: (5778) A will is the method of how a person can direct the location of his possessions after he completes his 120 years. It is important to write a will. I've seen families torn apart because of *machlokes* of how one's possessions should be divided. The more money it is, the more vicious the fights become. Some people are *zoche* to not leave much money over and don't have this problem. You can write, "I want these possessions to go to this child, these possessions to go to this child, etc." You can write, "I don't want to give this item to this child, and want to give this to another." Chazal say, "You shouldn't take away your possessions even from a bad child to a good child" (Bava Basra 133b)[396]. Rather, Chazal say you should treat all your children equally. Rav Moshe (Igros Moshe CM 2:50) says that only refers to an *ehrliche* yid. If he's a *frum yid* who slips up in some things then fine, but if he is no longer a *frum yid* at all then it is permitted to leave out him from the will – and in some cases recommended.

Q2. At what age should one write a will?

A: (5778) Rav Sternhell was a big *posek* and said you should make a will when you are 50 years old. Of course it's not assur to make it at 40, but you should do so at 50.

Q3. Can someone bequeath money to a company?

A: (5777) Although I don't know what the legal system allows, in Jewish law one can only bequeath property to a person. Therefore, an inheritance cannot be given to an LLC, a dog, or a corporation since they are not people. The only way a corporation possesses money is because they are a partnership of multiple people who decided to create a business together. The only condition of their

---

[396] Bava Basra (133b) - מאי הוי עלה ת"ש דאמר ליה שמואל לרב יהודה שיננא לא תיהוי בי עבורי אחסנתא ואפילו מברא בישא לברא טבא וכ"ש מברא לברתא

partnership is that their liability is limited to the assets of this LLC. The moment a person dies, his money reverts straight to the inheritors and cannot be transferred to anyone else because dead people cannot own money according to Jewish law (Igros Moshe EH 1:104). Hence, the way the current legal will is worded would not work for transferring money to someone other than his inheritors who would get it without the will, but there are ways to make it work. While a person is still alive, he can do what he wants with the money. For instance, he can buy himself a house, he can buy a lottery ticket – there are certain forms of gambling which are not forbidden (Shulchan Aruch YD 370:3)[397] – he can even throw his money down the sewer. Who is going to tell him what to do with his money? He can give away all of his money during his lifetime and his inheritors don't have the ability to say anything. Therefore, a person can give his money to any charity he wants a few moments before he dies as well. A person is able to make a *kinyan* now and say it is not fully effective until five minutes before he dies. Nonetheless, such an individual is also allowed to insert a condition in the contract that he may renege on the agreement at any time during his lifetime if he wants to. For example, if he says, "The house on this street will belong to my oldest child and the house on that street will belong to my youngest child" and makes a *kinyan* to formalize the agreement, he can still retain the right to renege on the deal if he wants to do something else with the house if he stipulates this in the agreement. If you ask a lawyer to write such a will, it won't work unless you make a *kinyan* with a *frum* individual saying, "Everyone who I apportion money to in my will should receive those possessions based on the *kinyan* I make now which will take effect starting now and finalizing an hour before my death"

---

[397] Shulchan Aruch YD (370:3) - יש מי שאומר שהמשחק בקוביא עם העכו"ם אין בו משום גזל אבל יש בו איסור עוסק בדברים בטלים שאין ראוי לאדם שיעסוק כל ימיו אלא בדברי חכמה ויישובו של עולם וחלקו עליו לומר שאינו פסול אלא א"כ אין לו אומנות אחרת: הגה אבל אם יש לו אומנות אחרת אפי' משחק עם ישראל אינו פסול וכבר פשט המנהג כסברא האחרונה לשחוק בקוביא ואין פסול אלא מי שאין לו אומנות אלא הוא

Chapter 9: Halachic Will

(Teshuvos HaRosh 84:5)[398]. Then the will would be valid according to the *din* of the Torah. This may even have legal ramifications since if the inheritance tax is higher than the gift tax, then you can save money by giving your possessions moments before death since it's given as a gift and not an inheritance.

Q4. Are there any other methods of bequeathing money to one's daughters?

A: (5777) - Yes, a person can make himself obligated to give five million dollars to one daughter, but say that he will only give the money to that daughter if she will give her mother and other siblings a certain amount of money – like $500,000 each. The same concept applies as before where all the money is technically given while the father is still alive, but say that it won't transfer until moments before dying. Nonetheless, there are some differences between the two methods. For instance, according to the first method, any extra money added to the estate after the time of the *kinyan* is not included in the will. You cannot make a *kinyan* on something which you don't currently possess (Shulchan Aruch CM 209:4)[399]. Nonetheless, you can include text in the will which takes future earnings into account, though you need to continue updating it. On the other hand, the second method might become more of a burden taxwise on the daughter since she technically possesses all the money and is apportioning out the money to her siblings, but I'm not sure about the legal matters of this question.

(5778) - Women live statistically longer than men. According to the strict halacha, a person must give all his possessions to his sons. His *bechor* gets *pi shnayim* (Shulchan Aruch CM 277:1)[400].

---

[398] Teshuvos HaRosh (84:5) - אמר רב ששת יטול יזכה יטול יחזיק כלן לשון מתנה הן במתניתא תנא אף יחסין בראוי ליורשו ור' יוחנן בן ברוקא היא והאי יפול לישנא דיחסין הוא וביחסין אין שייך מעכשיו דהא מעכשיו ושעה אחת קודם למיתתו אינו ראוי לירש דירושה בגמר מיתה הוא

[399] Shulchan Aruch CM (209:4) - אין אדם מקנה דבר שלא בא לעולם בין במכר בין במתנת בריא בין במתנת שכיב מרע

[400] Shulchan Aruch CM (277:1) - הבכור נוטל פי שנים בנכסי אביו כיצד הניח חמשה בנים ואחד מהם בכור הבכור נוטל שליש הממון וכל אחד מהארבעה

Chapter 9: Halachic Will

If you have three sons and one of them is a *bechor*, then you divide the property into four parts and give two parts to the *bechor* and the other two children get one part each. Already in earlier generations, when a person would marry off his daughter, they wrote a *tenai* at the wedding that the daughter would get half of whatever the son is entitled to in the inheritance (Rema CM 281:7)[401]. There is a way to write your will in a kosher way which will divide all of your property in the way you want everything divided. The wife technically inherits nothing, but when you get married with a *kesuva*, then Chazal (Kesubos 52b)[402] were *mesaken* that you support her in your home from your possessions until she gets remarried. However, until she remarries you must maintain her financial level she was used to while she was married. The inheritors must give her that money to support her at the same standard of living as when she was married to you (Shulchan Aruch EH 93:3)[403]. That is the *tenai* made at the marriage. Once she remarries, you no longer need to support her, but you must pay the *kesuva*. Rav Moshe *poskins* (Igros Moshe EH 4:91) it's the value of 100 pounds of pure silver at the time the *kesuva* would be paid. Before she remarries, since it's not really such a pleasant thing for a widow to go to her children saying, "I

פשוטים נוטל שתות הניח תשעה בנים הרי האחד הבכור נוטל חמישותו וכל א'
מהשמונה פשוטים נוטל עשירית וכן על דרך החלוקה הזאת חולקים לעולם
[401] Rema CM (281:7) - הכותב לבתו שתקח לאחר מותו כחצי חלק זכר דינו
כירושה בעלמא ובעל חוב וכתובה קודמין למתנה זו וכן עשור נכסי הבת וכל ימי
חיי הנותן יכול למכור הנכסים אע"פ שכתב לה מהיום ולאחר מיתה ואין הבת
נוטלת אלא בנכסים שהיו לו בשעת נתינה אבל לא אח"כ דאין אדם יכול להקנות
דבר שלא בא לעולם מיהו נ"ל דמה שנוהגין לכתוב שטר חוב לבתו
ולהתנות שאם יתן לבתו חלק חצי זכר יפטור מן החוב צריך ליתן לה בכל אשר
לו דעיקר הוא החוב ולכן צריך לקיים תנאו או ישלמו החוב וכן המנהג
[402] Kesubos (52b) - את תהא יתבא בביתי ומיתזנא מנכסי כל ימי מיגר
אלמנותיך בביתי חייב שהוא תנאי בית דין כך היו אנשי ירושלים כותבין אנשי
גליל היו כותבין כאנשי ירושלים אנשי יהודה היו כותבין עד שירצו היורשין ליתן
לך כתובתיך לפיכך אם רצו יורשין נותנין לה כתובתה ופוטרין אותה
[403] Shulchan Aruch EH (93:3) - אלמנה ניזונית מנכסי יורשין כ"ז אלמנותה
אפי' אם לא נכתב בכתובה ואפי' אם צוה בשעת מיתה אל תיזון אלמנותי מנכסי
אין שומעין לו ואין היורשים יכולין לפרוע לה כתובתה ולסלקה מהמזונות אלא
היא ניזונית על כרחם כל זמן שלא תתבע תתבע כתובתה אא"כ התנו כן בפירוש שלא
תזון אלמנתו מנכסיו או שהיה מנהג המקום כן

187

had 5,000 expenses" and drag it out of the children. Therefore, I think it's the right thing that if the husband has limited funds then he should give all of his property to his wife. Perhaps there is a child with special needs or struggling with parnasa, so they may be a reason to give one child more than the others as long as it will be the normal thing for all the children to understand why this was done. But I'm speaking in general terms. Don't make your wife go to the children for money. Assign the inheritance to her instead.

Q5. Are those methods *lechatchila*? They seem to circumvent the Torah's directive to bequeath everything to the son.

A: (5777) Although those methods are completely valid, the correct thing to do is to leave over a דבר חשוב – let's say $10,000, but it really depends on how much money you have – set aside to be bequeathed only in accordance with the *din* of the Torah. Meaning, the *bechor* takes פי שנים of that money which was set aside, the other sons each get their portion, and the daughters receive nothing. That way, you fulfill the *seder hayerusha* of the Torah as well. Some people leave over their *seforim* to their sons since for many people their set of *seforim* is a דבר חשוב. Even though the sons-in-law might also want to receive some of the *seforim*, a father has the right to only bequeath them to his sons in accordance with the *din* of the Torah. Nonetheless, when the Torah says כִּי אֶת־הַבְּכֹר בֶּן־הַשְּׂנוּאָה יַכִּיר לָתֶת לוֹ פִּי שְׁנַיִם בְּכֹל אֲשֶׁר־יִמָּצֵא לוֹ כִּי־הוּא רֵאשִׁית אֹנוֹ לוֹ מִשְׁפַּט הַבְּכֹרָה (Devarim 21:17), it's not so black-and-white since there are other factors to consider. If the father is owed money from creditors, then the *bechor* doesn't receive פי שנים. Additionally, if someone has a life insurance policy, that money is not considered בְּכֹל אֲשֶׁר־יִמָּצֵא לוֹ because the father did not possess that money before death. I don't even think any money from the life insurance is affected by the *yerusha* because the father never possessed that money. Anyone he included as part of his list of beneficiaries receives the money since dead individuals cannot possess anything.

Q6. May one give one child more than the other?

188

Chapter 9: Halachic Will

A: (5777) If one of the children has special needs and it's difficult for them to make a *parnasa* or one of the children has a draining expense where all of the other children would understand why one sibling receives more of the inheritance than the others, then it is permitted to give one child extra money. In general, Chazal say not to make one child more special than the others because we see from Yaakov giving a כתונת פסים to Yosef made the other brothers jealous and thereby send him down to Mitzrayim (Shabbos 10b)[404]. This even includes a case where someone has one son who does everything right and another son who doesn't do everything right where Chazal still say (Bava Basra 133b)[405] in such a case not to make one son more special than the other בן בישא because maybe the son who is not following in the path of the Torah will have a child who eventually will be a *tzaddik*. If there is no chance that the child will return to Torah, then you are allowed to disinherit him. Rav Moshe Feinstein (Igros Moshe CM 2:50:3)[406] writes in a *teshuva* that this Gemara only refers to a case

---

[404] Shabbos (10b) - ואמר רבא בר מחסיא אמר רב חמא בר גוריא אמר רב לעולם אל ישנה אדם בנו בין הבנים שבשביל משקל שני סלעים מילת שנתן יעקב ליוסף יותר משאר בניו נתקנאו בו אחיו ונתגלגל הדבר וירדו אבותינו למצרים

[405] Bava Basra (133b) - מאי הוי עלה ת"ש דאמר ליה שמואל לרב יהודה שיננא לא תיהוי בי עבורי אחסנתא ואפילו מברא בישא לברא טבא and כל הנותן נכסיו לאחרים והניח היורשים - Shulchan Aruch CM (282:1) - אע"פ שאין היורשים נוהגים בו כשורה אין רוח חכמים נוחה הימנו וזכו האחרים בכל מה שנתן להם ומדת חסידות שלא להעיד בצואה שמעבירין בה הירושה מהיורש אפי' מבן שאינו נוהג כשורה לאחיו חכם ונוהג כשורה

[406] Igros Moshe CM (2:50:3) - והנה בבנין דלא מעלי פשוט שהוא רק בברא בישא בעלמא דאינו זהיר כל כך במצות אבל הוא מאמין בה' ובתורתו ומחנך את בניו ללכת בתורת ה' ולשמר מצותיו שבזה יש ודאי ספק דיפקו מיניה זרעא מעליא, ואף אם הוא חוטא היותר גדול בין אדם לחברו כמסור נמי כיון דהוא נזהר בדברים שבין אדם למקום מחנך את בניו לתורה ומצות לכן יש ספק לזרעא מעליא כדאיתא בסוף ב"ק קי"ט ע"א אבל המומרים לחלל שבתות בפרהסיא ועוברים על איסורי התורה ואין מחנכים את בניהם לתורה ומצות אין להסתפק בזרעא מעליא ואף שאירע לפעמים שגם ממומרים לשבת ולכל התורה נפיק בן שומר תורה ודאי הוא רק מיעוט שלא מצוי ואין לחוש לזה שלכן ודאי רשאי לא רק ליתן לצדקה אלא אף ליתן לאחרים רשאי ורוח חכמים נוחה מזה וגם זכור לטוב שבזה לא יפלגו על רשב"ג. וגם יותר מזה אף במסור שיש ספק דליפוק מיניה זרעא מעליא

189

where the child not following the ways of the Torah is still an *erhliche yid* but struggles with keeping some of the *mitzvos* or isn't a *baal middos tovos* – but in general keeps the rest of the *mitzvos*. In such a case Chazal say not to exclude such a child from the will. However, Rav Moshe explains that a parent does not need to give anything to a child who has left the Torah. In fact, Rav Moshe says the parent should exclude that child from the will so that he knows that his actions did not find favor in his parents' eyes. A parent once approached me about their child who was put into prison and asked if he should keep up the relationship. I told him that one of the Chassidishe Rebbes had a child who stopped keeping the Torah yet continued to give him money and honor him. The Rebbe's other children asked why their father continued a relationship with his son, and he replied, "When I return to the Olam HaEmes after 120 years and the Ribono Shel Olam will ask, 'How come you didn't do this? How come you didn't do that?' then I will reply, 'I am not worthy of Your mercy, but I had a son who wasn't worthy of my רחמנות yet I still showed him mercy – please show me רחמנות too מדה כנגד מדה.'" That's what the *posuk* in Bereishis (25:28)[407] means וַיֶּאֱהַב יִצְחָק אֶת־עֵשָׂו כִּי־צַיִד בְּפִיו – Yitzchak now has the ability to claim to the Ribono Shel Olam, "Look, I also had a son who wasn't *frum*, but I was still מקרב him. So too you should be מקרב Klal Yisroel." Therefore, there is room to give one child more than the other children as long as they all can understand the disproportionate inheritance.

Q7. What do you do if a son says, "I keep all the *mitzvos*, but I just won't listen to this one *mitzva*"?

A: (5778) It's not correct to do so, but he could technically say that. Therefore, in such a situation it's better to make a regular will with whatever you want. Keep in mind that the standard today is to give daughters and sons equally otherwise there is tension

---

שמטעם זה אסור לאבד ממונו ביד מסתבר שהוא רק שלא לאבד מה שיש לו כבר אבל רשאי להעביר נחלה ממנו

[407] Bereishis (25:28) - וַיֶּאֱהַב יִצְחָק אֶת־עֵשָׂו כִּי־צַיִד בְּפִיו וְרִבְקָה אֹהֶבֶת אֶת־ יַעֲקֹב

Chapter 9: Halachic Will

(Rema CM 281:7)[408]. You can give your money to whomever and whatever you want. You can give all your money to a Kollel if you want. A person can say "I want to give $\frac{1}{3}$ of my money to this son, $\frac{1}{3}$ of my money to my daughter, and $\frac{1}{3}$ of my money to *tzedakah* (Rema YD 249:1 - ואל יבזבז אדם יותר מחומש שלא יצטרך לבריות ודוקא כל ימי חייו אבל בשעת מותו יכול אדם ליתן צדקה כל מה שירצה)." Whatever you want to do. What happens if a minute before you pass away, you give your money as a present? (Peah 3:7)[409] That is valid. So how do you make that take effect? קנין מעכשיו לאחר זמן – you can make a transaction which begins now and ends at a later time. As long as you make a *kinyan sudar*, even though it's not here anymore, it still has an effect. Therefore, you can write whatever you want in the will and then say "Whatever is outlined in my will is given over as a present to whoever is named in this will - it should begin now and will take effect a moment before I pass away." It doesn't matter whether the will comes into effect an hour or a minute before dying. However, you should say, "I want to keep a certain amount of money - let's say $10,000 - which should be given to my heirs in accordance with the halacha." Since all the money that he owns has been given away a minute before he passed away, all the money that he has is this $10,000. That $10,000 would be divided according to the halacha. That's done in order to fulfill the *mitzva* of *yerusha*. You

---

[408] Rema CM (281:7) - הכותב לבתו שתקח לאחר מותו כחצי חלק זכר דינו כירושה בעלמא ובעל חוב וכתובה קודמין למתנה זו וכן עשור נכסי הבת וכל ימי חיי הנותן יכול למכור הנכסים אע"פ שכתב לה מהיום ולאחר מיתה ואין הבת נוטלת אלא בנכסים שהיו לו בשעת נתינה אבל לא אח"כ דאין אדם יכול להקנות דבר שלא בא לעולם מיהו נ"ל דמה שנוהגין עכשיו לכתוב שטר חוב לבתו ולהתנות שאם יתן לבתו חלק חצי זכר יפטור מן החוב צריך ליתן לה בכל אשר לו דעיקר הוא החוב ולכן צריך לקיים תנאו או ישלמו החוב וכן המנהג כתב לבתו שטר חצי זכר וכתב לה וייוצאי חלציה בנותיה ובניה נוטלין בשוה הואיל ולא כ' יורשי יוצאי חלציה התנה שלא יהא חלק לבתו בספרים והלוה על הספרים אין בעל חוב קונה משכון ולכן יש לבת חלק בהן אבל אם הוחלטו הספרים בידו אין לבת חלק בהן

[409] Peah (3:7) - הַכּוֹתֵב נְכָסָיו שְׁכִיב מְרַע שִׁיֵּר קַרְקַע כָּל שֶׁהוּא מַתְּנָתוֹ מַתָּנָה לֹא שִׁיֵּר קַרְקַע כָּל שֶׁהוּא אֵין מַתְּנָתוֹ מַתָּנָה הַכּוֹתֵב נְכָסָיו לְבָנָיו וְכָתַב לְאִשְׁתּוֹ קַרְקַע כָּל שֶׁהוּא אִבְּדָה כְתֻבָּתָהּ רַבִּי יוֹסֵי אוֹמֵר אִם קִבְּלָה עָלֶיהָ אַף עַל פִּי שֶׁלֹּא כָתַב לָהּ אִבְּדָה כְתֻבָּתָהּ

fulfill a *mitzva d'oraysa* by giving that money to your inheritors (Sefer HaChinuch 400)[410]. Also, you can say "my *seforim* will be the *yerusha*" since the daughters probably don't want the *seforim* anyway and the sons probably do want them. The amount that you leave over for *yerusha* should be a *davar choshuv*. The Rav can give you his pen as the *kinyan sudar*, and he is the agent for everyone mentioned in the will.

Q8. Can you assign the money to a different inheritor before dying?

A: (5778) Since the *halacha* is that the money goes to the inheritors - which we said is officially the sons - the second a person dies the possessions automatically go to the inheritors. Saying anything differently about where the money should go after one dies won't help since he doesn't own his property once he has left this world. However, Chazal say it's a *mitzva* to listen to the *meis* (Kesubos 70a)[411], so if you command your will to apportion your money elsewhere, it's a *mitzva* for the family to listen to your directives (Shulchan Aruch CM 252:2)[412].

Q9. How long are children considered *yesomim* (orphans)?

A: (5777) Children are considered *yesomim* as long they need their parents. There are some places where children work in the family business at 13 years old and no longer need their parents. At that point, parents *halachically* have a right to tell their children, "You have a job now, so we don't need to support you." Of course that is a little bit of an אכזריות because how will he become a *talmid chacham* if in his younger years he already needs to go to work? Until that age, Beis Din will force the father to

---

[410] Sefer HaChinuch (400) - מצות דיני נחלות שנצטוינו בדיני נחלות כלומר שמצוה עלינו לעשות ולדון בענין הנחלה כאשר דנה התורה עליה שנאמר (במדבר כז:ח-ט) כי ימות ובן אין לו והעברתם את נחלתו לבתו ואם אין לו בת וגו' וסוף הפרשה (שם יא) והיתה לבני ישראל לחקת עולם כאשר צוה יי את משה

[411] Kesubos (70a) - רבי מאיר היא דאמר מצוה לקיים דברי המת

[412] Shulchan Aruch CM (252:2) - מצוה לקיים דברי המת אפי' בריא שצוה ומת והוא שנותנו עכשיו לשליש לשם כך

support that child (Shulchan Aruch EH 71:1)[413]. In fact, a person is not allowed to say he cannot find a job since he obligated himself in the *kesuva*[414]. Beis Din will find him a job as a garbage collector – or sanitation engineer as they're called nowadays. The father might reject the notion of going to work in such a capacity and say he wants to learn all day, but Beis Din tells him, "You can learn on your own *cheshbon*, but you cannot learn on your wife's *cheshbon*." Each husband is obligated to support his wife according to the standards of living of either he or she was accustomed to – whichever one is higher. He is also obligated to give his wife enough money to give a respectable amount to anyone collecting money so that she does not receive a bad name for being stingy (Kesubos 72a)[415]. That is part of the husband's obligation to his wife mentioned in the Gemara, aside from the jewelry he must buy her as part of the *minhag hamakom*. There are things which a husband is obligated to provide for his wife which he may not have realized before getting married, and are not necessarily outlined in the *kesuva*. Moreover, he must honor her more than himself (Yevamos 62b)[416] so that if they only have one coat, he must give her the coat to wear outside. On the other

---

[413] Shulchan Aruch EH (71:1) - חייב אדם לזון בניו ובנותיו עד שיהיו בני שש אפילו יש להם נכסים שנפלו להם מבית אבי אמם ומשם ואילך זנן כתקנת חכמים עד שיגדלו ואם לא רצה גוערין בו ומכלימין אותו ופוצרין בו ואם לא רצה מכריזין עליו בצבור ואומרים פלוני אכזרי הוא ואינו רוצה לזון בניו והרי הוא פחות מעוף טמא שהוא זן אפרוחיו ואין כופין אותו לזונן בד"א בשאינו אמוד אבל אם היה אמוד שיש לו ממון הראוי ליתן צדקה המספקת להם מוציאי' ממנו בעל כרחו משום צדקה וזנין אותם עד שיגדלו

[414] Kesuva - הוי לי לאנתו כדת משה וישראל ואנא אפלח ואוקיר ואיזון ואפרנס יתיכי ליכי כהלכות גוברין יהודאין דפלחין ומוקרין וזנין ומפרנסין לנשיהון בקושטא

[415] Kesubos (72a) - המדיר את אשתו שלא תשאל ושלא תשאיל נפה וכברה ריחים ותנור יוציא ויתן כתובה מפני שמשיאה שם רע בשכינותיה וכן היא שנדרה שלא תשאל ושלא תשאיל נפה וכברה וריחים ותנור ושלא תארוג בגדים נאים לבניו תצא שלא בכתובה מפני שמשיאתו שם רע בשכיניו

[416] Yevamos (62b) - ת"ר האוהב את אשתו כגופו והמכבדה יותר מגופו והמדריך בניו ובנותיו בדרך ישרה והמשיאן סמוך לפירקן עליו הכתוב אומר וידעת כי שלום אהלך

hand, the wife has responsibilities to her husband like cooking, cleaning, and laundry (Shulchan Aruch EH 80:6)[417]. It used to be that washing your clothing would be a whole day's work where she would need to wash each piece of clothing and figure out how to dry them if it wasn't a sunny day. Most people would pay for someone to do the laundry. Nowadays women often bring enough money into the marriage to pay for a washing machine the same way as they would bring in a maidservant to wash the clothing (Kesubos 59b)[418].

Q10. Is money in one's bank account considered בְּכֹל אֲשֶׁר־יִמָּצֵא לוֹ which is bequeathed to the children?

A: (5777) No, the money in your bank account is lent to the bank – as opposed to money in your safety deposit box. The banks make money by taking your money and spending it on investments, mortgages, and whatever else they want. You lend the money to them. I don't think that money in the bank would be considered בְּכֹל אֲשֶׁר־יִמָּצֵא לוֹ. There is even a question in the Shulchan Aruch whether or not a ship or a cow in a *hefker* property is considered בְּכֹל אֲשֶׁר־יִמָּצֵא לוֹ to the person bequeathing the property. Those items are not necessarily in your possession and would be a *machlokes haposkim* whether a *bechor* receives פי שנים for them. On the other hand, maybe you can say a bank is like a *pikadon* because you can always withdraw your money from the bank. Even though it's technically a loan to the bank, the money might still be considered in your possession. Moreover, even a CD might still be considered in your possession despite the penalty of receiving a lower interest rate if you withdraw your money earlier. However, the fact that banks have a certain level of ownership on

---

[417] Shulchan Aruch EH (80:6) - יש מלאכות שהאשה עושה לבעלה בזמן שהם עניים ואלו הם מטחנת ואופה ומכבסת ומניקה את בנה ונותנת תבן לפני בהמתו אבל לא לפני בקרו

[418] Kesubos (59b) - ואלו מלאכות שהאשה עושה לבעלה טוחנת ואופה ומכבסת מבשלת ומניקה את בנה מצעת לו המטה ועושה בצמר הכניסה לו שפחה אחת לא טוחנת ולא אופה ולא מכבסת שתים אין מבשלת ואין מניקה את בנה שלש אין מצעת לו המטה ואין עושה בצמר ארבע יושבת בקתדרא

the money since the funds are not available to be returned on certain days and times - along with the other factors mentioned earlier - I think money in your bank is not considered בְּכֹל אֲשֶׁר־יִמָּצֵא לוֹ.

Q11. Is a stock or pension plan considered בְּכֹל אֲשֶׁר־יִמָּצֵא לוֹ?

A: (5777) If you have a stock in General Motors, then you technically own part of General Motors and it should be considered בְּכֹל אֲשֶׁר־יִמָּצֵא לוֹ. However, Rav Moshe has a *teshuva* discussing whether you are obligated to sell your stock in General Motors before Pesach since the company has chametz in their cafeterias. Since you own part of the company, that should be considered as if you own a percentage of the chametz as well. Rav Moshe explains that having stock in a company does not make you a partial owner. When you walk into the corporation, they don't roll out a red carpet for you. You might be an owner on paper, but neither you nor the company believe you are a partial owner. Therefore, you are not obligated to sell your stocks before Pesach. Similarly, a stock would not be considered בְּכֹל אֲשֶׁר־יִמָּצֵא לוֹ. Nonetheless, Rav Moshe (Igros Moshe EH 1:7) says if you own a significant amount of the stock – like 2% of Pepsi Cola or AT&T – then you would be a multimillionaire and they might in fact roll out the red carpet for you. In such a case, Rav Moshe says you would need to sell the stock before Pesach because then you are considered to own a portion of the chametz in the company. You should ask a Rav knowledgeable in these *halachos* about this because questions about stocks can become complex.

Q12. Can you change your mind with your will?

A: (5778) Yes, that is included in this deal. You are able to say, "I am giving this money mentioned in my will as a present מעכשיו ושעה קודם מיתה to those people or institutions mentioned in my will with the condition that I may change my mind." Perhaps you want to change your mind to give more or less to one of your inheritors for some reason in the future – you are allowed to do that.

Q13. Must one specifically include his wife in his will?

Chapter 9: Halachic Will

A: (5777) A husband does not need to include his wife in his will because supporting one's widow is part of the *kesuva* which the husband obligated himself to pay at their wedding. He must provide everything his wife needs both during marriage and after he leaves this world until she gets remarried (Kesubos 52b)[419]. The children who receive the inheritance are required to pay for their mother's expenses. However, it's degrading for a mother to send a bill of her expenses to her children in order to receive the funds. Therefore, it would be better for a husband to include his wife in the will so that she is supported until 120 years, and whatever money is leftover he can leave for the children.

Q14. If a husband bequeathed all of his money to his wife, and then the wife later dies, does the *bechor* now receive פי שנים of his mother's inheritance?

A: (5777) The basis of this question is that the *bechor* only receives פי שנים if his father dies כִּי־הוּא רֵאשִׁית אֹנוֹ לוֹ מִשְׁפַּט הַבְּכֹרָה (Devarim 21:17)[420], while a mother doesn't cause a *din* of פי שנים. The Gemara says if someone leaves everything to his wife, she is considered an אפוטרופוס – in charge of administering the finances. Whatever money he owes to other people, including her and her children, are apportioned out through her. If she feels it is appropriate to give a Sefer Torah in his honor, then she was given the right to do so for her husband. However, if she is only an אפוטרופוס, then the *bechor* should have received פי שנים when his father died. It's not simple, but my advice to the *bechor* is that he should keep quiet. If they want to give him פי שנים then he should take it, but if they don't give it to him then he shouldn't make a

---

[419] Kesubos (52b) - את תהא יתבא בביתי ומיתזנא מנכסי כל ימי מיגר אלמנותיך and the Kesuva - חתן דנן אחריות שטר כתובתא דא נדוניא דן ותוספתא דא קבלית עלי ועל ירתי בתראי להתפרע מכל שפר ארג נכסין וקנינין דאית לי תחות כל שמיא דקנאי ודעתיד אנא למקני נכסין דאית להון אחריות ודלית להון אחריות כלהון יהון אחראין וערבאין לפרוע מנהון שטר כתובתא דא נדוניא דן ותוספתא דא מנאי ואפילו מן גלימא דעל כתפאי בחיי ובתר חיי מן יומא דנן ולעלם

[420] Devarim (21:17) - כִּי אֶת־הַבְּכֹר בֶּן־הַשְּׂנוּאָה יַכִּיר לָתֶת לוֹ פִּי שְׁנַיִם בְּכֹל אֲשֶׁר־יִמָּצֵא לוֹ כִּי־הוּא רֵאשִׁית אֹנוֹ לוֹ מִשְׁפַּט הַבְּכֹרָה

fuss about it. Don't use the Torah for *machlokes* – that is קרדום לחפור בה (Avos 4:5)[421], digging up more money through *machlokes*.

Q15. What else must one have in the process of creating the kosher will?

A: (5777) Since this is a kosher *shtar*, you must have two kosher witnesses who sign it or who watch the *shtar* being given (Rambam Eidus 3:4)[422]. Moreover, the witnesses only help for transferring property but not movable objects.

Q16. If you receive a large amount of money subsequent to writing your initial will, must you write another one?

A: (5778) Let's say you will eventually get a lot of money in a *yerusha* from a parent. That's not included in the original *kinyan*, so you can't include that in your will made last year. You need to redo the *kinyan* in order to include those additional possessions afterwards.

Q17. How do you make a *kinyan*?

A: (5778) You can tell a friend of yours to be an agent for your heirs by saying, "I want to give my heirs my money or property as designated in my will that it should start to take effect now and be finalized an hour before my death with the condition that I can

---

[421] Avos (4:5) - רַבִּי צָדוֹק אוֹמֵר אַל תַּעֲשֵׂם עֲטָרָה לְהִתְגַּדֵּל בָּהֶם וְלֹא קַרְדֹּם לַחְפֹּר בָּהֶם

[422] Rambam Eidus (3:4) - דִּין תּוֹרָה שֶׁאֵין מְקַבְּלִין עֵדוּת לֹא בְּדִינֵי מָמוֹנוֹת וְלֹא בְּדִינֵי נְפָשׁוֹת אֶלָּא מִפִּי הָעֵדִים שֶׁנֶּאֱמַר (דברים יז:ו) עַל פִּי שְׁנַיִם עֵדִים מִפִּיהֶם וְלֹא מִכְּתַב יָדָן. אֲבָל מִדִּבְרֵי סוֹפְרִים שֶׁחוֹתְכִין דִּינֵי מָמוֹנוֹת בְּעֵדוּת שֶׁבַּשְּׁטָר אַף עַל פִּי שֶׁאֵין הָעֵדִים קַיָּמִים כְּדֵי שֶׁלֹּא תִּנְעֹל דֶּלֶת בִּפְנֵי לֹוִין and Sefer Chasidim כ"ש - (718) כשיקרבו ימי האדם למות יצוה לפני עדים ואפי' לאביו לא יאמין לבניו ולאשתו ואם יודע שאביו אינו נאמן לא יעזוב ביד אביו רק ביד ירא שמים נאמן שאם לא כן אתה פושע וקשה יותר מן הגזל שהרי הגזלן יכול להשיב הגזילה אבל זה לאחר מיתה אין תשובה ואין כפרה ועליו נאמר (קהלת ז:יג) כי מי יוכל לתקן את אשר עותו מעוות לא יוכל לתקון וזהו שנאמר (משלי יט:כ) למען תחכם באחריתך

change my mind in the future." The friend would give you a pen, *yarmulke*, or handkerchief. Then you pick it up and that makes the *kinyan* be accomplished. However, the drawback of this option is that you need to make a new *kinyan* every few years to cover everything. There's an alternative will which gets around this issue and doesn't require you to make this *kinyan* every few years. Instead, you can go to the person with the least amount of rights to your possessions – either your wife or one of your daughters – and say, "I am obligating myself to give you one million dollars, but am only doing so on condition that you divide my estate in accordance with the way it's written in my will." Consequently, this heir will receive everything because she gets one million dollars despite the fact that the deceased doesn't have that much money – then in order to actually be able to keep the money, she must give out whatever money is available according to the will. Whatever is left over from the apportionment goes to this heir. This way has the advantage that you don't need to update it every couple of years. However, this method has a drawback too since the will is probably going to be registered with the Register of Wills. Therefore, they will make you pay high taxes on the estate since it's all going to the one heir who then apportions the money out to the rest of the heirs. You need to speak with your accountant or lawyer to consider all the various factors and decide what makes the most sense. You should be considerate of your wife's needs and give her enough to support her for the rest of her life at least until 100 years old according to the standard of living she was used to when you were married together. Then your wife should write a will in whichever way she would like to apportion out the money. You can suggest what you would like her to do, but at the end of the day she can decide whatever she wants to do with the money.

Q18. What is a living will?

A: (5778) If a person is in a situation where he cannot make his own decision about his health care – whether because his mental capacity was compromised due to Alzheimer's, was put in a position under anesthetics, or just doesn't want to make the decision – is he allowed to let himself die or do we say that he must live? If your next of kin is *frum*, then it's not such a concern to sign a living will since your child will ask the Rav what to do. However, it's important to say that a person isn't the one in charge of his life. A person committing suicide transgresses לא תרצח (Shemos 20:13)[423]. He would receive *sekila* if he was still alive (Rambam Rotze'ach 2:2)[424]. It's a very severe *aveira* written in the *Aseres HaDibros*. In fact, the Chasam Sofer (Teshuvas Chasam Sofer YD 326:3) says it's much worse to kill yourself than to kill someone else. If you kill yourself, you have no portion in Olam Haba. The Mishna Yoma (8:8)[425] says you can do *teshuva* for many things to receive a *kapara*, then there are worse *aveiros* which you can only receive a *kapara* through pain and *teshuva*, and there are worse *aveiros* which require a combination of *teshuva*, pain, and Yom Kippur. Finally, there are a few *aveiros* which only the day of death is able to provide a complete *kapara* (Mechilta D'Rebbi Yishmael 20:7)[426]. The Ramban (Vayikra 1:9)[427] says that when someone does an *aveira b'shogeg*, he

---

[423] Shemos (20:13) - לֹא תִּרְצָח: לֹא תִּנְאָף: לֹא תִּגְנֹב: לֹא־תַעֲנֶה בְרֵעֲךָ עֵד שָׁקֶר

[424] Rambam Rotze'ach (2:2) - וּמִנַּיִן שֶׁכֵּן הוּא הַדִּין שֶׁנֶּאֱמַר (בראשית ט:ו) שֹׁפֵךְ דַּם הָאָדָם בָּאָדָם דָּמוֹ יִשָּׁפֵךְ זֶה הַהוֹרֵג בְּעַצְמוֹ שֶׁלֹּא עַל יְדֵי שָׁלִיחַ (בראשית ט:ה) אֶת דְּמְכֶם לְנַפְשֹׁתֵיכֶם אֶדְרֹשׁ זֶה הוֹרֵג זֶה הוֹרֵג עַצְמוֹ

[425] Yoma (8:8) - חַטָּאת וְאָשָׁם וַדַּאי מְכַפְּרִין מִיתָה וְיוֹם הַכִּפּוּרִים מְכַפְּרִין עִם הַתְּשׁוּבָה הַתְּשׁוּבָה מְכַפֶּרֶת עַל עֲבֵרוֹת קַלּוֹת עַל עֲשֵׂה וְעַל לֹא תַעֲשֶׂה וְעַל הַחֲמוּרוֹת הִיא תוֹלָה עַד שֶׁיָּבֹא יוֹם הַכִּפּוּרִים וִיכַפֵּר

[426] Mechilta D'Rebbi Yishmael (20:7) - העובר על מצות עשה ועשה תשובה אינו זז משם עד שמוחלין לו ועל זה נאמר שובו בנים שובבים והעובר על מצות לא תעשה ועשה תשובה אין כח בתשובה לכפר אלא התשובה תולה ויום הכפורים מכפר ועל זה נאמר כי ביום הזה יכפר עליכם והמזיד על כריתות ועל מיתת בית דין ועשה תשובה אין כח בתשובה לתלות ויום הכפורים לכפר אלא תשובה ויום הכפורים מכפרין מחצה ויסורין ממרקין ומכפרין מחצה ועל זה נאמר ופקדתי בשבט פשעם ובנגעים עונם מי שמחלל שם שמים ועשה תשובה אין כח בתשובה לתלות ולא יום הכפורים מכפר ולא ייסורין בלבד ממרקין אלא התשובה ויום הכיפורים תולין ויום המיתה ויסורין ממרקין

[427] Ramban (Vayikra 1:9) - ויותר ראוי לשמוע הטעם שאומרים בהם כי בעבור שמעשי בני אדם נגמרים במחשבה ובדבור ובמעשה צוה השם כי כאשר יחטא יביא קרבן יסמוך ידיו עליו כנגד המעשה ויתודה בפיו כנגד הדבור וישרוף באש הקרב והכליות שהם כלי המחשבה והתאוה והכרעים כנגד ידיו ורגליו של אדם העושים כל מלאכתו ויזרוק הדם על המזבח כנגד דמו בנפשו כדי שיחשוב אדם בעשותו כל אלה כי חטא לאלהיו בגופו ובנפשו וראוי לו שישפך דמו וישרף

should think whatever is happening to the animal being brought as a *korban* should really be happening to him instead. Therefore, there is a *kapara* for a person when he dies. However, when a person takes his life by suicide by turning the *kapara* into an *aveira*, then there is no *kapara*. A person has no right to say, "kill me". We find an exception in the Chochmas Adam that a person can take his life if he will be tortured to death (Tosfos Avoda Zara 18a)[428] and that was the reason Shaul HaMelech told his shield bearer to kill him (Shmuel I 31:4)[429], but otherwise a person may not take his own life. However, there is a difference between taking your life and letting yourself die. Maybe you don't need to take medicine to continue living. The Gemara Nedarim (Nedarim 40a)[430] says it's a *mitzva* to visit the sick because anyone who doesn't visit the sick doesn't *daven* for him not to live or not to die. You see there are times to *daven* for someone to die (Aruch Hashulchan YD 335:3)[431]. The Ran (Nedarim 40a)[432] says that

---

גופו לולא חסד הבורא שלקח ממנו תמורה וכפר הקרבן הזה שיהא דמו תחת דמו נפש תחת נפש וראשי אברי הקרבן כנגד ראשי אבריו והמנות להחיות בהן מורי התורה שיתפללו עליו וקרבן התמיד בעבור שלא ינצלו הרבים מחטוא תמיד ואלה דברים מתקבלים מושכים את הלב כדברי אגדה

[428] Tosfos Avoda Zara (18a) - אור"ת דהיכא שיראים פן ואל יחבל עצמו יעבירום עובדי כוכבים לעבירה כגון ע"י יסורין שלא יוכל לעמוד בהם אז הוא מצוה לחבל בעצמו כי ההיא דגיטין (דף נז:) גבי ילדים שנשבו לקלון שהטילו עצמם לים

[429] Shmuel I (31:4) - וַיֹּאמֶר שָׁאוּל לְנֹשֵׂא כֵלָיו שְׁלֹף חַרְבְּךָ וְדָקְרֵנִי בָהּ פֶּן־ יָבוֹאוּ הָעֲרֵלִים הָאֵלֶּה וּדְקָרֻנִי וְהִתְעַלְּלוּ־בִי וְלֹא אָבָה נֹשֵׂא כֵלָיו כִּי יָרֵא מְאֹד וַיִּקַּח שָׁאוּל אֶת־הַחֶרֶב וַיִּפֹּל עָלֶיהָ

[430] Nedarim (40a) - רב חלבו באיש לא איכא דקא אתי אמר להו לא כך היה מעשה בתלמיד אחד מתלמידי ר' עקיבא שחלה לא נכנסו חכמים לבקרו ונכנס ר' עקיבא לבקרו ובשביל שכיבדו וריבצו לפניו חיה א"ל רבי החייתני יצא ר' עקיבא ודרש כל מי שאין מבקר חולים כאילו שופך דמים כי אתא רב דימי אמר כל המבקר את החולה גורם לו שיחיה וכל שאינו מבקר את החולה גורם לו שימות מאי גרמא אילימא כל המבקר את החולה מבקש עליו רחמים שיחיה וכל שאין מבקר את החולה מבקש עליו רחמים שימות ס"ד אלא כל שאין מבקר חולה אין מבקש עליו רחמים לא שיחיה ולא שימות

[431] Aruch Hashulchan YD (335:3) - דלפעמים יש לבקש רחמים שימות כגון שיש לו יסורים הרבה בחליו ואי אפשר לו שיחיה

[432] Ran Nedarim (40a) - אין מבקש עליו רחמים לא שיחיה ולא שימות נראה בעיני דה"ק פעמים שצריך לבקש רחמים על החולה שימות כגון שמצטער

Chapter 9: Halachic Will

when Rabbenu HaKadosh was sick, the people on this earth forced Beis Din shel maaleh to grant him more life. However, the maidservant of Rebbi's house – who we learn a lot of *halachos* from because she learned so much from being in Rebbi's house – said 'May the will of the Beis Din shel maaleh overpower the Beis Din shel mata' (Kesubos 104a)[433]. The Ran says if there is no hope to live and the person is in pain, you should *daven* that the person should die. Rav Moshe (Igros Moshe CM 2:74) says it doesn't make sense to say there is a *mitzva* to *daven* for someone to die yet there also be a *mitzva* to keep that person alive. I remember when Rav Yaakov Kamenetsky's first Rebbetzin was sick, the mother of Rav Shmuel, he was not *mispalel* that she should continue living. He felt that if he would *daven* for her to live when there was no hope then he would be *davening* for a miracle – and we're not allowed to *daven* for a miracle. Therefore, he wasn't *mispalel* for her to continue living. Nonetheless, Rav Yaakov wasn't *mispalel* for her to die either. I asked my Rosh Yeshiva what to do when posed with a question about someone suffering from cancer, and he said "Since there are so many places which are working on cures for cancer, your tefilla will help them find a cure for cancer – so you should *daven*." There are many researchers today who are finding cures. I'm not sure whether this is a *machlokes* between Rav Yaakov and my Rosh Yeshiva or not.

החולה בחליו הרבה ואי אפשר לו שיחיה כדאמרינן בפרק הנושא (כתובות קד) דכיון דחזאי אמתיה דרבי דעל כמה זימנין לבית הכסא ואנח תפילין וקא מצטער אמרה יהי רצון שיכופו העליונים את התחתונים כלומר דלימות רבי ומשה קאמר דהמבקר חולה מועילו בתפלתו אפי' לחיות מפני שהיא תפלה יותר מועלת ומי שאינו מבקרו אין צריך לומר שאינו מועילו לחיות אלא אפי' היכא דאיכא הנאה במיתה אפי' אותה זוטרתי אינו מהנהו

[433] Kesubos (104a) - ההוא יומא דנח נפשיה דרבי גזרו רבנן תעניתא ובעו רחמי ואמרי כל מאן דאמר נח נפשיה דר' ידקר בחרב סליקא אמתיה דרבי לאיגרא אמרה עליוני' מבקשין את רבי והתחתוני' מבקשין את רבי יהי רצון שיכופו תחתונים את העליונים כיון דחזאי כמה זימני דעייל לבית הכסא וחלץ תפילין ומנח להו וקמצטער אמרה יהי רצון שיכופו עליונים את התחתונים ולא הוו שתקי רבנן מלמיבעי רחמי שקלה כוזא שדייא מאיגרא [לארעא] אישתיקו מרחמי ונח נפשיה דרבי

201

Chapter 9: Halachic Will

Q19. If a person didn't know he was supposed to write a *halachic* will, what should the inheritors do?

A: (5777) There is a *halacha* of מצוה לקיים דברי המת (Shulchan Aruch CM 252:2)[434]. Although this person wasn't a *talmid chacham* or didn't realize that a legal will wouldn't help, we know what his wishes were based on the will. Even though according to the *din* of the Torah his will is not enforceable, it is still a *mitzva* to be מקיים דברי המת for the children to follow their father's wishes and not go to Beis Din over the inheritance. I have seen many families broken apart because of the *yerusha* of their parents. So many people have not talked to one another for years – sometimes forever – because they felt they were shortchanged. Whatever your parent wanted, it's a *mitzva* to follow those wishes. Don't make a fight about it.

---

[434] Shulchan Aruch CM (252:2) - מצוה לקיים דברי המת אפי' בריא שצוה
ומת והוא שנותנו עכשיו לשליש לשם כך

Chapter 10: Mourning

Q1. If an extra name is added to a חולה but he doesn't get better, is the extra name kept?

A: (5769) - You only change the name of a חולה if he's in סכנה. Adding a name is like major surgery. It is brought in the Sefer Rachamei Av that there's a מעשה with Rav Shmelke of Nikolsburg regarding Rav Shmuel, the brother of the Haflaah, who learned by the Mezricher Maggid and became very sick at 52 years old. The doctors gave up hope on Reb Shmuel, so they changed his name to Shmuel Shmelke and he recovered. However, when he got better he got very upset that they changed his name because he said his *neshama* was a *nitzutz* of Shmuel HaNavi who died at 52 as well. "Now that my name was changed to Shmuel Shmelke, I remained just Shmelke no longer being connected to Shmuel HaNavi." Nonetheless, we have a general rule that *pikuach nefesh* is דוחה כל התורה כולה – including the *issur* of changing names. He was upset because he felt he went down in *madrega* from being a *nitutz* of Shmuel HaNavi to become a סתם person. Still, we don't consider that when deciding cases of *pikuach nefashos*. The reason he recovered with a new name is because the decree to die at 52 was on Shmuel, not Shmuel Shmelke. Just like Avram and Sarai could not have children, but Avraham and Sarah could have children as different people with changed names. On the other hand, if this חולה dies, then the name isn't kept because the name didn't help. The name only helps if he was able to walk around in the street like a normal healthy person for 30 days. In such a case the person would keep the added name. When my Rosh Yeshiva זכר צדיק לברכה got sick, they changed his name to Refael Aharon, but he never recovered. Therefore, he remained just Aharon.

Q2. Must one wash his hands after a *levaya* if he was not in the same *ohel* as the *meis*?

A: (5769) - The מנהג is that you must wash your hands if you are in the same *ohel* as the *meis*. Also, if someone participated in the *levaya* and escorted the *meis* without being in the same *ohel*, then he must wash his hands even though he's not necessarily *tameh* (Shulchan Aruch 4:18)[435].

Q3. Must one wash his hands after going to a cemetery if he didn't become *tameh*?

A: (5769) - If a person entered a cemetery and didn't come within *daled amos* of the *kevarim*, and there were no tree branches that were above him and the *kevarim*, then he does not need to wash his hands.

Q4. What buildings may one not enter before washing his hands?

A: (5769) - The מנהג is not to enter any building which people live in before washing your hands. You may be able to walk into a Yeshiva building because people don't live there.

Q5. Should you wash your face after entering a cemetery?

A: (5769) - No, you do not need to wash your face.

Q6. Why can't you dry your hands after washing after the cemetery (Gesher HaChaim 1:14:21)?

A: (5769) - I think the reason you can't dry your hands is because there's a *ruach tumah* on the water which washed your hands which is going to spread to the towel. You want the *tumah* to stay with the water on your hands. Nonetheless, according to that it would be OK to use disposable towels.

Q7. Why are we not required to go to every *levaya* held down the block at Levinsons?

---

[435] Shulchan Aruch (4:18) - אלו דברים צריך נטילה במים הקם מהמטה והיוצא מבית הכסא ומבית המרחץ והנוטל צפורניו והחולץ מנעליו והנוגע ברגליו והחופף ראשו וי"א אף ההולך בין המתים ומי שנגע במת ומי שמפליא כליו והמשמש מטתו והנוגע בכנה והנוגע בגופו בידו ומי שעשה אחת מכל אלו ולא נטל אם ת"ח הוא תלמודו משתכח ואם אינו ת"ח יוצא מדעתו

Chapter 10: Mourning

A: (5769) - The Gemara (Megilla 29a)[436] says that someone who is קרי ותני should have a *levaya* of 600,000. Someone who was קרי ומתני - he taught Torah - has no limit. However, you don't have an obligation to attend the *levaya* of someone who isn't *frum* to begin with. That takes away most of the *levayos* at Levinsons, so you're not obligated to go. If they are *frum* people, then as long the נפטר has a *levaya lefi k'vodo* – it's not a *meis mitzva* where no one is attending – then there is no obligation for you to go if you're learning. Also, you have no obligation to be *choker u'doresh* whether there's a *levaya* taking place or not. What you don't know doesn't hurt you, so if you aren't aware of the *levaya* then you don't need to go.

Q8. What is the definition of a *talmid chacham* that you must go to his *levaya*?

A: (5769) - In general, a *talmid chacham* for these things is someone who is respected in his surroundings as a *talmid chacham*. Meaning, he is a higher level of *talmid chacham* than the regular people. That varies from place to place and time to time. In one place a person might be a *talmid chacham* but if he lived elsewhere he wouldn't be considered a *talmid chacham*. For instance, if a *talmid* of the Yeshiva who went through the shiurim moved out to San Antonio, Texas, then he would probably be considered a *talmid chacham*. If he moves to B'nei Brak then he would be a nobody. The Gemara (Nedarim 78a)[437] says that a *chacham* can be *matir neder* by himself without requiring two others to join a Beis Din of three people. You only need three people if there isn't a *talmid chacham* among them. The Mechaber says nowadays we don't have a *talmid chacham* for the *halacha* of being *matir neder* as a *yachid* (Shulchan Aruch YD 228:1)[438].

---

[436] Megilla (29a) - רב ששת אמר כנתינתה כך נטילתה מה נתינתה בששים ריבוא אף נטילתה בס' ריבוא ה"מ למאן דקרי ותני אבל למאן דמתני לית ליה שיעורא

[437] Nedarim (78a) - בפרשת נדרים למאי הלכתא אמר רב אחא בר יעקב להכשיר שלשה הדיוטות והא (במדבר ל:ב) ראשי המטות כתיב רב חסדא ואיתימא ר' יוחנן ביחיד מומחה

[438] Shulchan Aruch YD (228:1) - מי שנדר ונתחרט יש תקנה ע"י חרטה ואפילו נדר באלהי ישראל כיצד יעשה ילך אצל חכם מומחה דגמיר וסביר ואם

We don't have such a *talmid chacham* who could answer the halacha in every single case. The Chofetz Chaim who wrote the Mishna Berura wrote on Orach Chaim but doesn't come out with *psak* on every single case. The Mishna Berura will sometimes leave the *shailah* as a *machlokes haposkim*. The Vilna Gaon would *poskin* what the *halacha* is like in each case, but פשטות nowadays we don't have someone like that. Therefore, there is no *talmid chacham* nowadays. Even though we have a lot of *choshuv yidden* – like Rav Elyashiv who was considered to be the *posek hador* – he too doesn't have a *psak* on every single case as he brings a *machlokes* and says to be stringent or lenient depending on the case without being clear on what the *psak* is. On the other hand, for attending the *levaya* of a *talmid chacham*, he only needs to be someone who is above everyone else in the erudition of his learning. Nonetheless, if you have other *shibudim*, like you have a *chavrusa* who doesn't know this *talmid chacham*, then it's not so simple for you to leave your *chavrusa*. You need to ask your Rebbi or Rosh Yeshiva what to do in each situation.

Q9. If one is walking down the street and a hearse drives by, must he follow it for *daled amos*?

A: (5769) - You are only obligated to escort the נפטר four *amos* if you know it's a *frum yid* (Shulchan Aruch YD 361:3)[439]. If you don't know, then you you're not obligated to do so (Shulchan Aruch YD 361:1)[440].

Q10. Where does the עניין of following the hearse come from?

A: (5769) - We're talking about walking after the first car which is an עניין of escorting the *meis*. Driving after the hearse to the cemetery is the same as escorting the *meis*. I remember there were

---

אין יחיד מומחה ילך אצל שלשה הדיוטות והוא דגמירי להו וסבירי וגם יודעים לפתוח לו פתח ויתירו לו והאידנא אין מומחה שיהא ראוי להתיר ביחיד
[439] Shulchan Aruch YD (361:3) - הרואה את המת ואינו מלווהו עובר משום לועג לרש ובר נידוי הוא ולפחות ילוונו ד' אמות
[440] Shulchan Aruch YD (361:1) - ואין מבטלין ת"ת למת כשיש מי שיתעסק עמו כל צרכו אלא עוסק בתורה ואינו צריך לצאת ולראות אם יש עמו כל צרכו אם לאו אלא כיון שיש שם מי שיעשה מעשה תלמוד תורה שלו קודם

Chapter 10: Mourning

170 cars following my Rosh Yeshiva זכר צדיק לברכה at his *levaya* from Lakewood to New York. It caused major traffic problems because 170 cars through red lights causes issues.

Q11. May one hold a *sefer* at a *levaya*?

A: (5769) - You may hold a *sefer* in your hands. There's no מצוה to hold a *sefer*. A *meis* can hold a *sefer* too – the מצוה is learning from the *sefer* which you should not do during the *levaya*.

Q12. May one have his *tzitzis* out? Does that apply to Kohanim in the כהן room?

A: (5769) - You may not have your *tzitzis* out if the נפטר is a man. If the נפטר is a woman then you may leave your *tzitzis* out (Shulchan Aruch 23:1)[441]. Nonetheless, a כהן in the כהן room may keep his *tzitzis* out because he is in a different room.

Q13. May one talk or think in learning if he's more than *daled amos* away from the *meis*?

A: (5769) - Yes, there is no לועג לרש for thinking in learning even within *daled amos* since people cannot see that from the outside. You can be lenient to talk in learning beyond *daled amos*.

Q14. Can one fulfill the *mitzva* of *nichum aveilim* over the phone or by letter?

A: (5769) - The Chofetz Chaim writes in numerous places that the *mitzva* of *nichum aveilim* is a *mitzva* of *chesed* (Ahavas Chesed 3:5). *Chesed* is a *mitzva d'oraysa*, so if you can make him feel better over the phone or by writing a letter, then you were *mekayem* the *mitzva*. Maybe you would make him feel even better

---

[441] Shulchan Aruch (23:1) - מותר לכנס בבית הקברות והוא לבוש ציצית והוא שלא יהא נגרר על הקברות אבל אם הוא נגרר על הקברות אסור משום לועג לרש במה דברים אמורים בימיהם שהיו מטילים ציצית במלבוש שלובשים לצורך עצמם אבל אנו שאין אנו מכוונים בהם אלא לשם מצוה אסור אפילו אינם נגררים וה"מ כשהציציות מגולי' אבל אם הם מכסים מותר

by attending in person, but you're not obligated to do so and can be יוצא over the phone.

(5769) - The *mitzva* of *nichum aveilim* is a *mitzva* of *chesed* (Rambam Aveilus 14:1)[442]. This person had a big loss and feels bad, so you're coming to comfort him. Just by telling him that someone is thinking of him is a comfort – עִמּוֹ־אָנֹכִי בְצָרָה – I am with you and feel bad for you (Tehillim 91:15)[443]. That is a comfort for people. It says in the *posuk* (Eicha 2:13) מָה־אֲעִידֵךְ מָה אֲדַמֶּה־לָּךְ הַבַּת יְרוּשָׁלַם מָה אַשְׁוֶה־לָּךְ וַאֲנַחֲמֵךְ בְּתוּלַת בַּת־צִיּוֹן כִּי־גָדוֹל כַּיָּם שִׁבְרֵךְ מִי יִרְפָּא־לָךְ – what is there that I can compare you to in order to make you feel your loss isn't the biggest loss in the world since other people felt this loss too. Although it's better to be comfort mourners in person if possible, if it's not practical then you can be *yotzei* by phone as you're still providing some comfort. It's not a *halacha* that you must say the words המקום ינחם as a magical phrase. The fact that you came, and he knows you're thinking about him is a comfort (Igros Moshe OC 4:40:11)[444]. The words

---

[442] Rambam Aveilus (14:1) - מִצְוַת עֲשֵׂה שֶׁל דִּבְרֵיהֶם לְבַקֵּר חוֹלִים וּלְנַחֵם אֲבֵלִים וּלְהוֹצִיא הַמֵּת וּלְהַכְנִיס הַכַּלָּה וּלְלַוּוֹת הָאוֹרְחִים וּלְהִתְעַסֵּק בְּכָל צָרְכֵי הַקְּבוּרָה לָשֵׂאת עַל הַכָּתֵף וְלֵילֵךְ לְפָנָיו וְלִסְפֹּד וְלַחְפֹּר וְלִקְבֹּר וְכֵן לְשַׂמֵּחַ הַכַּלָּה וְהֶחָתָן וּלְסַעֲדָם בְּכָל צָרְכֵיהֶם וְאֵלוּ הֵן גְּמִילוּת חֲסָדִים שֶׁבְּגוּפוֹ שֶׁאֵין לָהֶם שִׁעוּר אַף עַל פִּי שֶׁכָּל מִצְוֹת אֵלּוּ מִדִּבְרֵיהֶם הֲרֵי הֵן בִּכְלָל וְאָהַבְתָּ לְרֵעֲךָ כָּמוֹךָ כָּל הַדְּבָרִים שֶׁאַתָּה רוֹצֶה שֶׁיַּעֲשׂוּ אוֹתָם לְךָ אֲחֵרִים עֲשֵׂה אַתָּה אוֹתָן לְאָחִיךָ בְּתוֹרָה וּבְמִצְוֹת:
[443] Tehillim (91:15) - יִקְרָאֵנִי וְאֶעֱנֵהוּ עִמּוֹ־אָנֹכִי בְצָרָה אֲחַלְּצֵהוּ וַאֲכַבְּדֵהוּ:
[444] Igros Moshe OC (4:40:11) – הנה בנחום אבלים איכא תרתי ענינים חדא לטובת אבלים החיים שהם טרודים מאד בצערם מחוייבין לדבר על לבו ולנחמו שבשביל זה הרי ג"כ מחוייבין לילך לביתו למקום שהוא נמצא ושנית לטובת המת כדאיתא בשבת דף קנ"ב א' בר' יהודה מת שאין לו מנחמין הולכין בנ"א ויושבין במקומו ומסיק עובדא דמת שאין לו מנחמין שבכל יומא הוה דבר ר' יהודה בי עשרה ותיתבי בדוכתיה ואיתחזי ליה בחלמו דר' יהודה וא"ל תנוח דעתך שהנחת את דעתי הרי דעתי ממילא ידעינן דכשיש מנחמין איכא בזה גם טובת המת ומטעם זה כתב הרמב"ם בפי"ד מאבל ה"ז יראה לי שנחמת אבלים קודם לבק"ח שנחום אבלים גמ"ח עם החיים ועם המתים וגו'...ומשמע לי שמצד האבל החי שייך לקיים גם ע"י הטעלעפאן אבל המצוה שמצד טובת המת לא שייך אלא דוקא כשיבא לשם במקום שמתנחמין או במקום שמת ואף מצד האבל החי נמי ודאי עדיף כשבא לשם שהוא גם מכבדו שזה עצמו הוא ג"כ ענין תנחומין כלשון ר"ע במו"ק דף כ"א כשמתו בניו והספידום כל ישראל עמד ר"ע ואמר אחב"י שמעו אפילו שני בנים חתנים מנוחם הוא בשביל כבוד שעשיתם וענין הכבוד לא שייך

המקום ינחם is telling him that he's not the only one in this *tzara* since we're all *aveilei Tzion*, which you can accomplish over the phone too.

Q15. Must the mourner start the conversation?

A: (5769) - The Shulchan Aruch (YD 376:1)[445] says the mourner must start the conversation first. Why? When a person is very depressed, sometimes he just wants to be left alone and doesn't want people interfering with his thoughts. If he'd rather be left alone, then what kind of *chesed* are you doing by starting a conversation with him? However, if he starts talking, then it's a sign that he wants to talk with people. If the mourner was talking with the person before you but is now quiet with you, you can still begin the conversation because evidently the אבל isn't dejected since he was talking before.

Q16. What should you do if the mourner doesn't say anything?

A: (5769) - If the mourner doesn't want to speak, then you can leave. You could sit there with him – יֵשֵׁב בָּדָד וְיִדֹּם כִּי נָטַל עָלָיו (Eicha 3:28) – there's such a thing as suffering in silence together. However, you don't need to sit there the whole day and can leave after about five minutes.

Q17. Should one initiate discussing the *niftar* when comforting a mourner over the phone?

ע"י הטעלעפאן דלכן למעשה אם אפשר לו ליל לבית האבלים שהוא קיום מצוה
שלמה לא שייך שיפטר בטעלעפאן אך קצת מצוה יש גם ע"י הטעלעפאן שלכן
אם א"א לו ללכת לבית האבלים כגון מחמת חולי או שהוא טרוד בטירדא דמצוה
יש עליו חיוב לקיים מה שאפשר לו יש לו לנחם ע"י הטעלעפאן דג"כ איכא בזה
מצוה ולא יאמר כי מאחר שאינו יכול ליל לבית האבלים אין עליו שוב שום חיוב
כלל
[445] Shulchan Aruch YD (376:1) - אין המנחמים רשאים לפתוח עד שיפתח
האבל תחלה

Chapter 10: Mourning

A: (5769) - I just saw a *chiddush* recently from Rav Shlomo Zalman[446] that the *halacha* of the mourner starting the discussion (Shulchan Aruch YD 376:1)[447] is not *noheg* nowadays because the mere fact that he opened a his door to allow others to enter his house is already enough of a *siman* that he wants to be comforted. The reason why the mourner has to start the conversation is because maybe he's not in the mood for *nechama*. However, why else would he have opened his door to let others in? Therefore, you don't need to wait for the mourner to begin speaking anymore. Similarly, you may initiate the conversation about the *niftar* over the phone with the mourner because he knew why you were calling and could have ignored the call – he knows it wasn't the electric company calling about why he didn't pay his bill otherwise they wouldn't have given him the phone. Therefore, you may start the conversation when comforting a mourner over the phone.

Q18. May one change the topic of conversation when comforting a mourner in person?

A: (5769) - The gist of the conversation should be about the *niftar*, about mourning in general, or the connection between the mourner and the *niftar*. It's not appropriate to discuss the stock market in the mourner's home since you're coming to comfort him.

Q19. What should one say to a mourner besides the פסוק of המקום?

A: (5769) - It all depends on the situation. Sometimes there's very little you can say. Do whatever you can do to make the mourner feel better.

Q20. Should you say the פסוק in *lashon rabim* if there is more than one mourner?

---

[446] See Toras Rabbeinu Shmuel MiSalant (I:16) and Tzitz Eliezer (17:45:4)

[447] Shulchan Aruch YD (376:1) - אין המנחמים רשאים לפתוח עד שיפתח האבל תחלה

Chapter 10: Mourning

A: (5769) - Yes, the מנהג is to say it *b'lashon rabim* - המקום ינחם אתכם. The rationale behind this מנהג is because the Ribono Shel Olam is עִמּוֹ־אָנֹכִי בְצָרָה (Tehillim 91:15)[448] – in pain with every *yid* who is in pain – so we say המקום ינחם אתכם in referring to the Ribono Shel Olam and the אבל. If you say המקום ינחם אותך, then you are also יוצא.

(5769) - There's a lot of talk about this. Even if there's only one person sitting *shiva* who you are comforting in person, perhaps you say המקום ינחם אתכם instead of המקום ינחם אותך or אותך. Some say that אתכם refers to the Ribono Shel Olam and the mourner together since there's an element of עִמּוֹ־אָנֹכִי בְצָרָה (Tehillim 91:15) as Hashem is in pain with the mourner. We're saying המקום - Hashem - should comfort Himself along with the mourner. Therefore, there's no *issur* of saying אתכם every time you comfort a mourner. If I comfort a mourner by himself, I say אוֹתָךְ (Igros Moshe OC 5:20:21)[449], but doing it the other way isn't *me'akev*.

Q21. When should a person say the פסוק of המקום on Friday night?

A: (5769) - When the אבל walks in at Kabbalas Shabbos, before מזמור שיר ליום השבת, then you say המקום ינחם. On Shabbos when you want to be comfort him, you say שבת היא מלנחם ונחמה קרבה לבא (Mishna Berura 287:3)[450].

Q22. Are you *yotzei bikur cholim* over the phone?

A: (5769) - There are two aspects to *bikur cholim*. One is similar to comforting a mourner that the person knows you're thinking about him. The other *inyan* is as the Kitzur Shulchan Aruch says

---

[448] Tehillim (91:15) - יִקְרָאֵנִי וְאֶעֱנֵהוּ עִמּוֹ־אָנֹכִי בְצָרָה אֲחַלְּצֵהוּ וַאֲכַבְּדֵהוּ
[449] Igros Moshe OC (5:20:21) - שאמירת המנחמים המקום ינחם אותך הוא רק גמר דברים של המנחמים להאבל
[450] Mishna Berura (287:3) - ובנחום אבלים יאמר לו שבת היא מלנחם ונחמה קרובה לבוא ויש מקילים דרשאי לומר המקום ינחמך כתב בפמ"ג אם בא האבל לבהכ"נ אחר אמירת מזמור שיר ליום השבת שוב לא יקרא השמש צאו נגד האבל דאין להזכיר אבילות בפרהסיא ומ"מ לילך בעצמו לו לומר שבת היא מלנחם וכו' רשאי

211

עִקַּר מִצְוַת בִּקּוּר חוֹלִים הוּא לְעַיֵּן בְּצָרְכֵי הַחוֹלֶה מַה הוּא צָרִיךְ לַעֲשׂוֹת (193:3)
you - לוֹ וְשֶׁיִּמְצָא נַחַת רוּחַ עִם חֲבֵרָיו וְגַם שֶׁיִּתֵּן דַּעְתּוֹ עָלָיו וִיבַקֵּשׁ רַחֲמִים עָלָיו
come to see if the *choleh* needs anything like calling a nurse or
getting something else at the hospital. The second aspect you can't
be *yotzei* over the phone, but it's still a *chesed* to call in order for
him to feel you're thinking of him (Igros Moshe YD 1:223)[451]. In
general, there's a rule that you're not obligated to travel out of
town to fulfill a מצות עשה. For instance, you have a *mitzva* to get
married – הָאִישׁ מצווה על פריה ורביה (Rambam Ishus 15:2 -
ורביה). You're not obligated to go out of town to find a *shidduch*
because it's no different than any other *mitzva*. I'm not saying you
shouldn't go out of town, but you're not obligated to leave even
after you've exhausted all the possibilities in town. I would think
such a person would be exempt from פריה ורביה after exhausting
all the possible *shidduchim* in his city. That doesn't mean I

---

[451] Igros Moshe YD (1:223) - הנה פשוט לע"ד שאף שמקיים מצוה דבק"ח
אבל אינו שייך לומר שיצא י"ח כיון שחסר בבקור זה ענינים האחרים שיש
בבק"ח. ורק יצא מזה שאם א"א לו לקיים בהליכה לשם לא נפטר לגמרי אלא
צריך לבקרו במה שאפשר לו לכל הפחות ענין אחד או שנים שהוא גם ע"י
הטעלעפאן. וזהו הדין דחלה בנו שואלו בשוק בנדרים דף ל"ט לא שיצא בזה כל
ענין בק"ח אלא שאף שלא יצא בזה הא פטור משום שאינו יכול לקיים כיון
דאדריה גם מן חיותיה דבנו אך השמיענו דמ"מ מחוייב לקיים במה שאפשר לו
דהוא לשאול עליו בשוק ובחלה הוא שלא אדריה מן חיותיה מחוייב ליכנס ולראות
ובעצמו כדי שיקיים בק"ח בכל הענינים ולא יצא בשאלה בשוק. וכן אינו כלום
הראיה שהביא כתר"ה מסעי' ח' דבחולה שקשה לו הדבור אין מבקרין אותו בפניו
אלא נכנסין בבית החיצון ושואלין אם צריכין לכבד ולרבץ ושומעין צערו
ומבקשין רחמים אלמא שא"צ להיות נוכח החולה בכדי לקיים המצוה דשם הא
הוא חולה שא"א בפניו דיש לחוש שידבר שקשה לו זה אך עכ"פ לא נפטר לגמרי
אלא צריך לבקרו ולשאול עליו בבית החיצון כדי לקיים מה שאפשר וזהו עיקר
החדוש דשם אבל בחולה שאפשר לבקרו בפניו מחוייבין לבקרו בפניו בשביל
הטעם שימצא נחת רוח זה שלא בפניו וגם מחמת שמהראיה
מתרגש המבקר יותר ומבקש ביותר תחנונים וכדכתבת גם כתר"ה וגם אולי
מתקבלת שם התפלה ביותר משום דהשכינה מצויה שם עם החולה. ומש"כ כתר"ה
דנראה דעיקר בק"ח היא התפלה שלזה גם בטעלעפאן הוא כראה יקשה א"כ למה
צריך בכלל לילך לשם יסגי לשם בשאלה מאחרים ויתפלל אלא צריך לומר שאם
לתפלה יותר טוב כשיראה בעצמו מטעם שיותר מתרגש ומטעם שהתפלה יותר
מקובלת

wouldn't advise him not to go out of town, but he's just not obligated to leave town.

Q23. If one first sees a mourner after he got up from *shiva*, should he comfort the mourner at that point?

A: (5769) - *Nichum aveilim* goes on for the entire year for one's parents and thirty days for other *kerovim*. As long as there is *aveilus*, there is an ענין of *nichum aveilim*. The *chesed* of making *aveilim* feel better doesn't end at the *shiva*. In general we assume that after a year the אבל is OK.

Q24. Why is one a mourner for twelve months for a parent?

A: (5769) - Everything else in the world is replaceable except for a parent. If you lost a sibling, your parents can have another child. The concept is that every loss is replaceable except for a parent. You can potentially have another sibling or another child *chas v'shalom* – Chava felt Sheis took the place of Hevel (Bereishis 4:25)[452]. However, you can never get another parent. Stepparents are not the same as your biological parents. Yes, it's tragic to lose one of your relatives, but it's not the same as losing your irreplaceable parent. Rav Moshe writes in a *teshuva* that the reason why *aveilus* for a parent is longer is a din in כיבוד אב ואם (Igros Moshe YD 1:255).

Q25. May one take an object out of the house of a mourner?

A: (5769) - There is a Rebbi Akiva Eiger in (376) which says we're *noheg* not to remove anything from a mourner's house. There is a Sefer Yosef Ometz (192) who brings from the Mahari Vayil that this whole idea is a mistake and says you may take something out of a mourner's home. The Yosef Ometz was written before Rebbi Akiva Eiger, but I'm not sure if Rebbi Akiva Eiger would've said anything differently because he says it's the מנהג. The Yosef Ometz agrees it's a מנהג, just that it's a mistake. I would suggest that the only time it's *shayach* to say the *ruach hatuma* is שורה שם כל ז is if the *meis* dies there. However, most of the time

---

[452] Bereishis (4:25) - שֵׁת אֶת־שְׁמוֹ וַתִּקְרָא בֵּן וַתֵּלֶד עוֹד אֶת־אִשְׁתּוֹ אָדָם וַיֵּדַע
קָיִן הָרְגוֹ כִּי הֶבֶל תַּחַת אַחֵר זֶרַע אֱלֹהִים לִי שָׁת כִּי

the *meis* dies in the hospital, so there's no *ruach tumah* in the house. In such a case, even Rebbi Akiva Eiger wouldn't say there's an issue.

Q26. Why do we cover mirrors in the mourner's home?

A: (5769) - That's a good question. The Chasam Sofer (Derashos Chasam Sofer 2:387) and many others ask the same question since it's not mentioned in any Gemara, Rishon, or Shulchan Aruch. However, it seems already in the time of the Chasam Sofer they had this מנהג because the Chasam Sofer explains the מנהג in the following way: The Gemara (Moed Katan 15a)[453] says a mourner is obligated to turn over the beds – the אבלים turn over their beds and sit on the other side (Shulchan Aruch YD 387:1)[454]. That's where the ענין of sitting low comes from because if you turn over the bed, then the legs are up in the air and the mattress is low on the floor. The Yerushalmi says the reason the Chachamim made this *kefiyas hamita* because most people are conceived on a bed (Yerushalmi Moed Katan 16b)[455]. Therefore, we're saying this bed upon which the נפטר was conceived has ended its purpose. It was instrumental in making this person alive, but now he's dead. The Chasam Sofer continues saying the *kiyor* was made ממראות

---

[453] Moed Katan (15a) - אבל חייב בכפיית המטה דתני בר קפרא דמות דיוקני נתתי בהן ובעונותיהם הפכתיה כפו מטותיהן עליה

[454] Shulchan Aruch YD (387:1) - אבל חייב בכפיית המטה ובשעת שינה ואכילה יושב על מטה כפויה אבל כל היום אינו יושב על מטה כפויה אלא על גבי קרקע וכן המנחמים אינן רשאים לישב אלא ע"ג קרקע

[455] Yerushalmi Moed Katan (16b) - ומנין לכפיית המיטות ר' קריספי בשם ר' יוחנן (איוב ב:יג) וישבו אתו לארץ על הארץ אין כתיב כאן אלא וישבו אתו לארץ אלא דבר שהוא סמוך לארץ מיכן שהיו ישנין על מיטות כפויות. בר קפרא אמר איקונין אחת טובה היתה לך בתוך ביתך וגרמתני לכפותה אף את כפה מיטתך ואית דמפקין לישנא יכפה הסרסיר רבי יונה ורבי יוסה תריהון בשם ר' שמעון בן לקיש חד אמר מפני מה הוא ישן על מטה כפויה כדי שיהא ניעור בלילה ונזכר שהוא אבל וחורנה אמר מתוך שהוא ישן על גבי מטה כפויה הוא ניעור בלילה ונזכר שהוא אבל אמר איני כופה את המטה הרי אני ישן על גבי הספסל אין שומעין לו מפני שאמר איני כופה את המטה אבל אם אמר הרי אני כופה את המטה שומעין לו

Chapter 10: Mourning

הצובאות (Shemos 38:8)[456]. What does that mean? Rashi explains the Ribono Shel Olam has a lot of הכרת הטוב for these mirrors which the women used in Mitzrayim to make their husbands want to continue having children even after being overtaxed (Rashi Shemos 38:8)[457]. If it wasn't for these mirrors, no children would have been born over the years Klal Yisroel was in *galus* Mitzrayim. Since these mirrors continued the existence of Klal Yisroel, the Ribono Shel Olam wanted the *kiyor* used to cleanse the *kohanim* each day to prepare for the *avoda* made from them. So too, now that the mirror has lost its purpose in the house of the mourner - as mirrors are used for *pirya v'ribya* - so the mirror is covered just like the bed is overturned. Although the Chasam Sofer is bending over backwards to come up with a reason, we have a rule that אִם אֵין נְבִיאִים הֵם בְּנֵי נְבִיאִים הֵם (Ein Yaakov Pesachim 6:1) – whatever Klal Yisroel does was probably done with the *haskama* of *gedolim* at one point. Otherwise, it would've never been started. Therefore, the מנהגים of Yisroel have a special קדושה.

Q27. Does the *din* of covering mirrors apply to other reflective surfaces?

A: (5769) - No, it does not apply to other reflective surfaces, but the Gesher HaChaim (1:50) - a *sefer* on *aveilus* - says you should not have paintings or pictures of people around on display in the mourner's home for the same reason we cover the mirrors. Since someone just died, you should not have pictures of people on

---

[456] Shemos (38:8) - וַיַּעַשׂ אֵת הַכִּיּוֹר נְחֹשֶׁת וְאֵת כַּנּוֹ נְחֹשֶׁת בְּמַרְאֹת הַצֹּבְאֹת אֲשֶׁר צָבְאוּ פֶּתַח אֹהֶל מוֹעֵד

[457] Rashi Shemos (38:8) - בְּנוֹת יִשְׂרָאֵל הָיוּ בְיָדָן מַרְאוֹת שֶׁרוֹאוֹת בָּהֶן כְּשֶׁהֵן מִתְקַשְּׁטוֹת וְאַף אוֹתָן לֹא עִכְּבוּ מִלְּהָבִיא לְנִדְבַת הַמִּשְׁכָּן וְהָיָה מוֹאֵס מֹשֶׁה בָּהֶן מִפְּנֵי שֶׁעֲשׂוּיִין לְיֵצֶר הָרָע אָמַר לוֹ הַקָּבָּ"ה קַבֵּל כִּי אֵלּוּ חֲבִיבִין עָלַי מִן הַכֹּל שֶׁעַל יְדֵיהֶם הֶעֱמִידוּ הַנָּשִׁים צְבָאוֹת רַבּוֹת בְּמִצְרַיִם כְּשֶׁהָיוּ בַּעֲלֵיהֶם יְגֵעִים בַּעֲבוֹדַת פֶּרֶךְ הָיוּ הוֹלְכוֹת וּמוֹלִיכוֹת לָהֶם מַאֲכָל וּמִשְׁתֶּה וּמַאֲכִילוֹת אוֹתָם וְנוֹטְלוֹת הַמַּרְאוֹת וְכָל אַחַת רוֹאָה עַצְמָהּ עִם בַּעְלָהּ בַּמַּרְאָה וּמְשַׁדַּלְתּוֹ בִּדְבָרִים לוֹמַר אֲנִי נָאָה מִמְּךָ וּמִתּוֹךְ כָּךְ מְבִיאוֹת לְבַעְלֵיהֶן לִידֵי תַאֲוָה וְנִזְקָקוֹת לָהֶם וּמִתְעַבְּרוֹת וְיוֹלְדוֹת שָׁם, שֶׁנֶּאֱמַר תַּחַת הַתַּפּוּחַ עוֹרַרְתִּיךָ (שיר השירים ח') וְזֶה שֶׁנֶּאֱמַר בְּמַרְאֹת הַצֹּבְאֹת וְנַעֲשָׂה הַכִּיּוֹר מֵהֶם שֶׁהוּא לָשׂוּם שָׁלוֹם בֵּין אִישׁ לְאִשְׁתּוֹ לְהַשְׁקוֹת מִמֶּנּוּ מַיִם שֶׁבְּתוֹכוֹ לְמִי שֶׁקִּנֵּא לָהּ בַּעְלָהּ וְנִסְתְּרָה

display – including pictures of the *meis*. It's not a universally kept מנהג, but the Gesher HaChaim does bring it.

Q28. May one use a small mirror to check the position of his *tefillin*?

A: (5769) – *B'dieved* you can be lenient. You really don't need a mirror to check the position of your *tefillin*. They never used to do that as the *tefillin* don't need to be exactly in the middle. The Gemara (Eruvin 95b)[458] says there is enough room for you to wear two pairs of *tefillin*. The כהן גדול would wear the *tzitz* and the *tefillin* in the same area without there being a problem. The Avnei Nezer says this Gemara doesn't mean wearing one behind the other, like Rabbenu Tam *tefillin* behind Rashi *tefillin*. Rather, the Avnei Nezer says to wear them next to one another. If you do that, then you can't ensure either are exactly in the middle. Therefore, it's fine for your תפילין to be a little on the side.

Q29. Can a mourner be lenient with the *shiur tefach* of the Chazon Ish regarding sitting on couches?

A: (5769) - Yes, a mourner may rely on the Chazon Ish. First of all, if the Chazon Ish said this as the *shiur*, then you may rely on it. Secondly, even if there's a *machlokes* on the *shiur*, we have a general rule that we follow the lenient opinions regarding mourning since *aveilus* is *d'rabanan*. Nonetheless, if you are always lenient not following the *shiur* of the Chazon Ish, then you should continue following the *shiur* you normally use.

Q30. What should a mourner do if he is uncomfortable sitting on a low stool for long periods of time?

A: (5769) - Too bad for him. If he's uncomfortable then he's uncomfortable. If he's older, then he might have an issue of blood clots developing in his veins. You are not obligated to get sick to be fulfill the *mitzva* of אבלות. The Chasam Sofer says it's a *mitzvas aseh* to sit low, not an *issur* to sit high. Therefore, we say you're

---

[458] Eruvin (95b) - אמר רב שמואל בר רב יצחק מקום יש בראש להניח בו שתי תפילין

not obligated to get sick to perform the *mitzva* nor are you required to be in pain.

Q31. Does an *onen* say Kaddish on Shabbos?

A: (5769) - In the Matzeves Moshe, written by the Chayei Adam, it says that an *onen* does say Kaddish on Shabbos.

(5769) - Yes, he does say Kiddush because there is no *aninus* on Shabbos.

Q32. May a mourner wear comfortable non-leather shoes?

A: (5769) - Yes. On Yom Kippur (Shulchan Aruch 614:2)[459] and Tisha B'Av (Shulchan Aruch 554:1)[460] there are opinions which say you should not wear comfortable shoes because it's a *din* in *inui*. We're more lenient with Tisha B'Av since not wearing shoes is *d'rabanan* in contrast to Yom Kippur. Therefore, since we're lenient with Tisha B'Av where there are *dinei aveilus d'rabim*, you can certainly be more lenient with *aveilus d'yachid*.

Q33. May one *daven* in a mourner's home if there are many pictures hanging on the walls?

A: (5769) - The question is whether you can *daven* if it appears as if you are bowing to the picture. I think you should hold the *siddur* in front of the picture and *daven*. Keep the *siddur* in front of you as you bow. If you don't have a *siddur*, then you can put your hat in front of the picture.

Q34. May one list multiple חולים מסוכנים in one *Mishaberach* or personal *tefillah*?

A: (5769) - Yes, you may list them in the same *Mishaberach* or personal *tefillah*.

---

[459] Shulchan Aruch (614:2) - אסור לנעול סנדל או מנעל של עור אפי' קב הקיטע וכיוצא בו אפי' של עץ ומחופה עור אסור אבל של גמי או של קש או של בגד או של שאר מינים מותר אפילו לצאת בהם לרשו' הרבים

[460] Shulchan Aruch (554:1) - תשעה באב אסור ברחיצה וסיכה ונעילת הסנדל

Q35. How long should you continue *davening* for *cholim* if you don't hear about them?

A: After a week you may assume the *choleh* got better as the Ribono Shel Olam listened to your *tefillah*. If you don't hear anything, then you can assume he's OK now and you don't need to make sure.

Q36. If someone doesn't have a good voice, should he still be a *chazan* for the *yahrtzeit* of his parent?

A: No, he's not doing his relative any favors if he cannot say the words well or have a pleasant voice. In fact, I don't daven from the *amud* for the *yahrtzeit* of my parents on Shabbos because why should I put the *tzibur* through pain in hearing me daven?

Index

Index

Index

Index

Index

Made in the USA
Middletown, DE
21 May 2025

75824871R00132